Disney ALICE IN WONDERLAND

GRAPHIC NOVEL

ADAPTED FROM THE MOVIE BY
TIM BURTON

"*It's only a dream...*"

ALICE

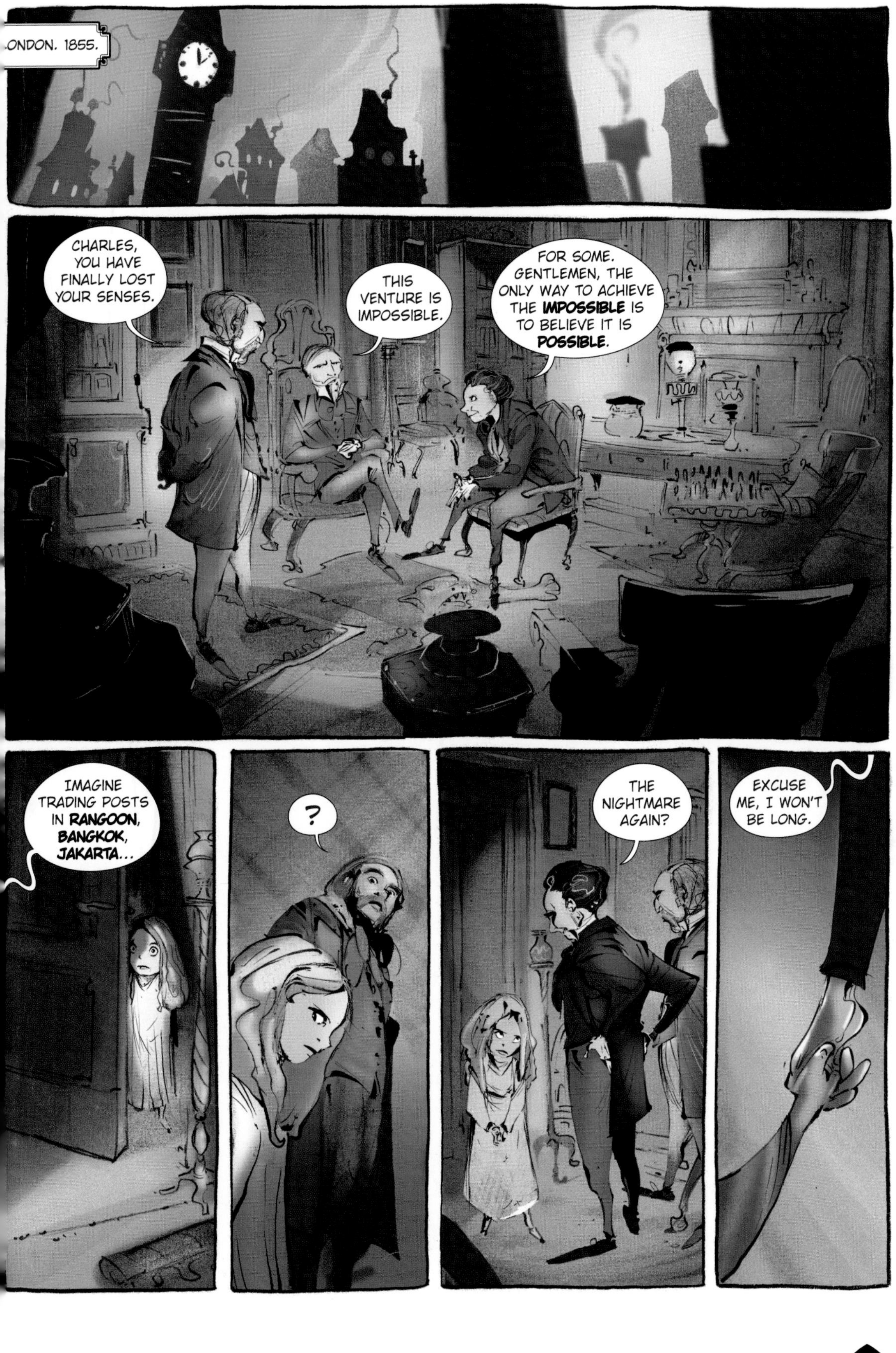

ONDON. 1855.
CHARLES, YOU HAVE FINALLY LOST YOUR SENSES.
THIS VENTURE IS IMPOSSIBLE.
FOR SOME. GENTLEMEN, THE ONLY WAY TO ACHIEVE THE IMPOSSIBLE IS TO BELIEVE IT IS POSSIBLE.
IMAGINE TRADING POSTS IN RANGOON, BANGKOK, JAKARTA...
?
THE NIGHTMARE AGAIN?
EXCUSE ME, I WON'T BE LONG.

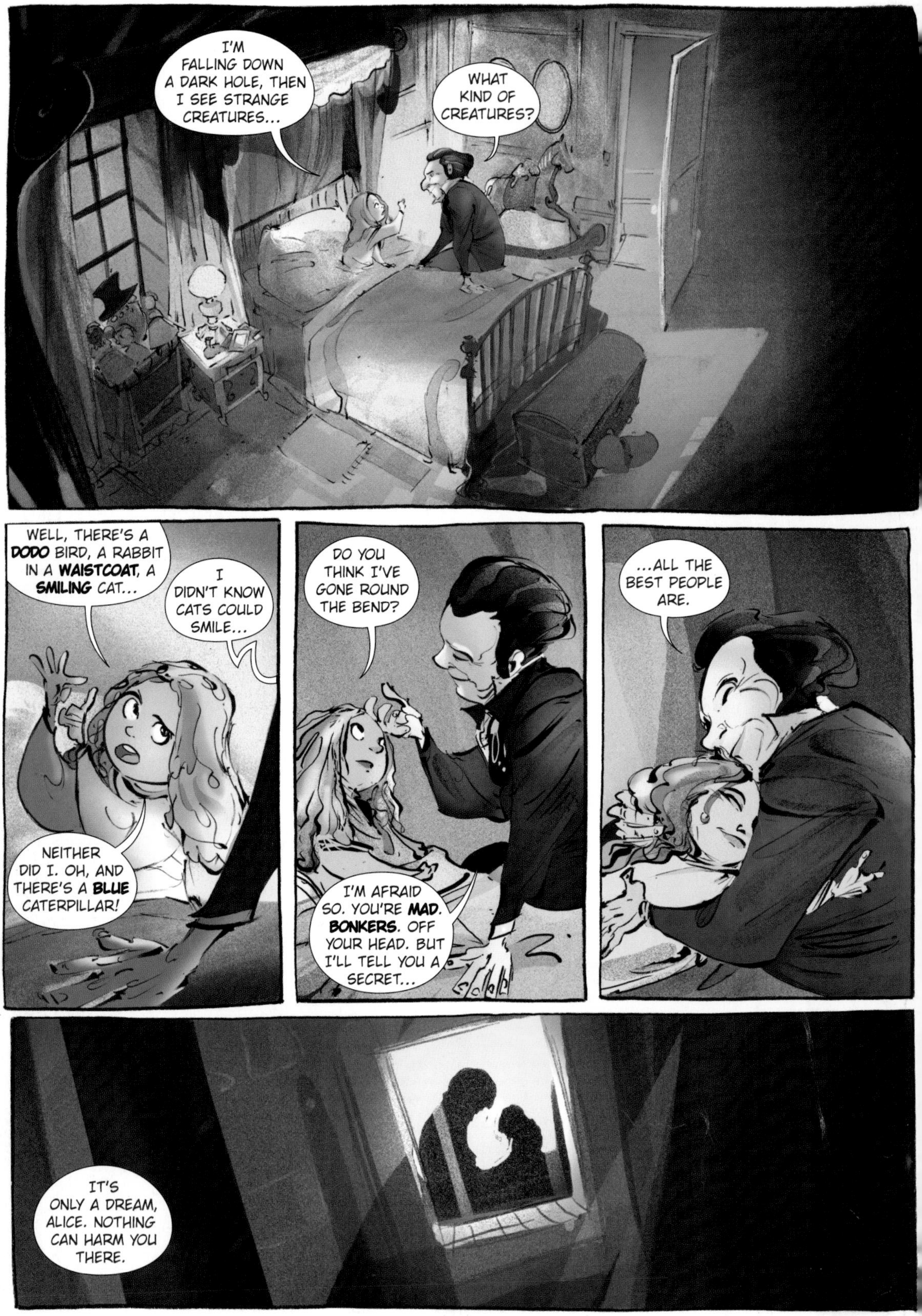
I'M FALLING DOWN A DARK HOLE, THEN I SEE STRANGE CREATURES...
WHAT KIND OF CREATURES?
WELL, THERE'S A DODO BIRD, A RABBIT IN A WAISTCOAT, A SMILING CAT...
I DIDN'T KNOW CATS COULD SMILE...
NEITHER DID I. OH, AND THERE'S A BLUE CATERPILLAR!
DO YOU THINK I'VE GONE ROUND THE BEND?
I'M AFRAID SO. YOU'RE MAD. BONKERS. OFF YOUR HEAD. BUT I'LL TELL YOU A SECRET...
...ALL THE BEST PEOPLE ARE.
IT'S ONLY A DREAM, ALICE. NOTHING CAN HARM YOU THERE.

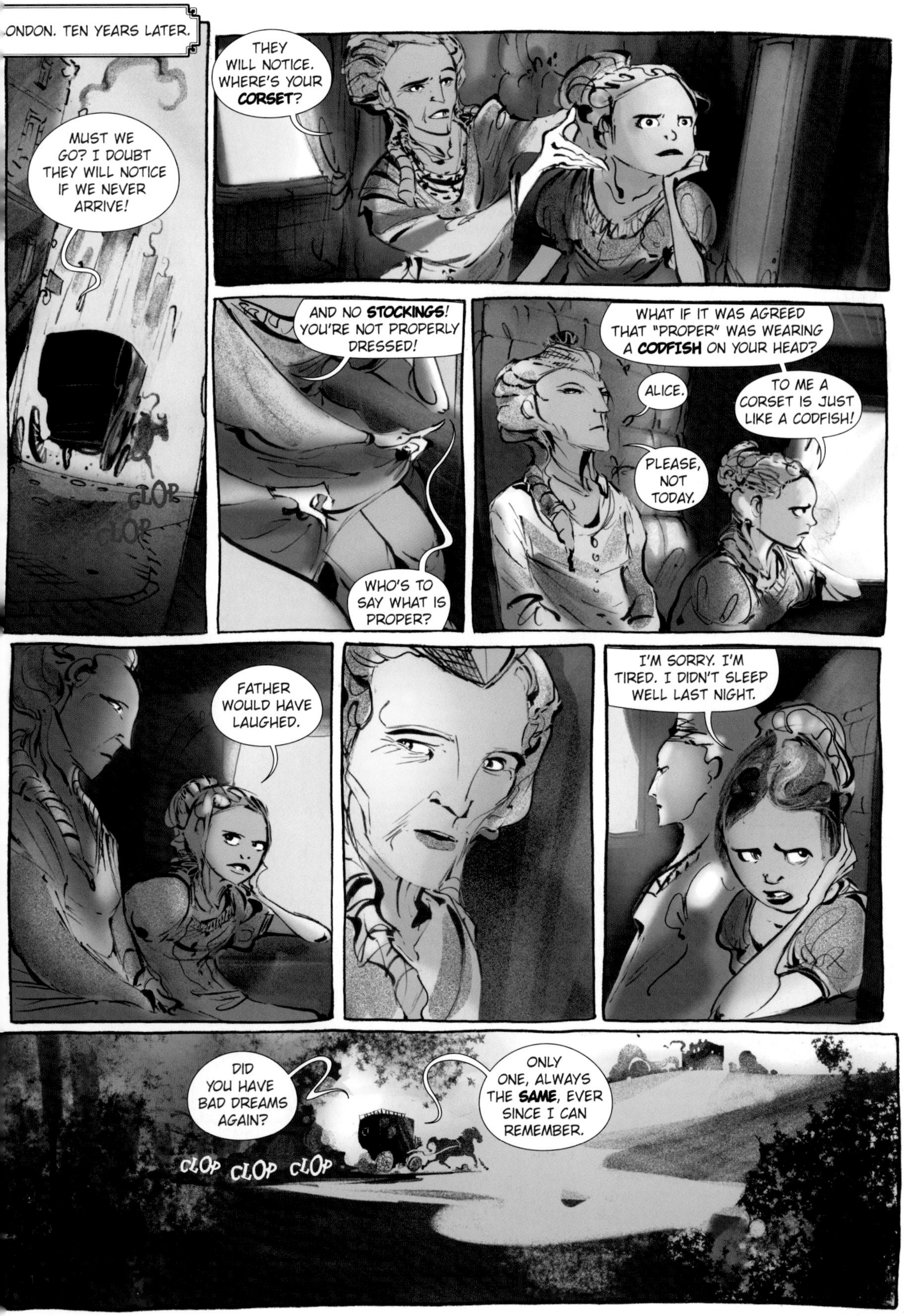
ONDON. TEN YEARS LATER.
MUST WE GO? I DOUBT THEY WILL NOTICE IF WE NEVER ARRIVE!
CLOP CLOP
THEY WILL NOTICE. WHERE'S YOUR CORSET?
AND NO STOCKINGS! YOU'RE NOT PROPERLY DRESSED!
WHO'S TO SAY WHAT IS PROPER?
WHAT IF IT WAS AGREED THAT "PROPER" WAS WEARING A CODFISH ON YOUR HEAD?
ALICE.
TO ME A CORSET IS JUST LIKE A CODFISH!
PLEASE, NOT TODAY.
FATHER WOULD HAVE LAUGHED.
I'M SORRY. I'M TIRED. I DIDN'T SLEEP WELL LAST NIGHT.
DID YOU HAVE BAD DREAMS AGAIN?
ONLY ONE, ALWAYS THE SAME, EVER SINCE I CAN REMEMBER.
CLOP CLOP CLOP

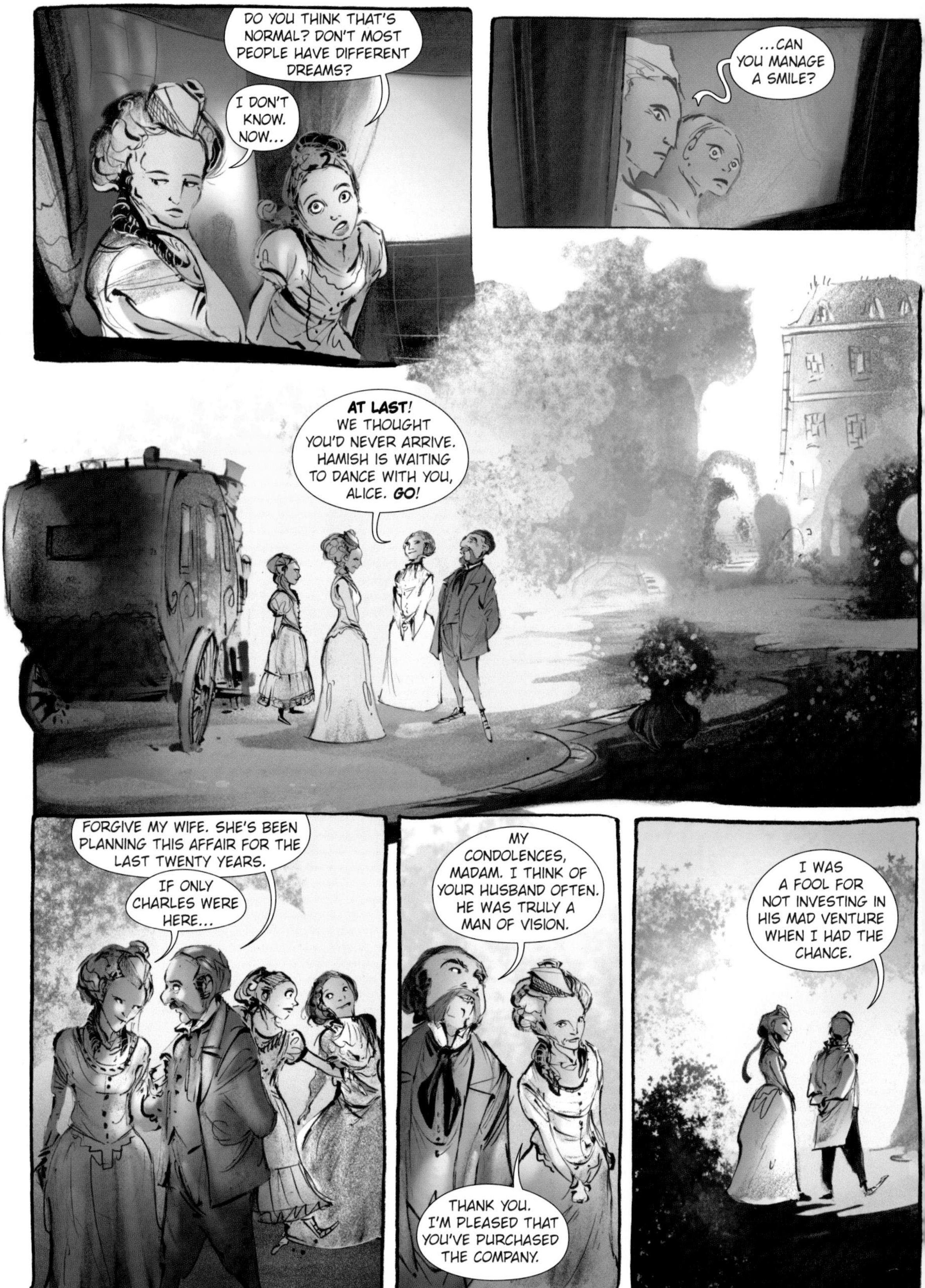
DO YOU THINK THAT'S NORMAL? DON'T MOST PEOPLE HAVE DIFFERENT DREAMS?
I DON'T KNOW. NOW...
...CAN YOU MANAGE A SMILE?
AT LAST! WE THOUGHT YOU'D NEVER ARRIVE. HAMISH IS WAITING TO DANCE WITH YOU, ALICE. GO!
FORGIVE MY WIFE. SHE'S BEEN PLANNING THIS AFFAIR FOR THE LAST TWENTY YEARS.
IF ONLY CHARLES WERE HERE...
MY CONDOLENCES, MADAM. I THINK OF YOUR HUSBAND OFTEN. HE WAS TRULY A MAN OF VISION.
THANK YOU. I'M PLEASED THAT YOU'VE PURCHASED THE COMPANY.
I WAS A FOOL FOR NOT INVESTING IN HIS MAD VENTURE WHEN I HAD THE CHANCE.

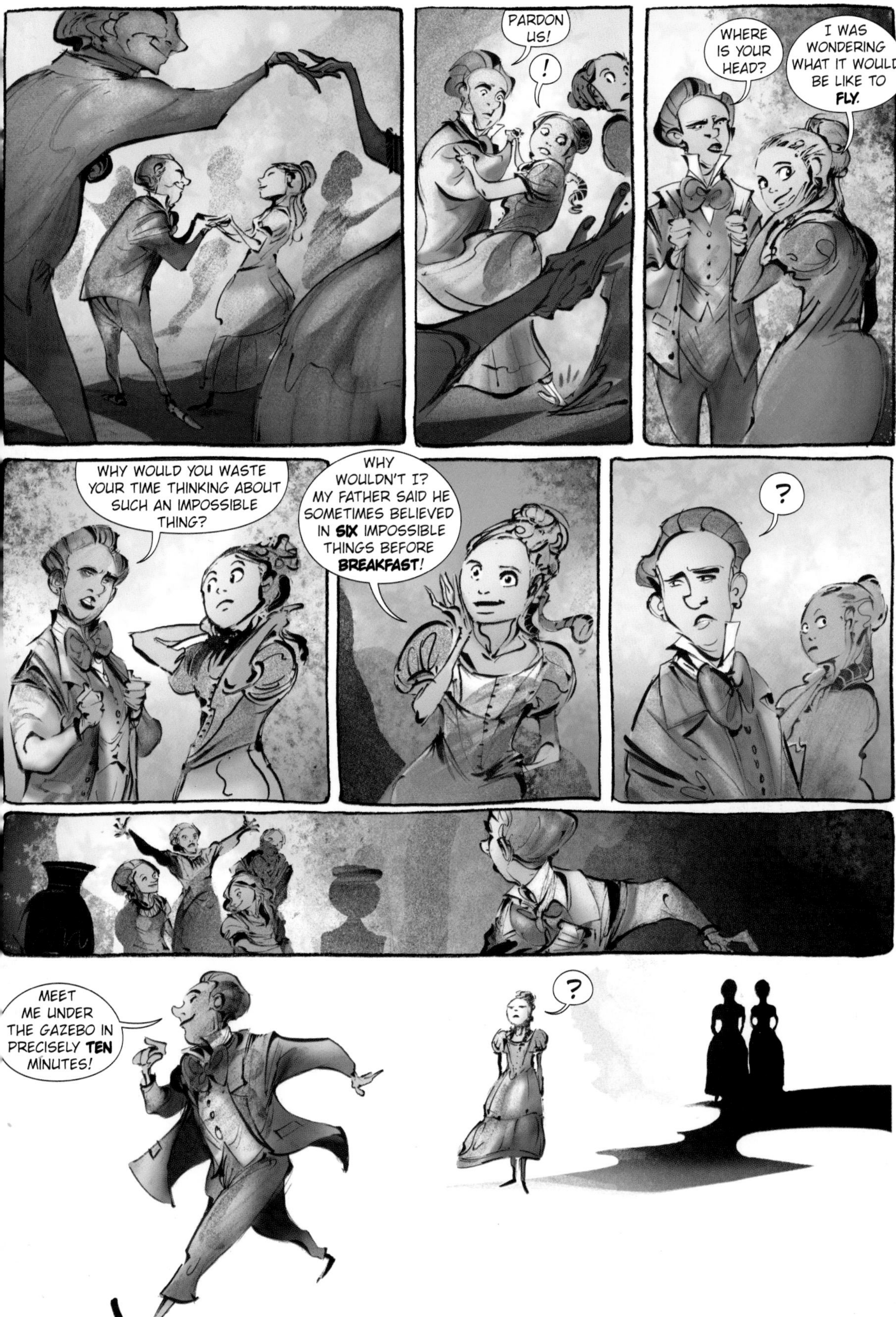
PARDON US!
!
WHERE IS YOUR HEAD?
I WAS WONDERING WHAT IT WOULD BE LIKE TO FLY.
WHY WOULD YOU WASTE YOUR TIME THINKING ABOUT SUCH AN IMPOSSIBLE THING?
WHY WOULDN'T I? MY FATHER SAID HE SOMETIMES BELIEVED IN SIX IMPOSSIBLE THINGS BEFORE BREAKFAST!
?
MEET ME UNDER THE GAZEBO IN PRECISELY TEN MINUTES!
?

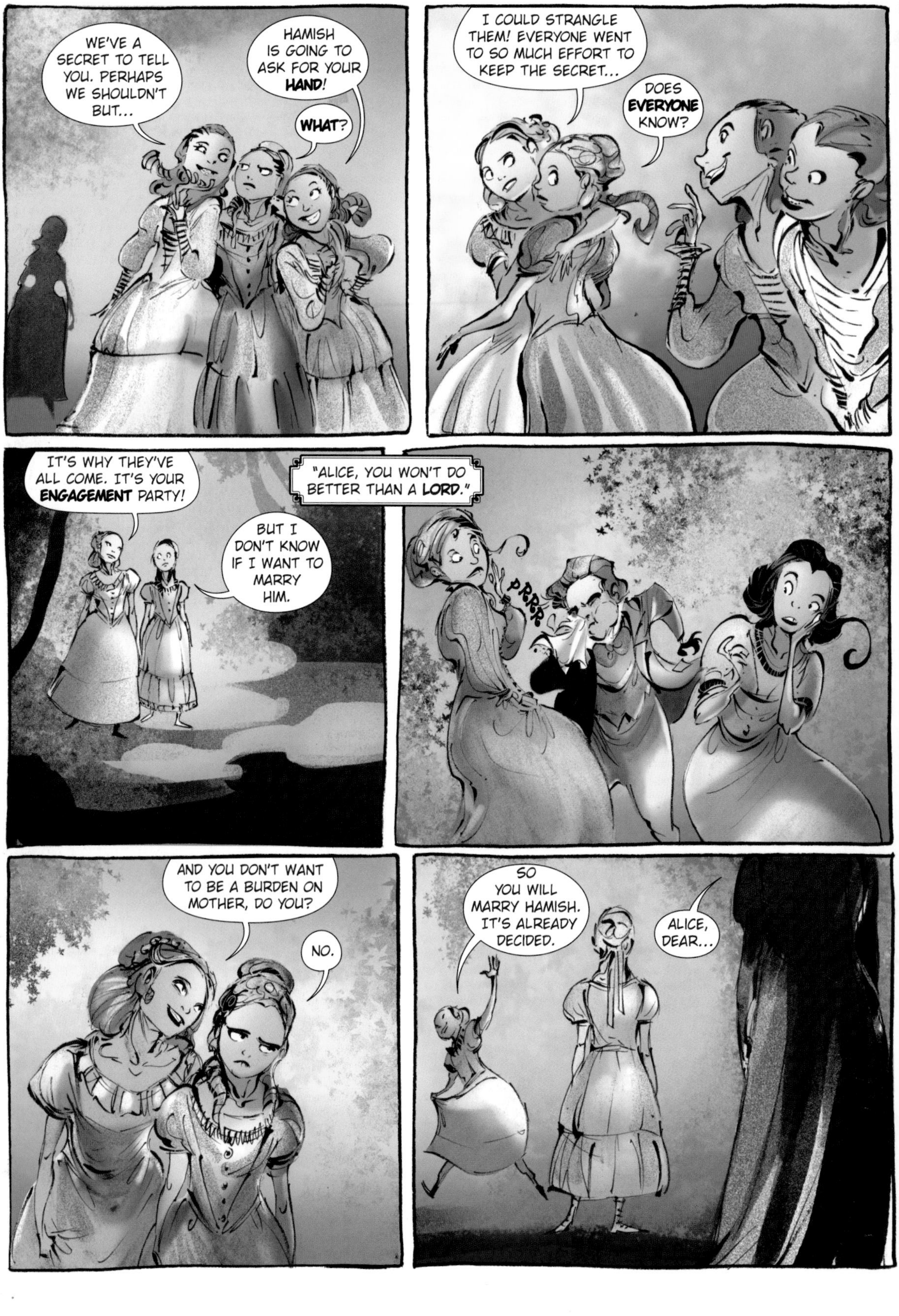
WE'VE A SECRET TO TELL YOU. PERHAPS WE SHOULDN'T BUT...
HAMISH IS GOING TO ASK FOR YOUR **HAND**!
WHAT?
I COULD STRANGLE THEM! EVERYONE WENT TO SO MUCH EFFORT TO KEEP THE SECRET...
DOES **EVERYONE** KNOW?
IT'S WHY THEY'VE ALL COME. IT'S YOUR **ENGAGEMENT** PARTY!
"ALICE, YOU WON'T DO BETTER THAN A **LORD**."
BUT I DON'T KNOW IF I WANT TO MARRY HIM.
PRRRR
AND YOU DON'T WANT TO BE A BURDEN ON MOTHER, DO YOU?
NO.
SO YOU WILL MARRY HAMISH. IT'S ALREADY DECIDED.
ALICE, DEAR...

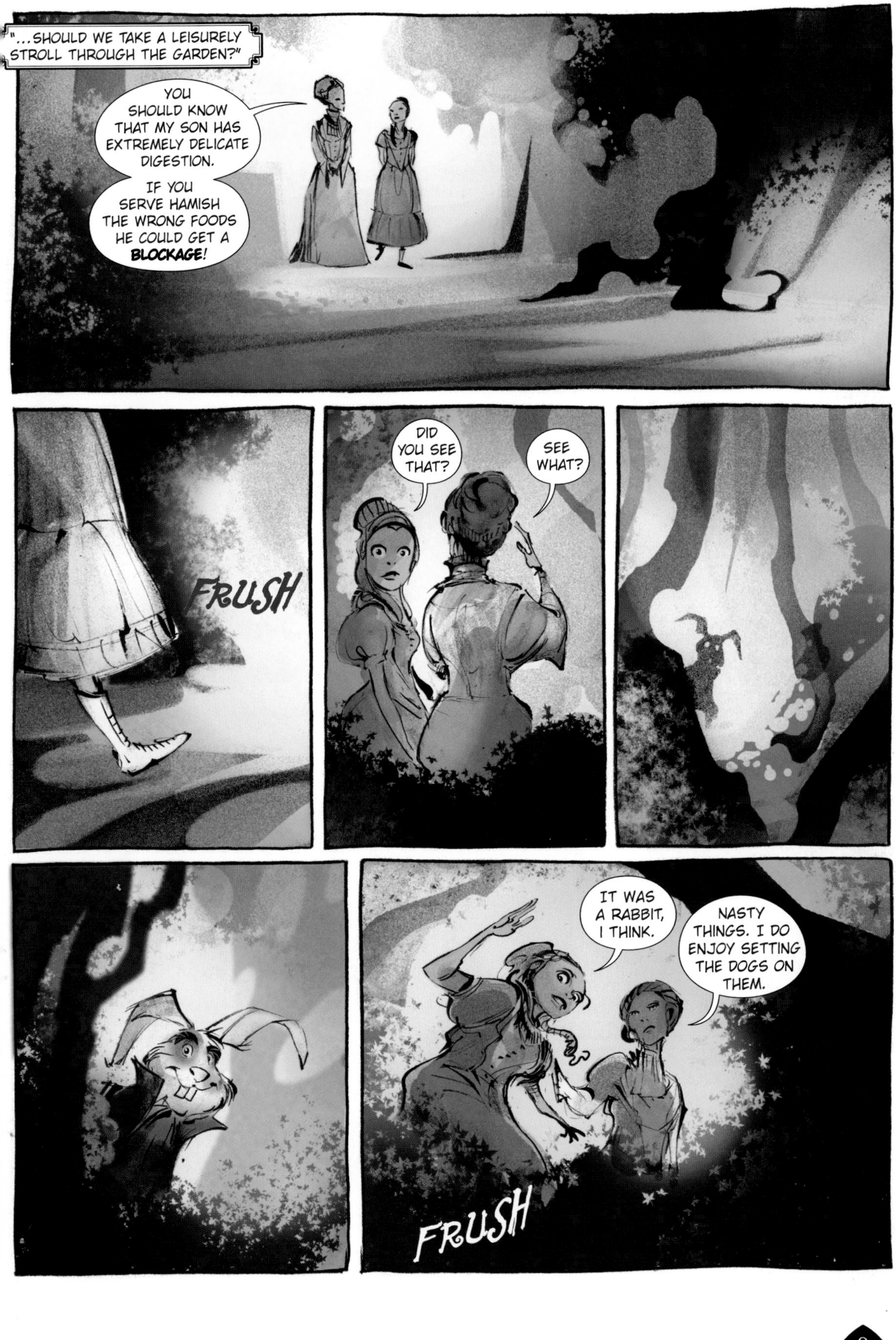
"...SHOULD WE TAKE A LEISURELY STROLL THROUGH THE GARDEN?"
YOU SHOULD KNOW THAT MY SON HAS EXTREMELY DELICATE DIGESTION.
IF YOU SERVE HAMISH THE WRONG FOODS HE COULD GET A **BLOCKAGE**!
FRUSH
DID YOU SEE THAT?
SEE WHAT?
IT WAS A RABBIT, I THINK.
NASTY THINGS. I DO ENJOY SETTING THE DOGS ON THEM.
FRUSH

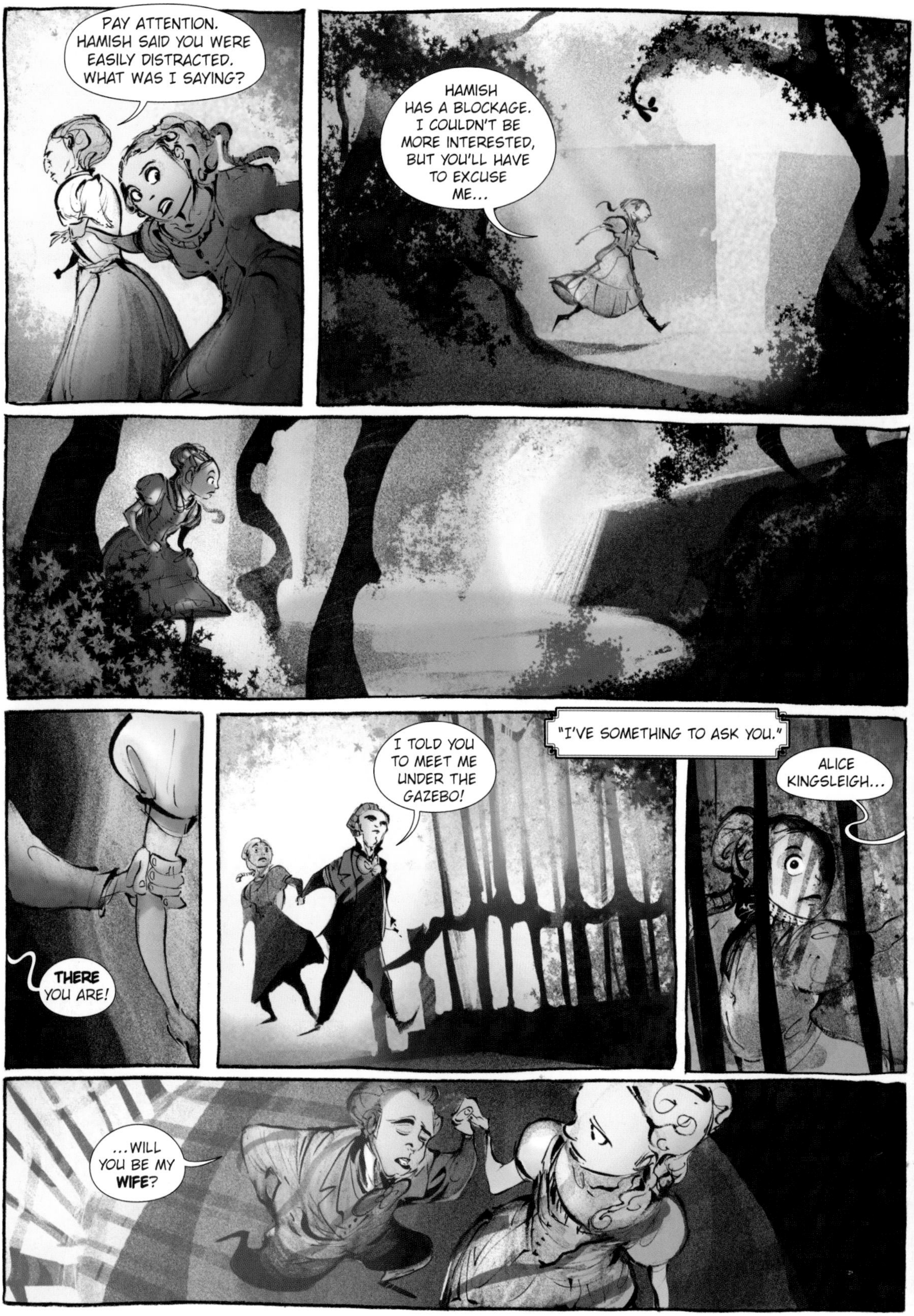
PAY ATTENTION. HAMISH SAID YOU WERE EASILY DISTRACTED. WHAT WAS I SAYING?
HAMISH HAS A BLOCKAGE. I COULDN'T BE MORE INTERESTED, BUT YOU'LL HAVE TO EXCUSE ME...
THERE YOU ARE!
I TOLD YOU TO MEET ME UNDER THE GAZEBO!
"I'VE SOMETHING TO ASK YOU."
ALICE KINGSLEIGH...
...WILL YOU BE MY WIFE?

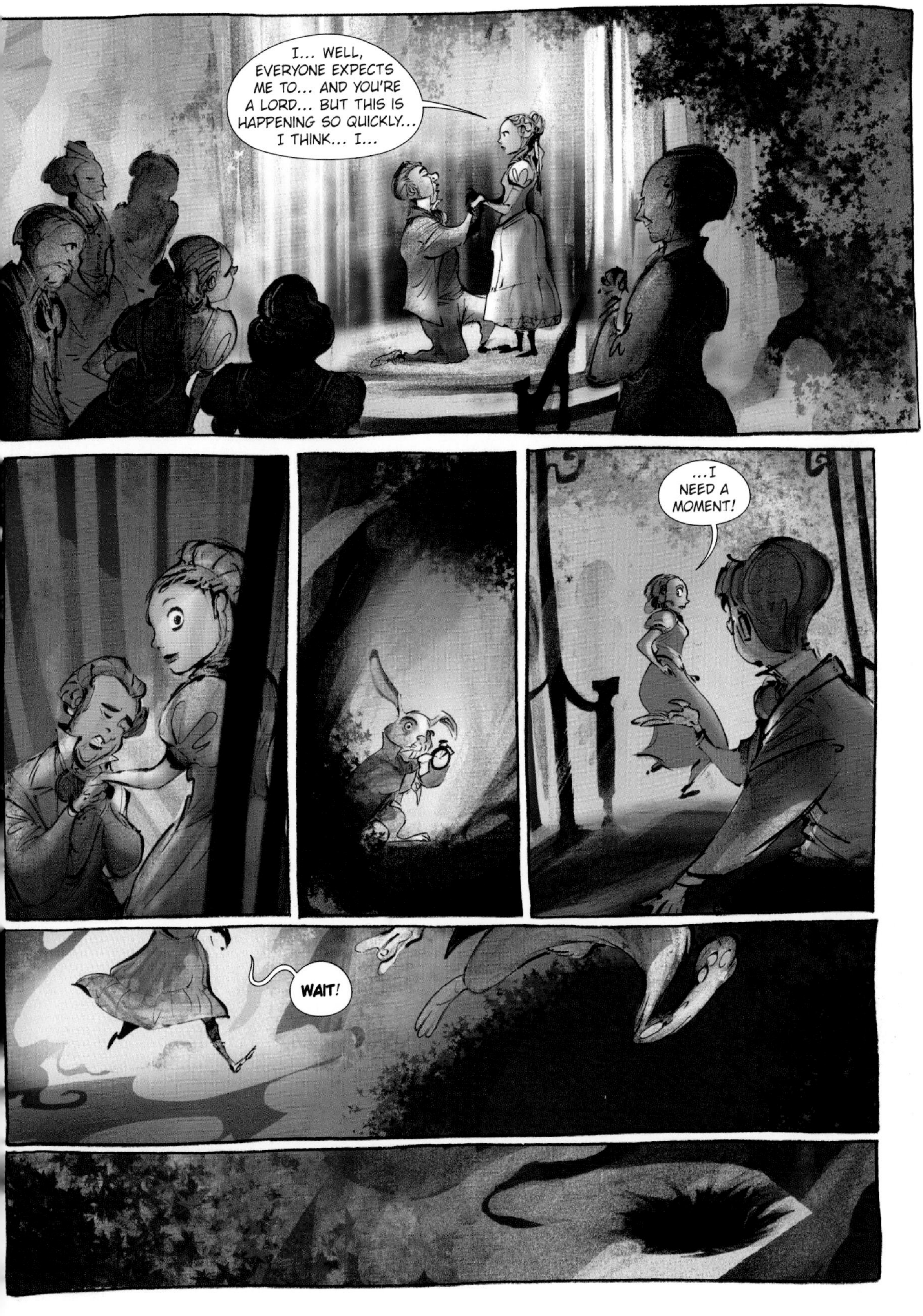
I... WELL, EVERYONE EXPECTS ME TO... AND YOU'RE A LORD... BUT THIS IS HAPPENING SO QUICKLY... I THINK... I...
...I NEED A MOMENT!
WAIT!

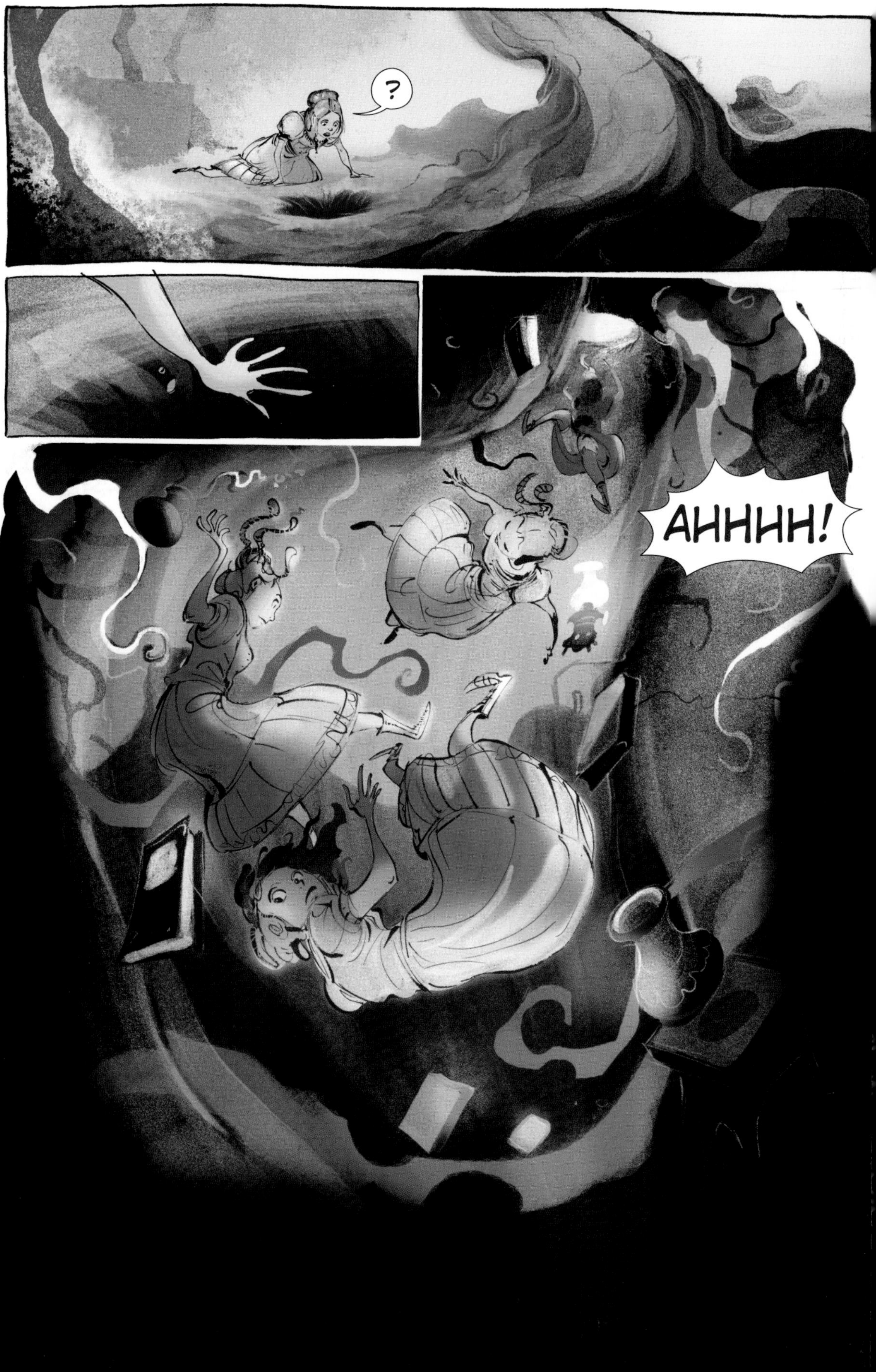
?
AHHHH!

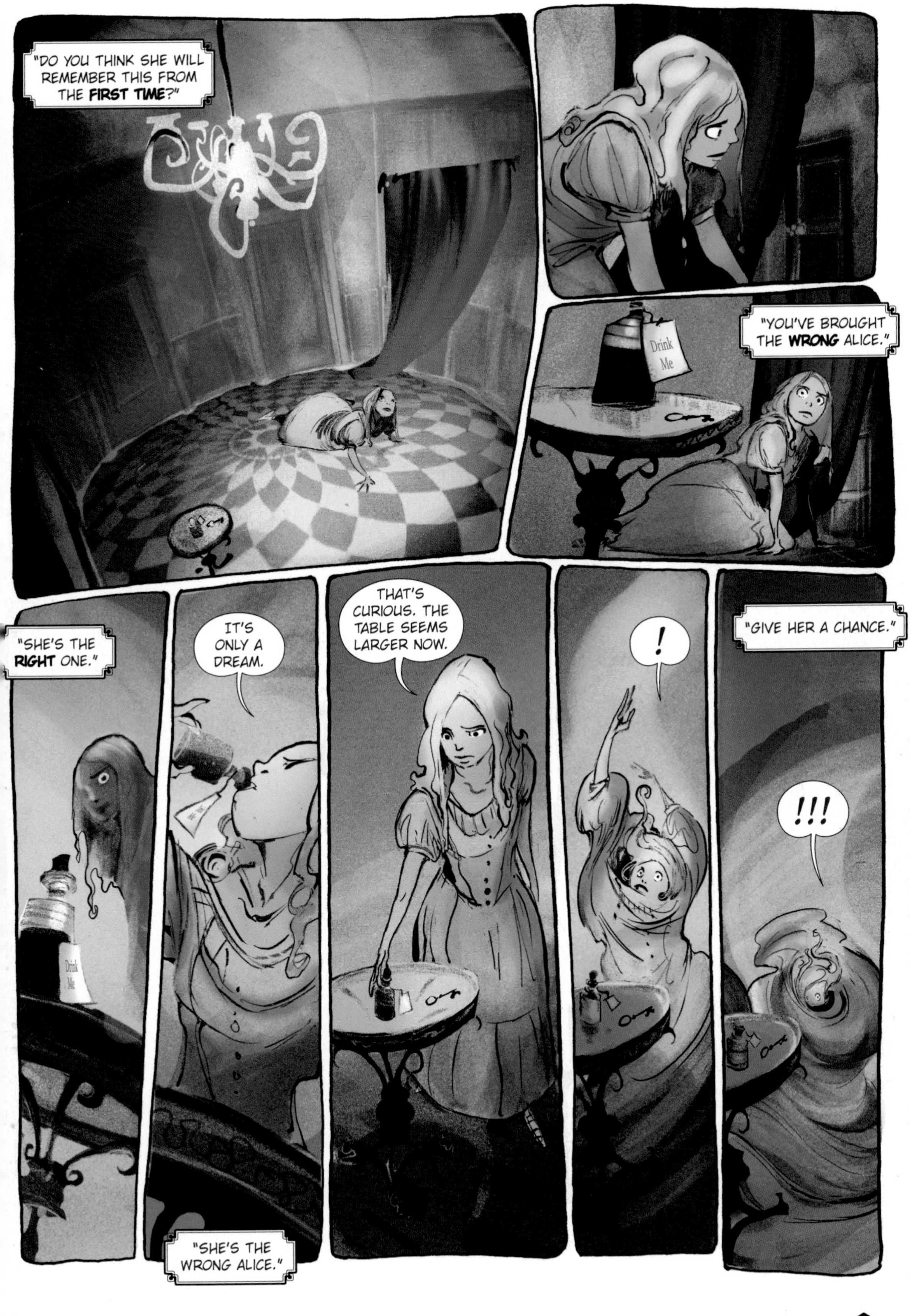
"DO YOU THINK SHE WILL REMEMBER THIS FROM THE **FIRST TIME**?"
"YOU'VE BROUGHT THE **WRONG** ALICE."
Drink Me
"SHE'S THE **RIGHT** ONE."
Drink Me
IT'S ONLY A DREAM.
"SHE'S THE WRONG ALICE."
THAT'S CURIOUS. THE TABLE SEEMS LARGER NOW.
!
"GIVE HER A CHANCE."
!!!

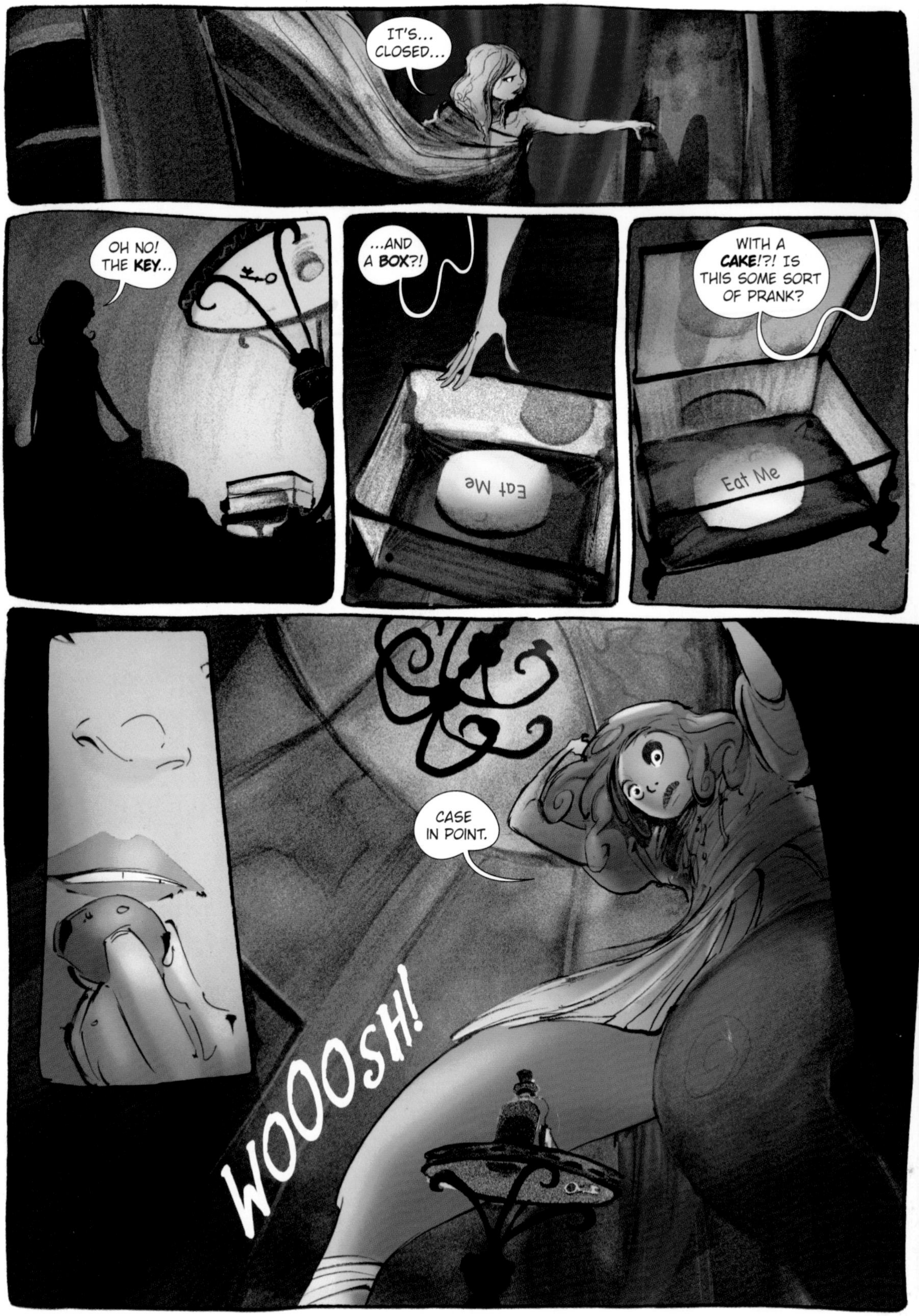
IT'S... CLOSED...
OH NO! THE **KEY**...
...AND A **BOX**?!
Eat Me
WITH A **CAKE**!?! IS THIS SOME SORT OF PRANK?
Eat Me
CASE IN POINT.
WOOOSH!

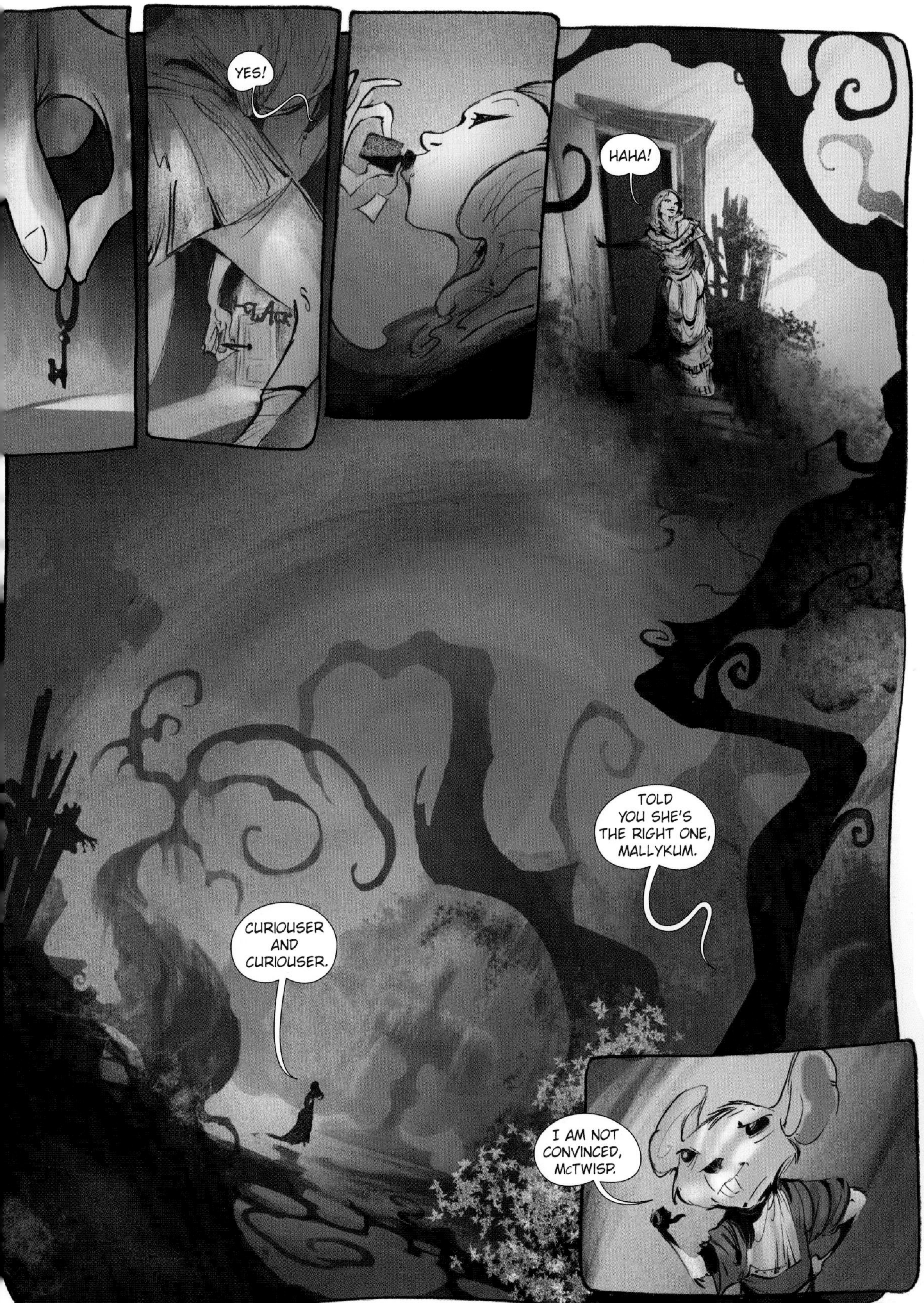
YES!
HAHA!
TOLD YOU SHE'S THE RIGHT ONE, MALLYKUM.
CURIOUSER AND CURIOUSER.
I AM NOT CONVINCED, McTWISP.

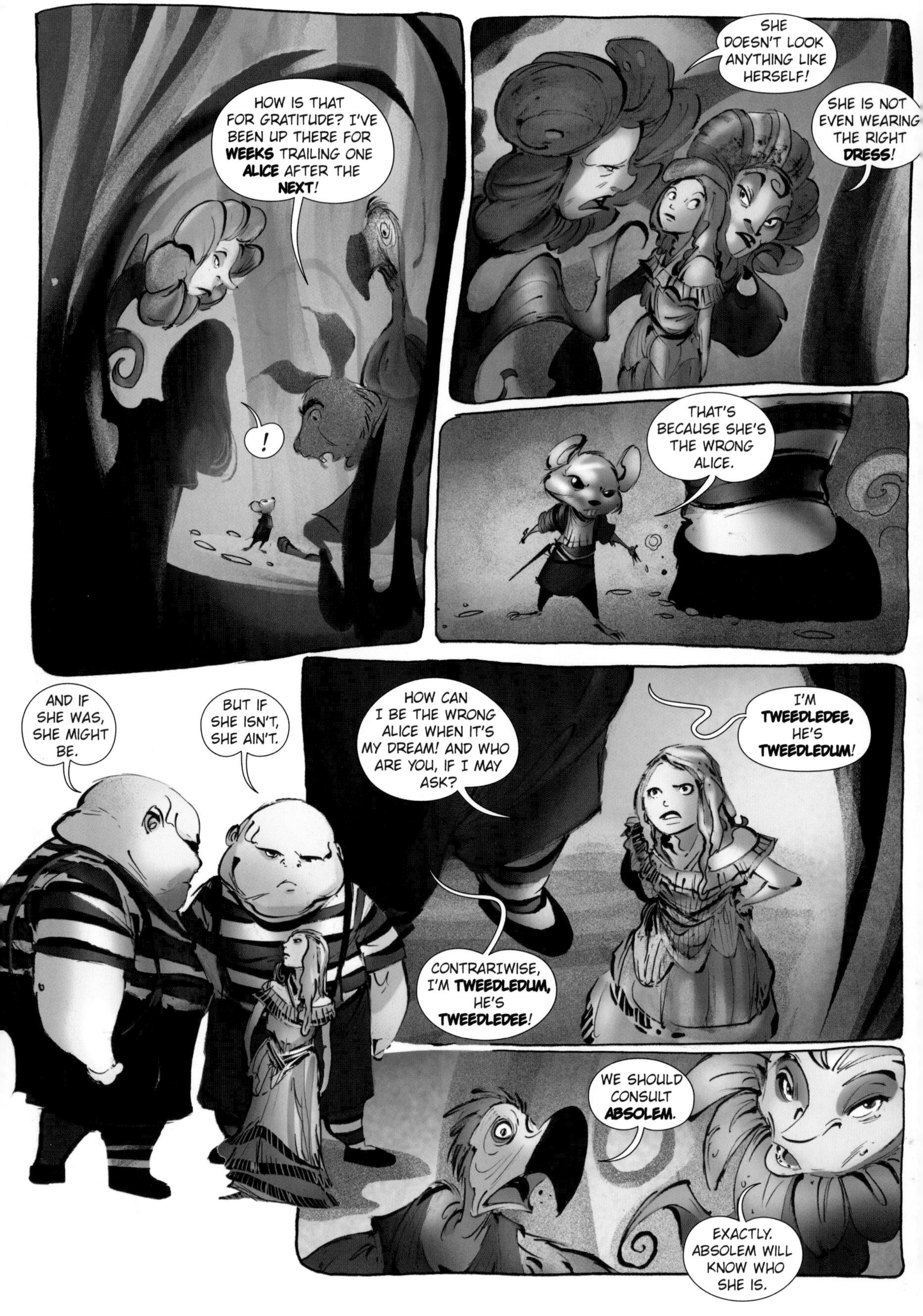
HOW IS THAT FOR GRATITUDE? I'VE BEEN UP THERE FOR **WEEKS** TRAILING ONE **ALICE** AFTER THE **NEXT**!
!
SHE DOESN'T LOOK ANYTHING LIKE HERSELF!
SHE IS NOT EVEN WEARING THE RIGHT **DRESS**!
THAT'S BECAUSE SHE'S THE WRONG ALICE.
AND IF SHE WAS, SHE MIGHT BE.
BUT IF SHE ISN'T, SHE AIN'T.
HOW CAN I BE THE WRONG ALICE WHEN IT'S MY DREAM! AND WHO ARE YOU, IF I MAY ASK?
I'M **TWEEDLEDEE,** HE'S **TWEEDLEDUM**!
CONTRARIWISE, I'M **TWEEDLEDUM,** HE'S **TWEEDLEDEE**!
WE SHOULD CONSULT **ABSOLEM**.
EXACTLY. ABSOLEM WILL KNOW WHO SHE IS.

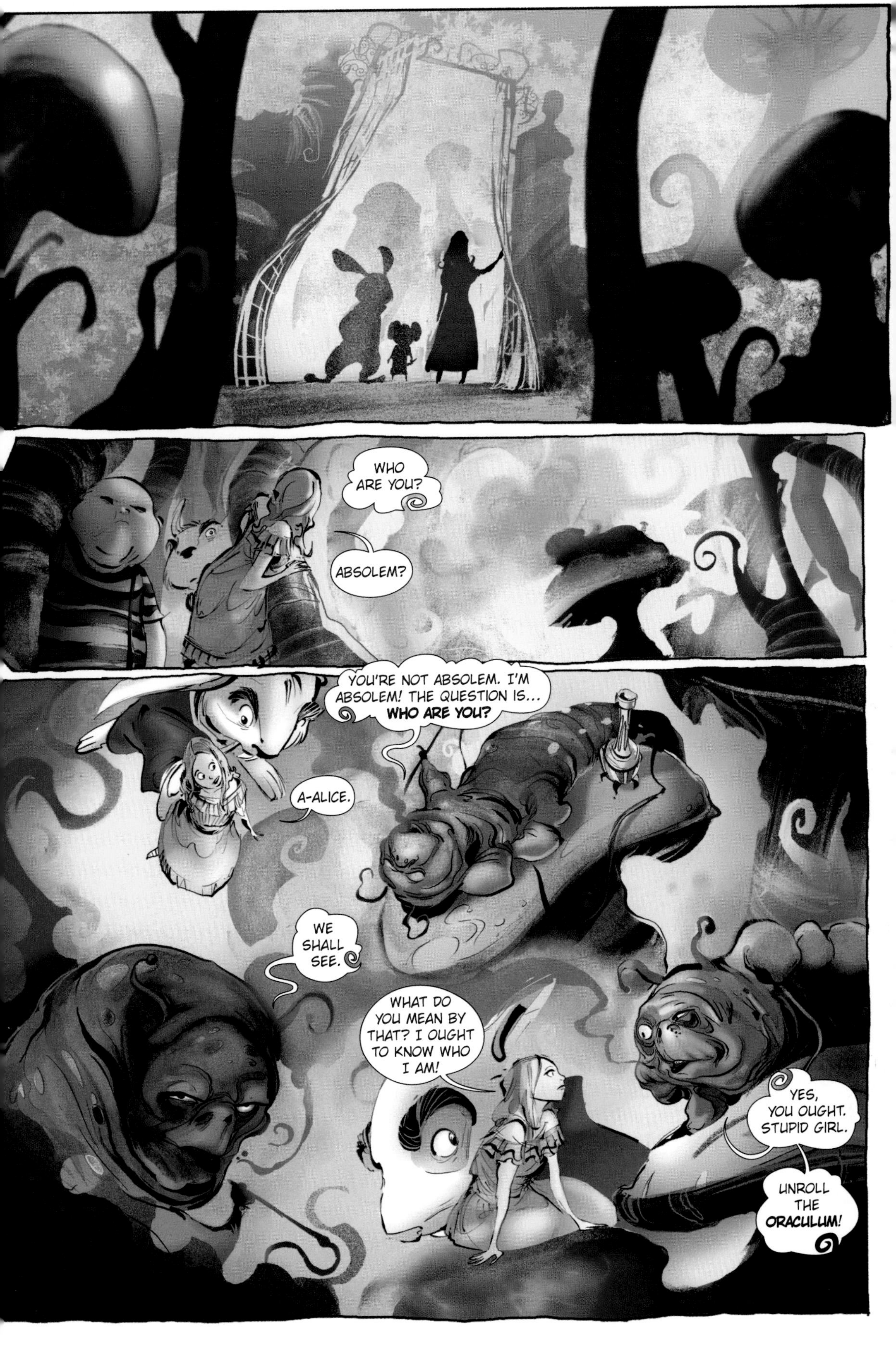
WHO ARE YOU?
ABSOLEM?
YOU'RE NOT ABSOLEM. I'M ABSOLEM! THE QUESTION IS... **WHO ARE YOU?**
A-ALICE.
WE SHALL SEE.
WHAT DO YOU MEAN BY THAT? I OUGHT TO KNOW WHO I AM!
YES, YOU OUGHT. STUPID GIRL.
UNROLL THE **ORACULUM!**

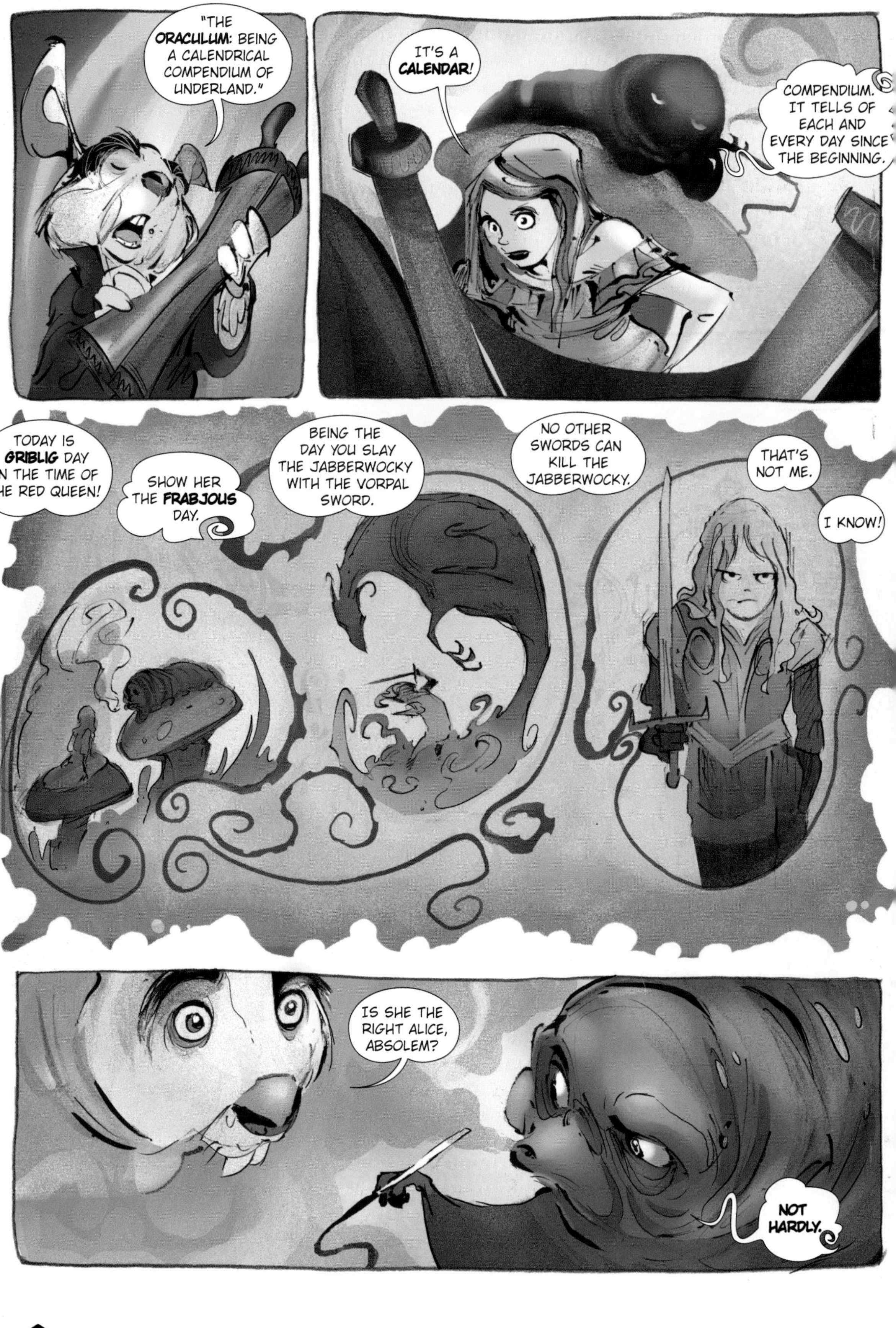
"THE ORACULUM: BEING A CALENDRICAL COMPENDIUM OF UNDERLAND."
IT'S A CALENDAR!
COMPENDIUM. IT TELLS OF EACH AND EVERY DAY SINCE THE BEGINNING.
TODAY IS GRIBLIG DAY IN THE TIME OF THE RED QUEEN!
SHOW HER THE FRABJOUS DAY.
BEING THE DAY YOU SLAY THE JABBERWOCKY WITH THE VORPAL SWORD.
NO OTHER SWORDS CAN KILL THE JABBERWOCKY.
THAT'S NOT ME.
I KNOW!
IS SHE THE RIGHT ALICE, ABSOLEM?
NOT HARDLY.

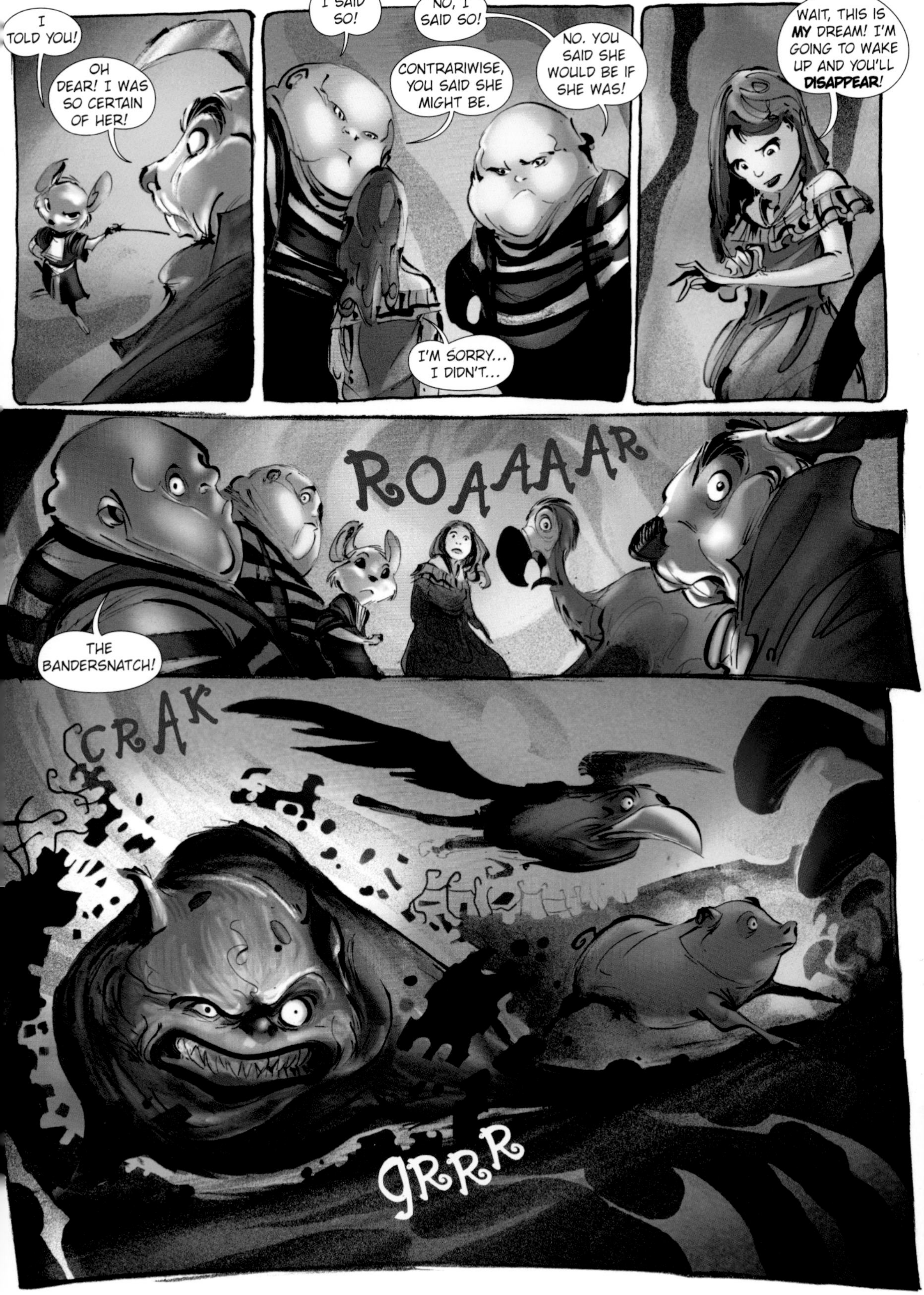

I TOLD YOU!
OH DEAR! I WAS SO CERTAIN OF HER!
I SAID SO!
NO, I SAID SO!
CONTRARIWISE, YOU SAID SHE MIGHT BE.
NO. YOU SAID SHE WOULD BE IF SHE WAS!
I'M SORRY... I DIDN'T...
WAIT, THIS IS **MY** DREAM! I'M GOING TO WAKE UP AND YOU'LL **DISAPPEAR**!
ROAAAAR
THE BANDERSNATCH!
CRAK
GRRR

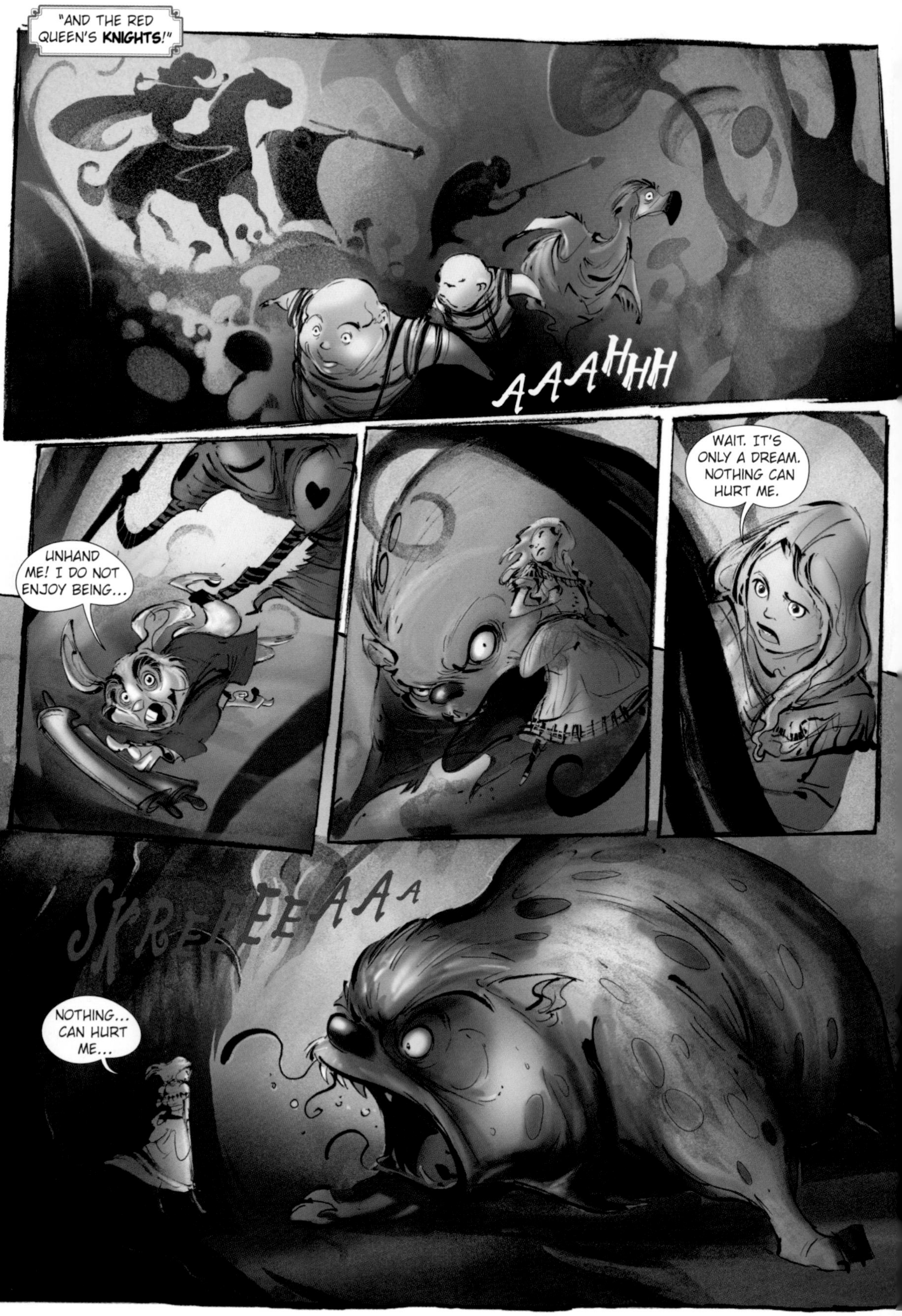
"AND THE RED QUEEN'S **KNIGHTS**!"
AAAHHH
UNHAND ME! I DO NOT ENJOY BEING...
WAIT. IT'S ONLY A DREAM. NOTHING CAN HURT ME.
SKREEEEAAAA
NOTHING... CAN HURT ME...

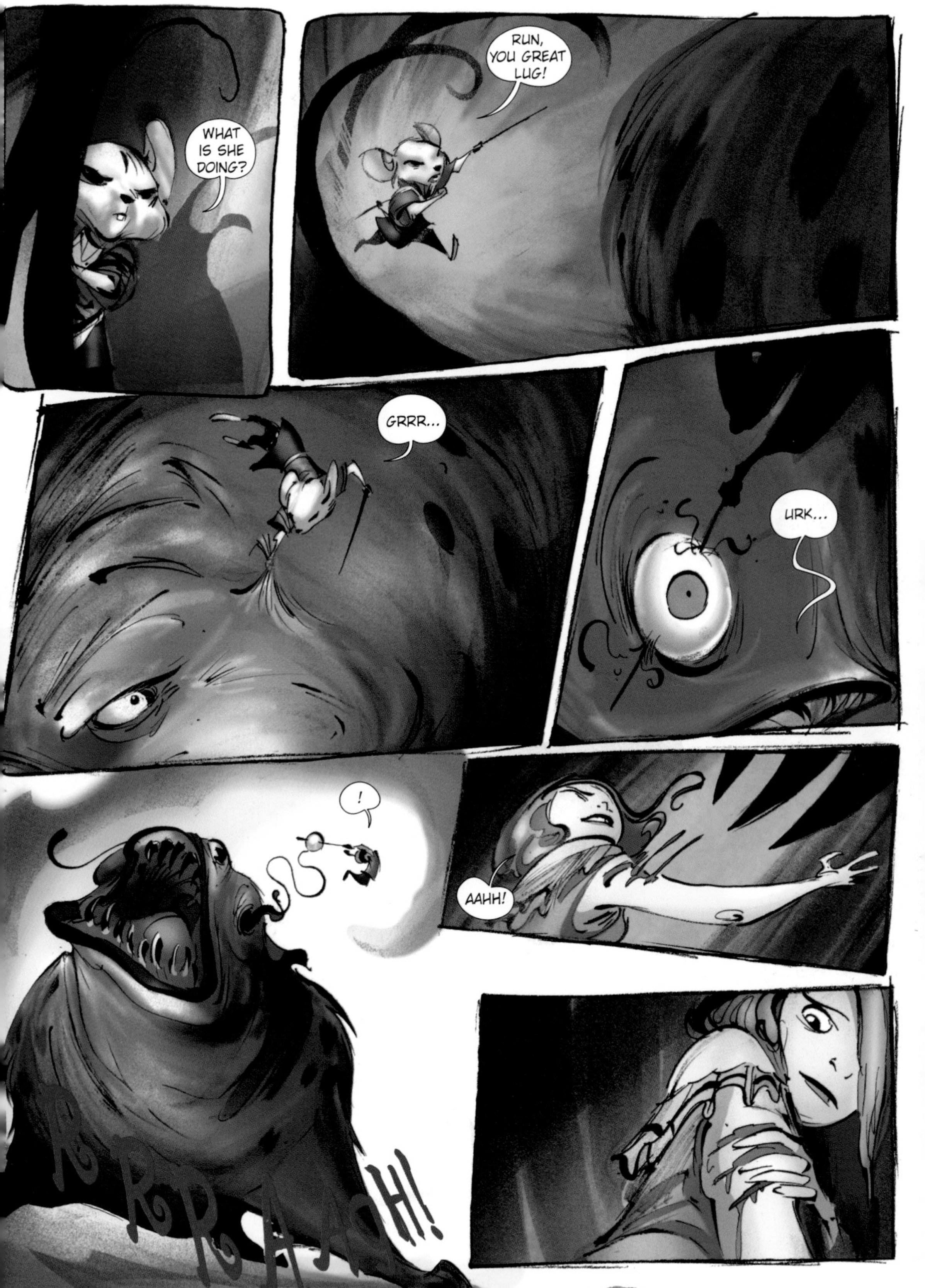
WHAT IS SHE DOING?
RUN, YOU GREAT LUG!
GRRR...
URK...
!
AAHH!
RRRAAH!

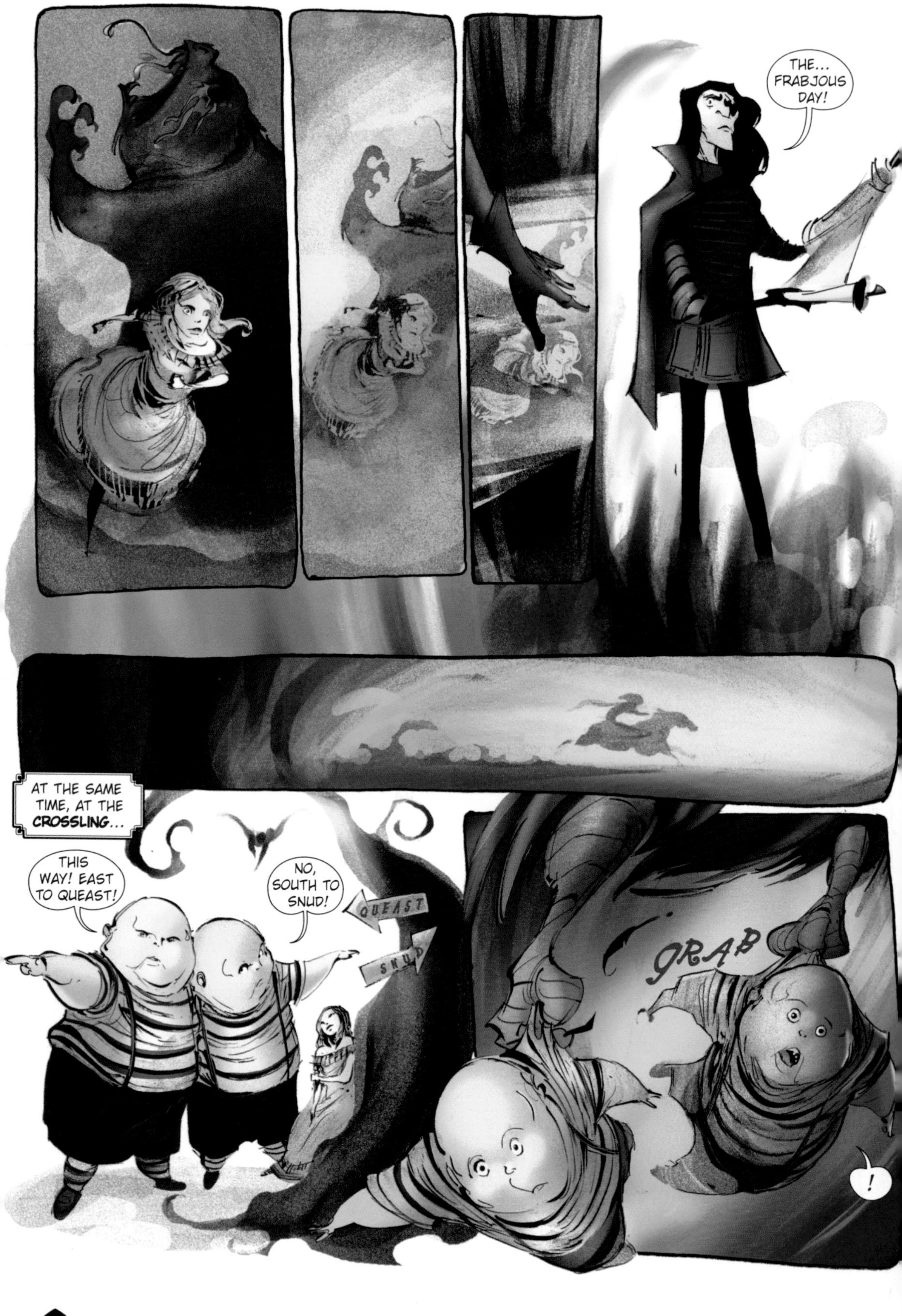
THE... FRABJOUS DAY!
AT THE SAME TIME, AT THE CROSSLING...
THIS WAY! EAST TO QUEAST!
NO, SOUTH TO SNUD!
QUEAST
SNUD
GRAB
!

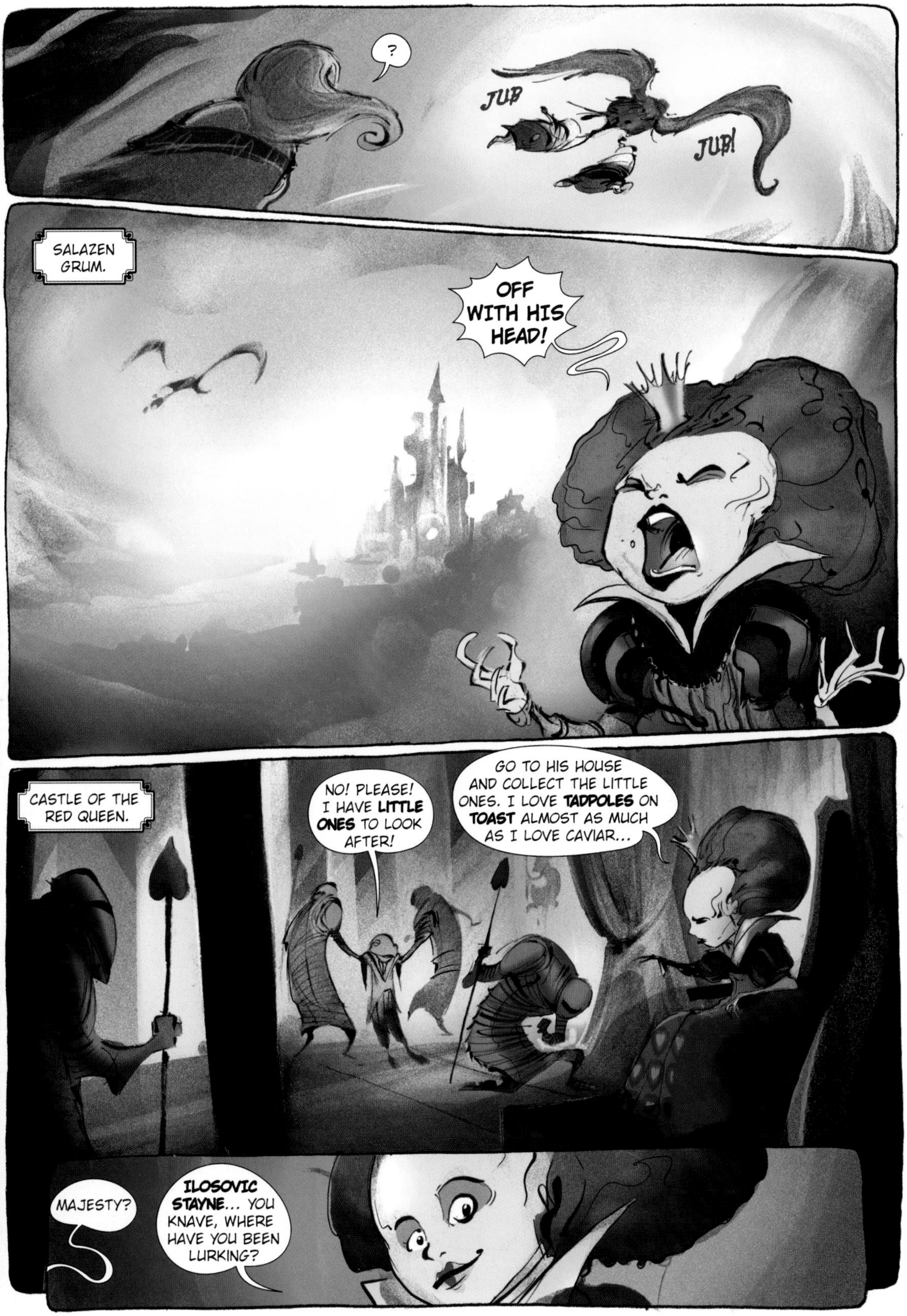
?
JUB
JUB!
SALAZEN GRUM.
OFF WITH HIS HEAD!
CASTLE OF THE RED QUEEN.
NO! PLEASE! I HAVE **LITTLE ONES** TO LOOK AFTER!
GO TO HIS HOUSE AND COLLECT THE LITTLE ONES. I LOVE **TADPOLES** ON **TOAST** ALMOST AS MUCH AS I LOVE CAVIAR...
MAJESTY?
ILOSOVIC STAYNE... YOU KNAVE, WHERE HAVE YOU BEEN LURKING?

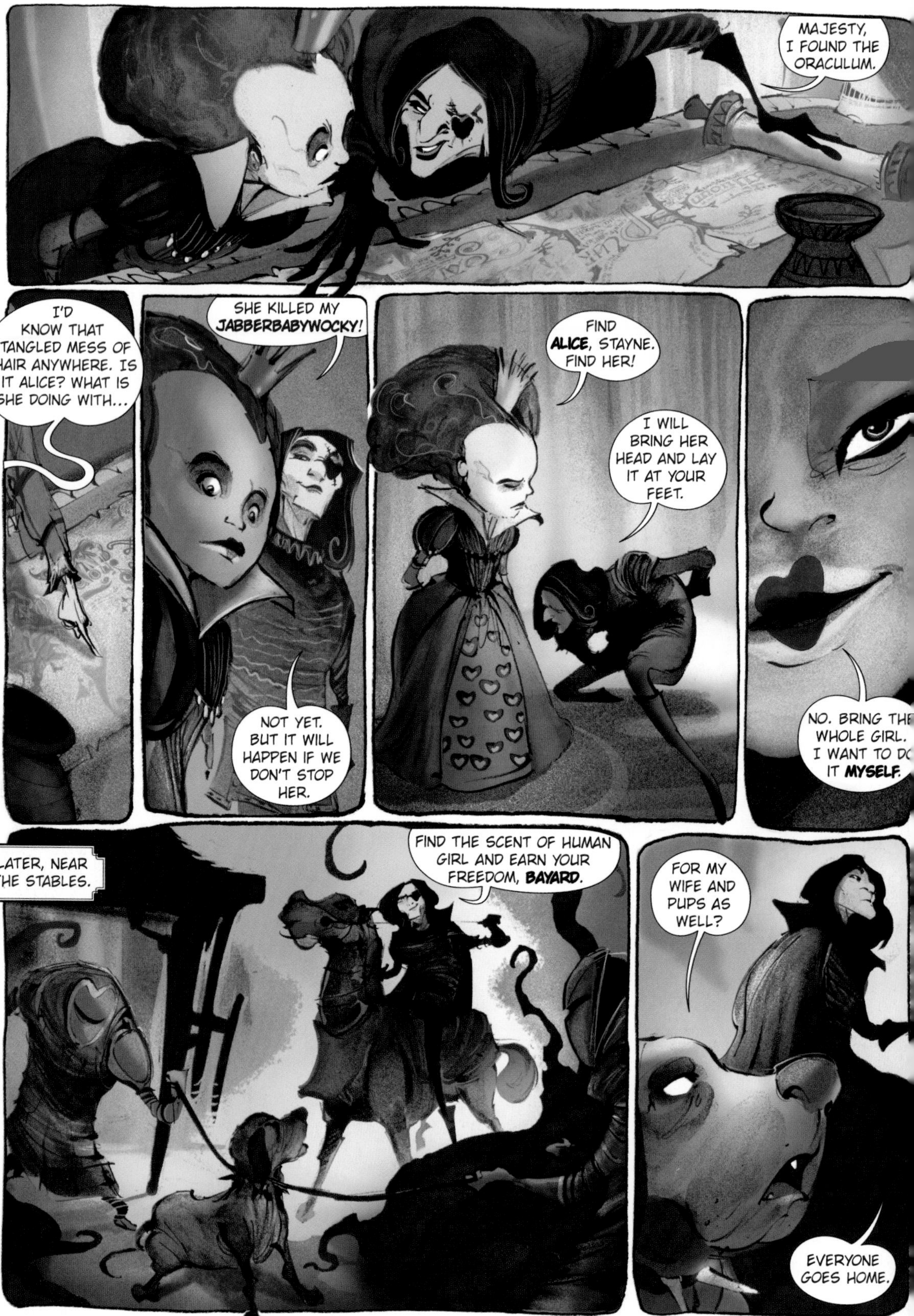
MAJESTY, I FOUND THE ORACULUM.
I'D KNOW THAT TANGLED MESS OF HAIR ANYWHERE. IS IT ALICE? WHAT IS SHE DOING WITH...
SHE KILLED MY JABBERBABYWOCKY!
NOT YET. BUT IT WILL HAPPEN IF WE DON'T STOP HER.
FIND ALICE, STAYNE. FIND HER!
I WILL BRING HER HEAD AND LAY IT AT YOUR FEET.
NO. BRING THE WHOLE GIRL. I WANT TO DO IT MYSELF.
LATER, NEAR THE STABLES.
FIND THE SCENT OF HUMAN GIRL AND EARN YOUR FREEDOM, BAYARD.
FOR MY WIFE AND PUPS AS WELL?
EVERYONE GOES HOME.

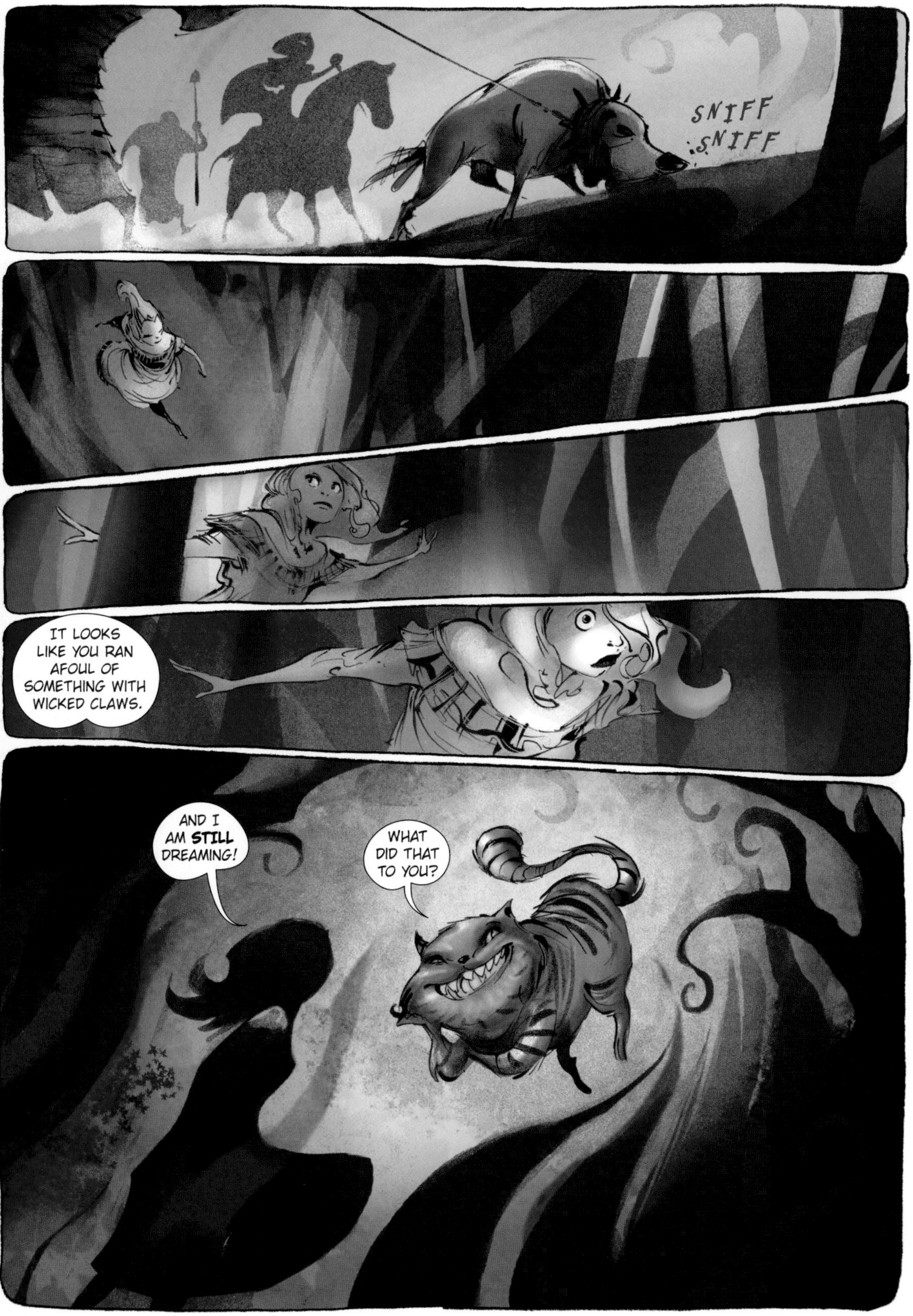
SNIFF
SNIFF
IT LOOKS LIKE YOU RAN AFOUL OF SOMETHING WITH WICKED CLAWS.
AND I AM **STILL** DREAMING!
WHAT DID THAT TO YOU?

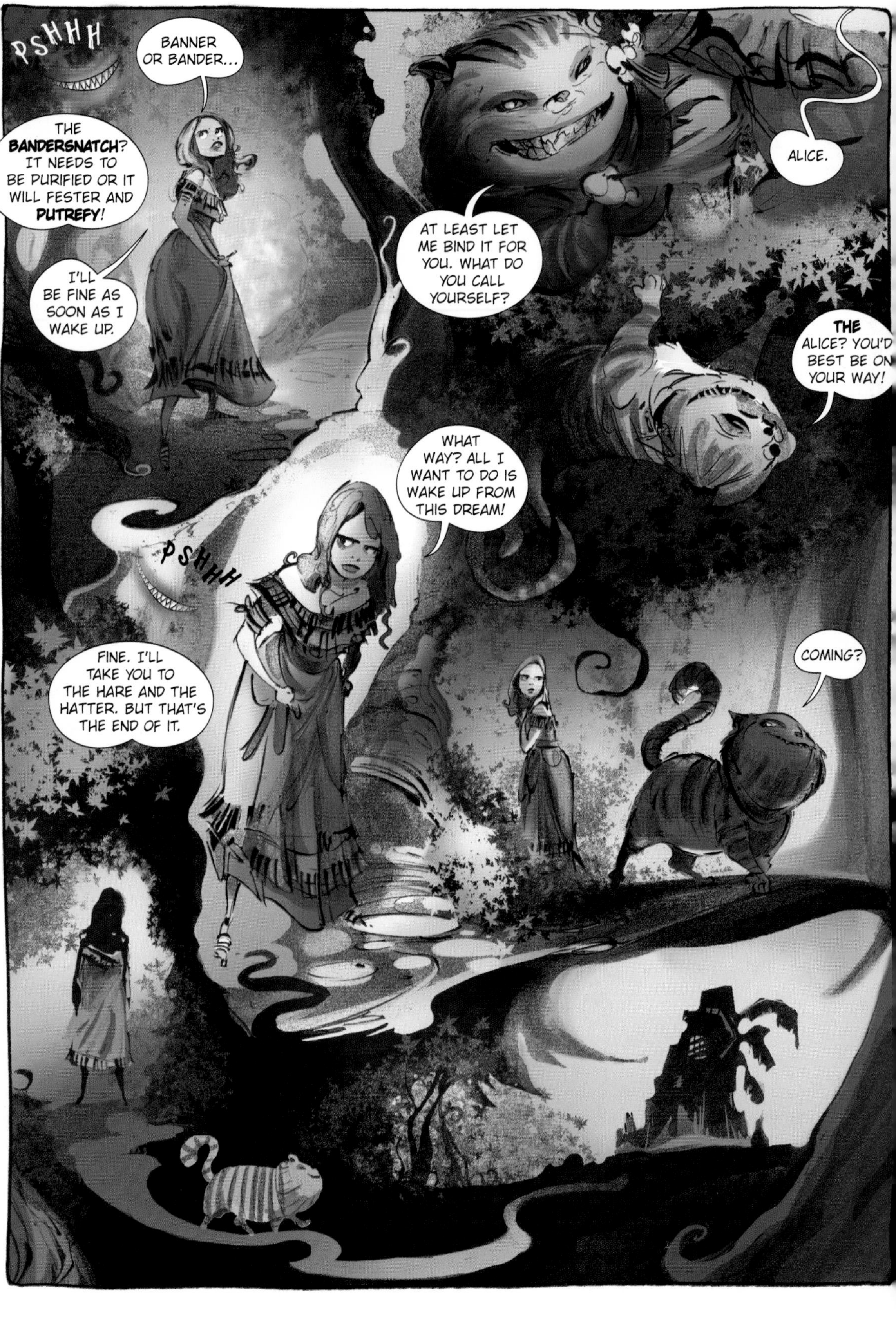
PSHHH
BANNER OR BANDER...
THE **BANDERSNATCH**? IT NEEDS TO BE PURIFIED OR IT WILL FESTER AND **PUTREFY**!
I'LL BE FINE AS SOON AS I WAKE UP.
AT LEAST LET ME BIND IT FOR YOU. WHAT DO YOU CALL YOURSELF?
ALICE.
THE ALICE? YOU'D BEST BE ON YOUR WAY!
WHAT WAY? ALL I WANT TO DO IS WAKE UP FROM THIS DREAM!
PSHHH
FINE. I'LL TAKE YOU TO THE HARE AND THE HATTER. BUT THAT'S THE END OF IT.
COMING?

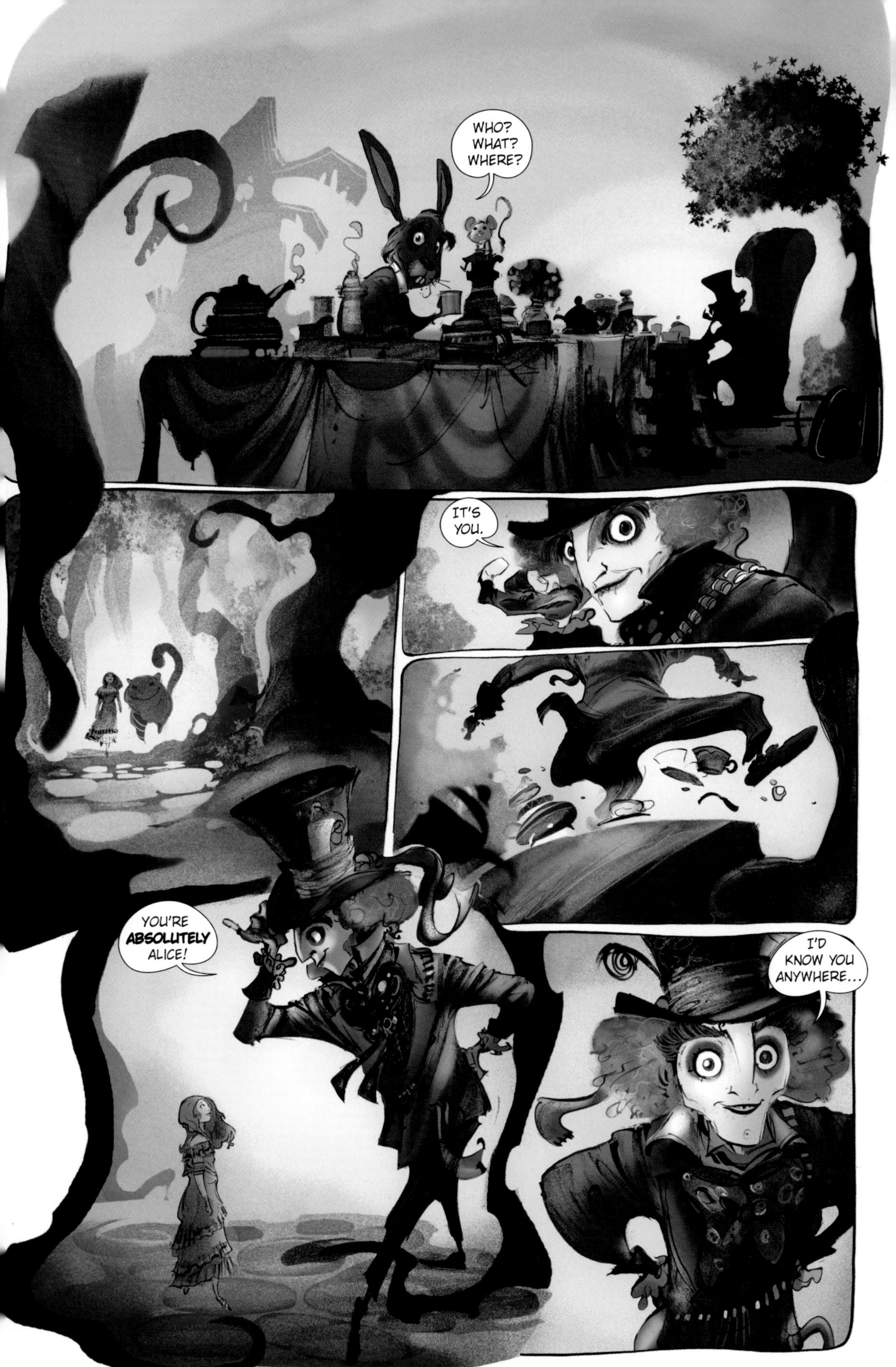
WHO?
WHAT?
WHERE?
IT'S YOU.
YOU'RE **ABSOLUTELY** ALICE!
I'D KNOW YOU ANYWHERE...

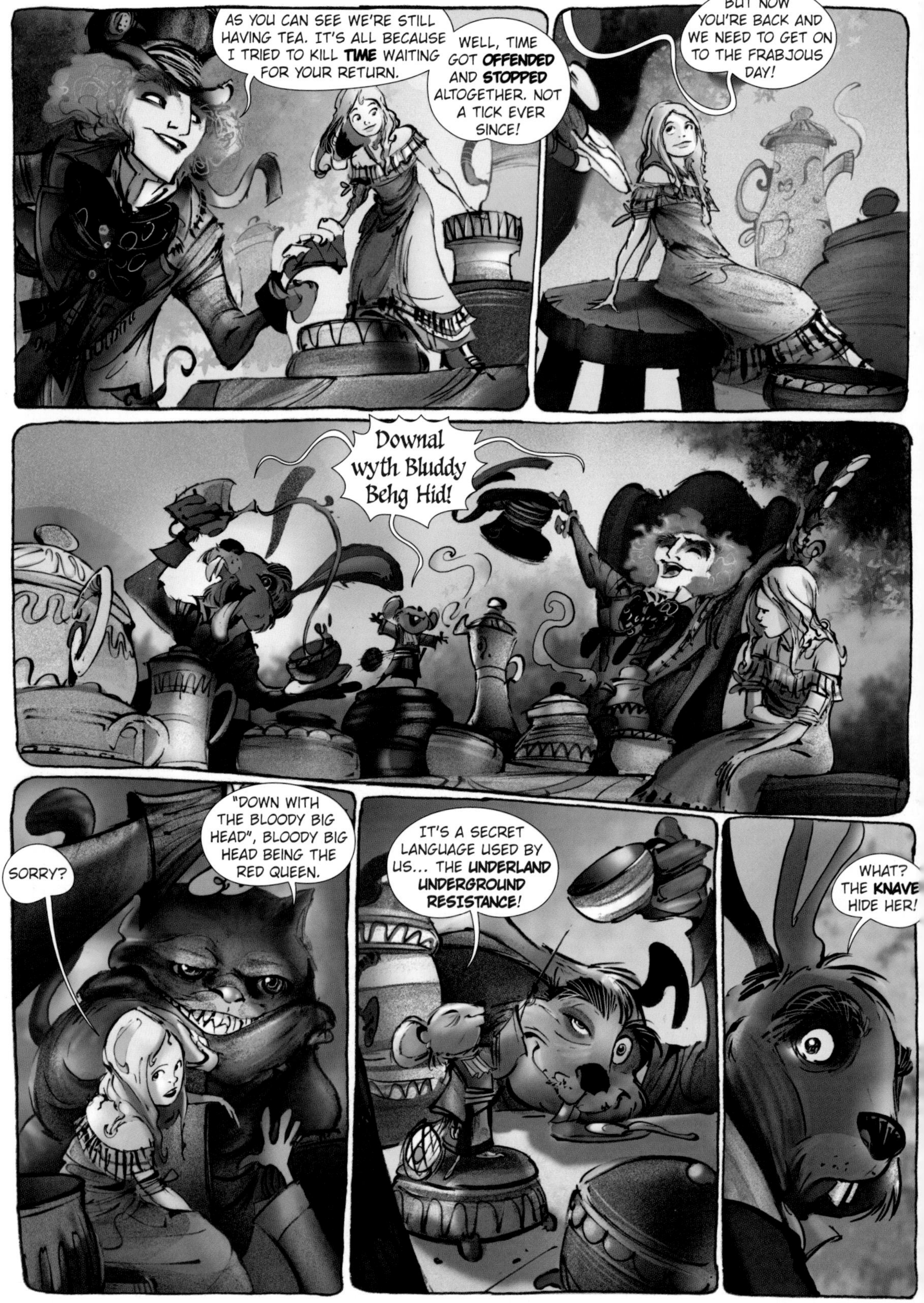
AS YOU CAN SEE WE'RE STILL HAVING TEA. IT'S ALL BECAUSE I TRIED TO KILL **TIME** WAITING FOR YOUR RETURN.
WELL, TIME GOT **OFFENDED** AND **STOPPED** ALTOGETHER. NOT A TICK EVER SINCE!
BUT NOW YOU'RE BACK AND WE NEED TO GET ON TO THE FRABJOUS DAY!
Downal wyth Bluddy Behg Hid!
SORRY?
"DOWN WITH THE BLOODY BIG HEAD", BLOODY BIG HEAD BEING THE RED QUEEN.
IT'S A SECRET LANGUAGE USED BY US... THE **UNDERLAND UNDERGROUND RESISTANCE**!
WHAT? THE **KNAVE** HIDE HER!

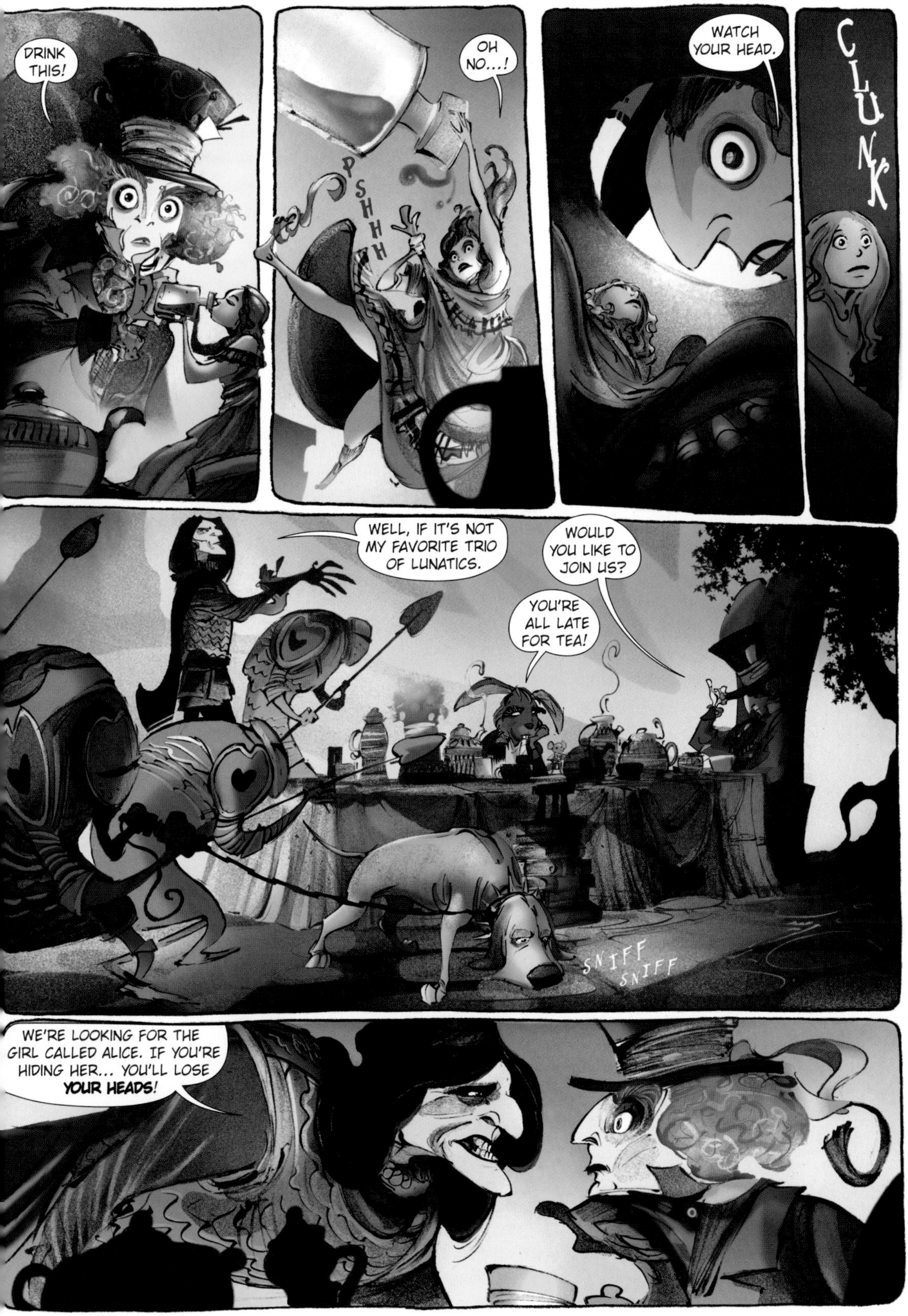
DRINK THIS!
OH NO...!
PSHHH
WATCH YOUR HEAD.
CLUNK
WELL, IF IT'S NOT MY FAVORITE TRIO OF LUNATICS.
WOULD YOU LIKE TO JOIN US?
YOU'RE ALL LATE FOR TEA!
SNIFF SNIFF
WE'RE LOOKING FOR THE GIRL CALLED ALICE. IF YOU'RE HIDING HER... YOU'LL LOSE **YOUR HEADS**!

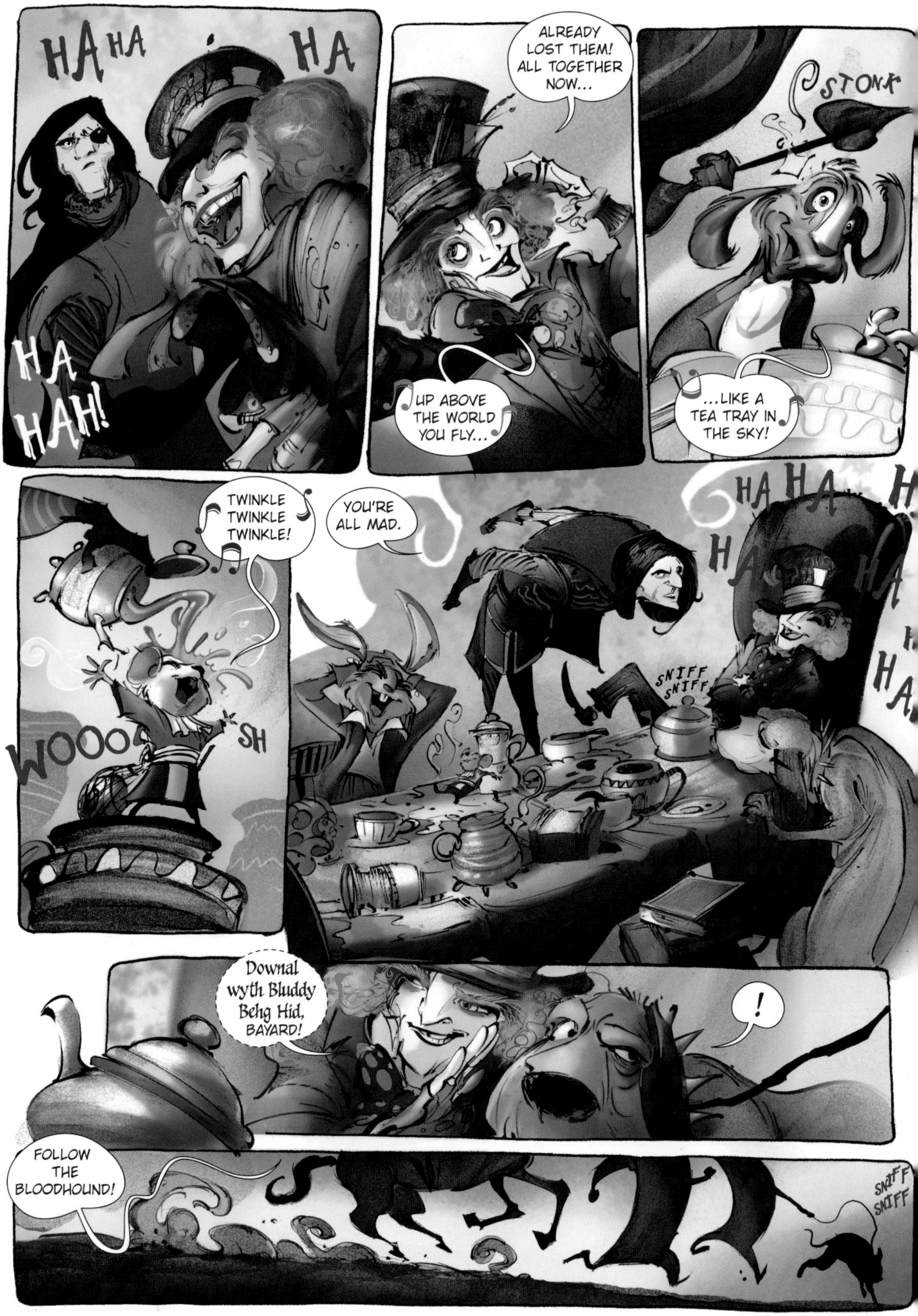
HA HA HA
HA HAH!
ALREADY LOST THEM! ALL TOGETHER NOW...
UP ABOVE THE WORLD YOU FLY...
STONK
...LIKE A TEA TRAY IN THE SKY!
TWINKLE TWINKLE TWINKLE!
WOOOSH
YOU'RE ALL MAD.
HA HA HA HA HA
SNIFF SNIFF
Downal wyth Bluddy Behg Hid, BAYARD!
!
FOLLOW THE BLOODHOUND!
SNIFF SNIFF

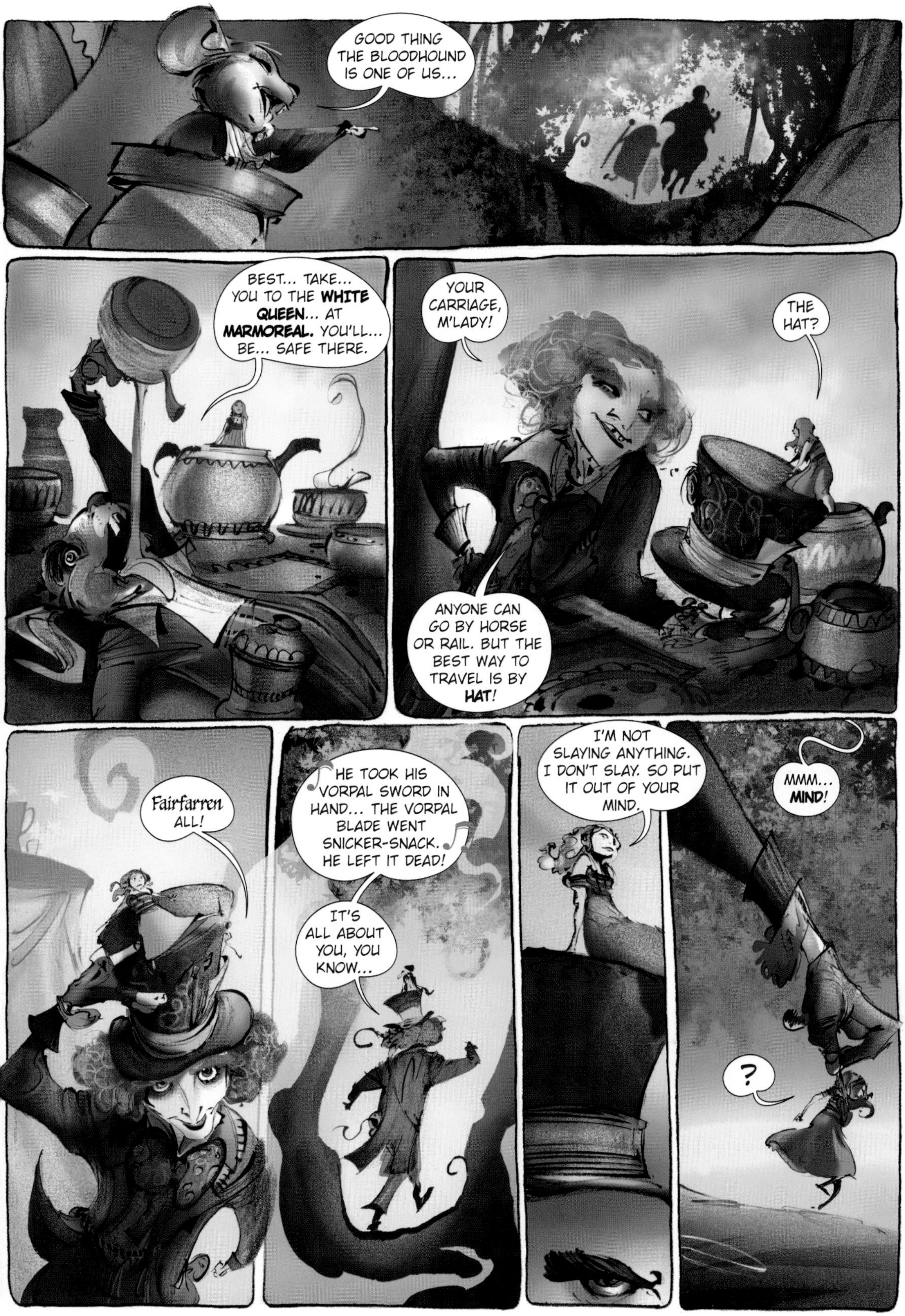
GOOD THING THE BLOODHOUND IS ONE OF US...
BEST... TAKE... YOU TO THE **WHITE QUEEN**... AT **MARMOREAL.** YOU'LL... BE... SAFE THERE.
YOUR CARRIAGE, M'LADY!
THE HAT?
ANYONE CAN GO BY HORSE OR RAIL. BUT THE BEST WAY TO TRAVEL IS BY **HAT**!
Fairfarren ALL!
HE TOOK HIS VORPAL SWORD IN HAND... THE VORPAL BLADE WENT SNICKER-SNACK. HE LEFT IT DEAD!
IT'S ALL ABOUT YOU, YOU KNOW...
I'M NOT SLAYING ANYTHING. I DON'T SLAY. SO PUT IT OUT OF YOUR MIND.
MMM... **MIND**!
?

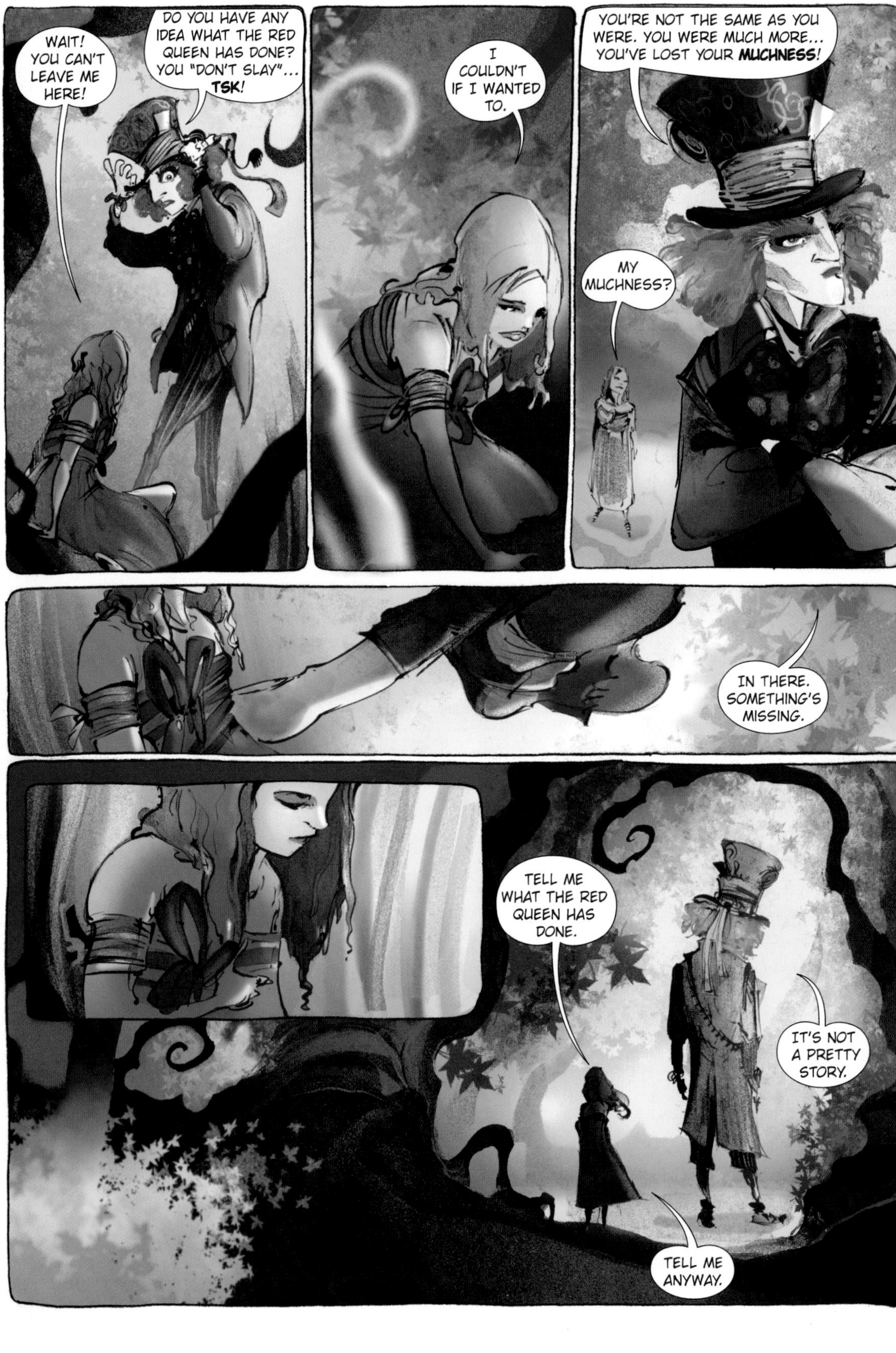
WAIT! YOU CAN'T LEAVE ME HERE!
DO YOU HAVE ANY IDEA WHAT THE RED QUEEN HAS DONE? YOU "DON'T SLAY"... **TSK**!
I COULDN'T IF I WANTED TO.
YOU'RE NOT THE SAME AS YOU WERE. YOU WERE MUCH MORE... YOU'VE LOST YOUR **MUCHNESS**!
MY MUCHNESS?
IN THERE. SOMETHING'S MISSING.
TELL ME WHAT THE RED QUEEN HAS DONE.
IT'S NOT A PRETTY STORY.
TELL ME ANYWAY.

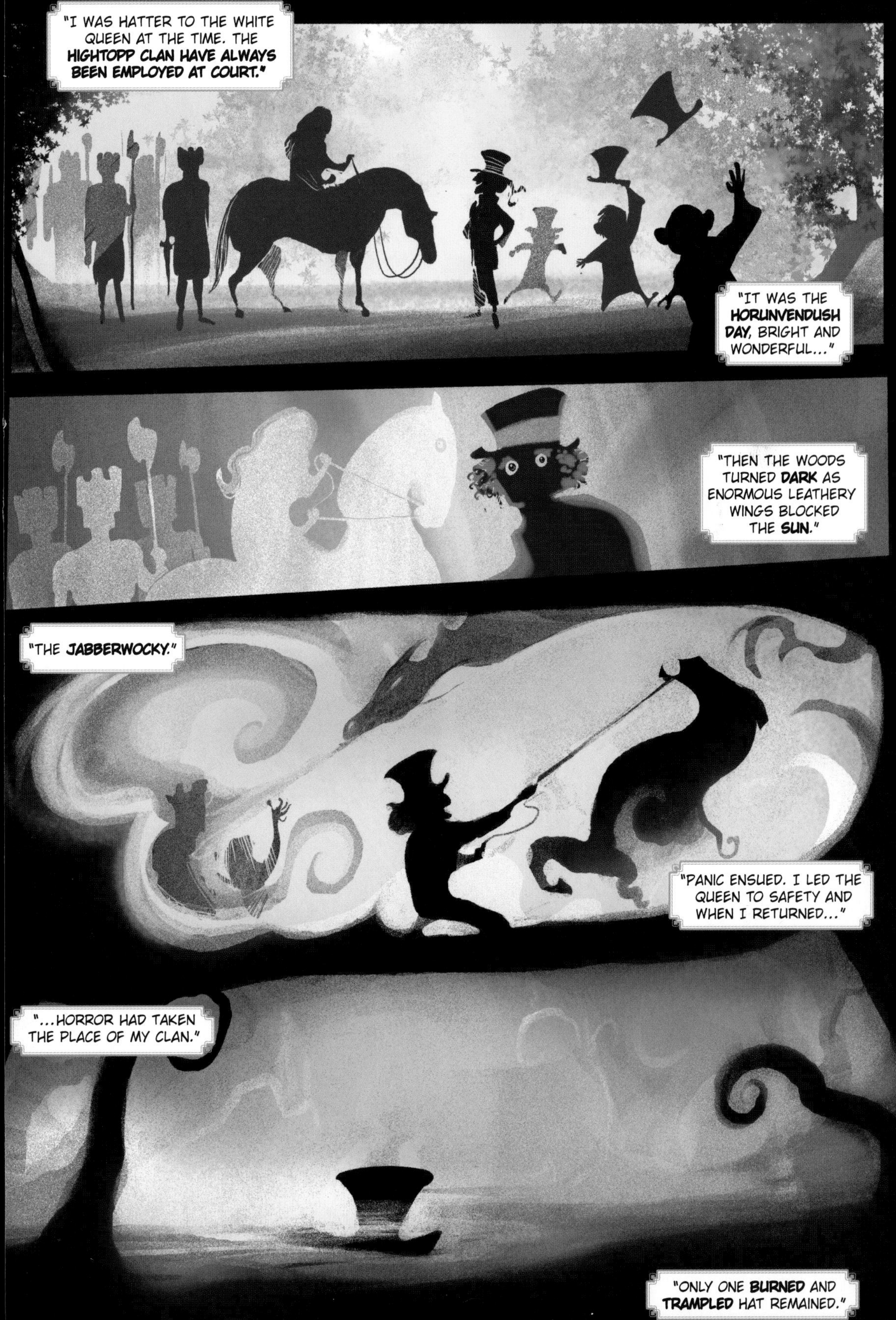
"I WAS HATTER TO THE WHITE QUEEN AT THE TIME. THE **HIGHTOPP CLAN HAVE ALWAYS BEEN EMPLOYED AT COURT.**"
"IT WAS THE **HORUNVENDUSH DAY**, BRIGHT AND WONDERFUL..."
"THEN THE WOODS TURNED **DARK** AS ENORMOUS LEATHERY WINGS BLOCKED THE **SUN**."
"THE **JABBERWOCKY**."
"PANIC ENSUED. I LED THE QUEEN TO SAFETY AND WHEN I RETURNED..."
"...HORROR HAD TAKEN THE PLACE OF MY CLAN."
"ONLY ONE **BURNED** AND **TRAMPLED** HAT REMAINED."

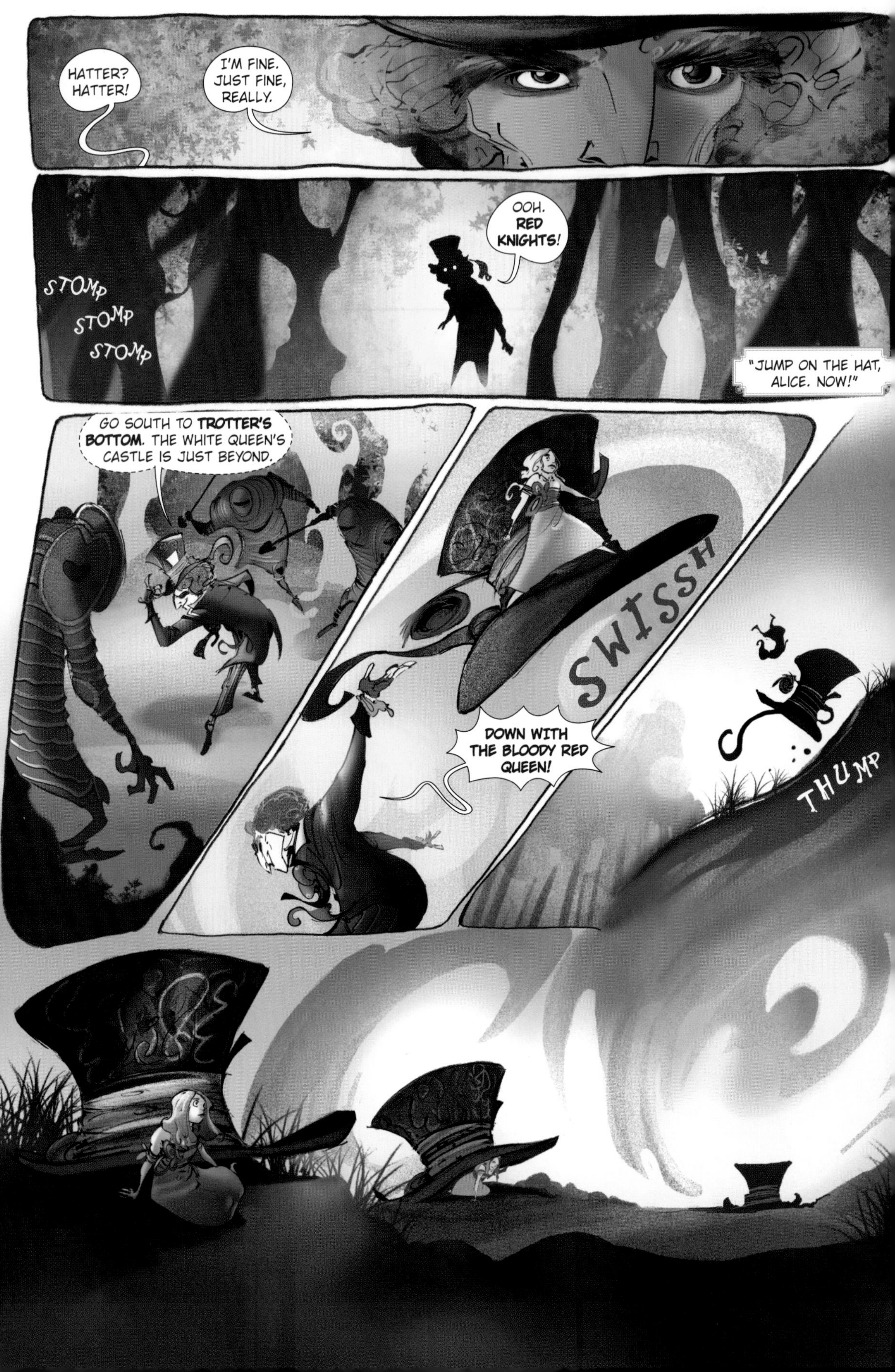
HATTER? HATTER!
I'M FINE. JUST FINE, REALLY.
STOMP
STOMP
STOMP
OOH. **RED KNIGHTS**!
"JUMP ON THE HAT, ALICE. NOW!"
GO SOUTH TO **TROTTER'S BOTTOM**. THE WHITE QUEEN'S CASTLE IS JUST BEYOND.
SWISSH
DOWN WITH THE BLOODY RED QUEEN!
THUMP

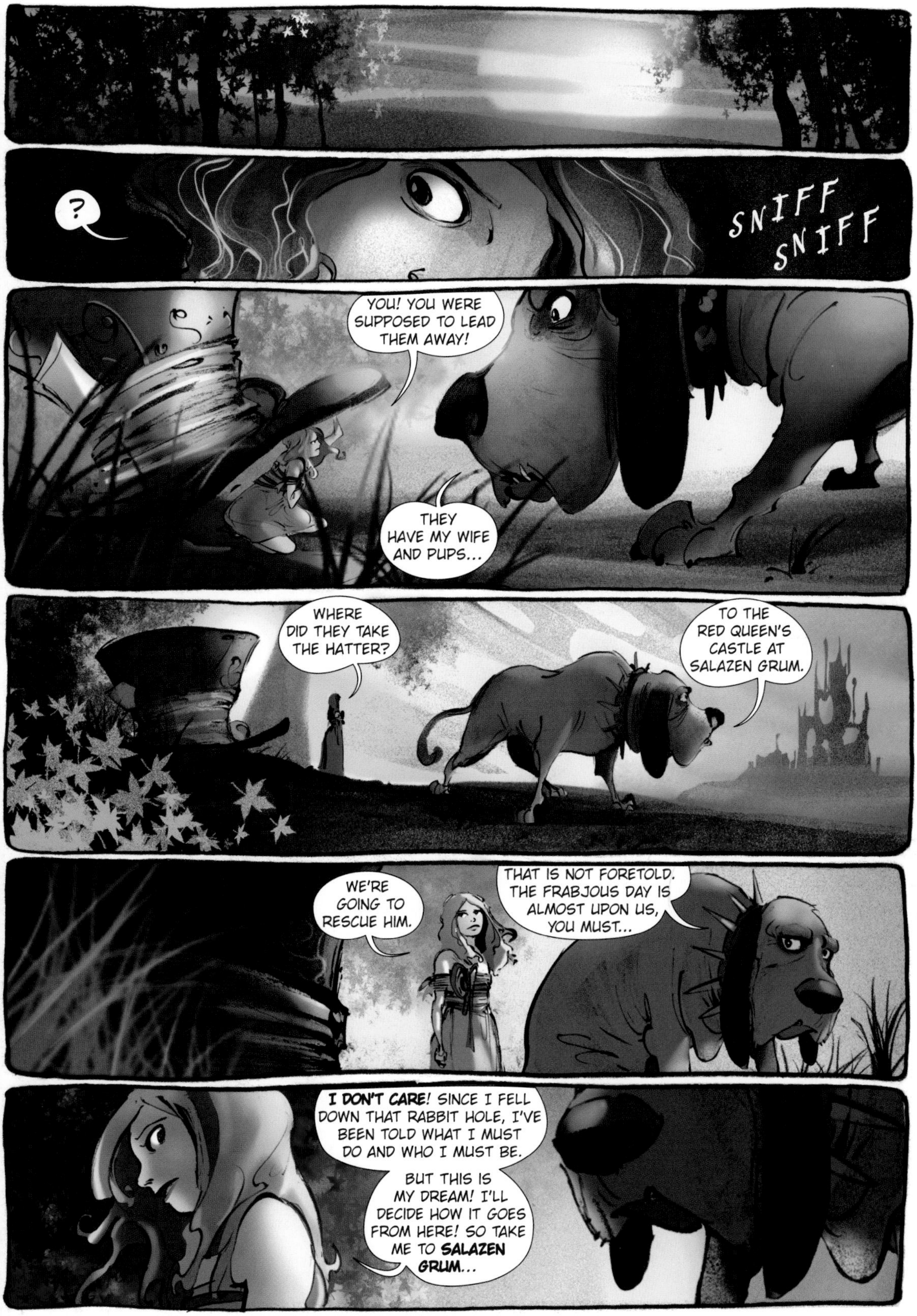
?
SNIFF SNIFF
YOU! YOU WERE SUPPOSED TO LEAD THEM AWAY!
THEY HAVE MY WIFE AND PUPS...
WHERE DID THEY TAKE THE HATTER?
TO THE RED QUEEN'S CASTLE AT SALAZEN GRUM.
WE'RE GOING TO RESCUE HIM.
THAT IS NOT FORETOLD. THE FRABJOUS DAY IS ALMOST UPON US, YOU MUST...
I DON'T CARE! SINCE I FELL DOWN THAT RABBIT HOLE, I'VE BEEN TOLD WHAT I MUST DO AND WHO I MUST BE.
BUT THIS IS MY DREAM! I'LL DECIDE HOW IT GOES FROM HERE! SO TAKE ME TO SALAZEN GRUM...

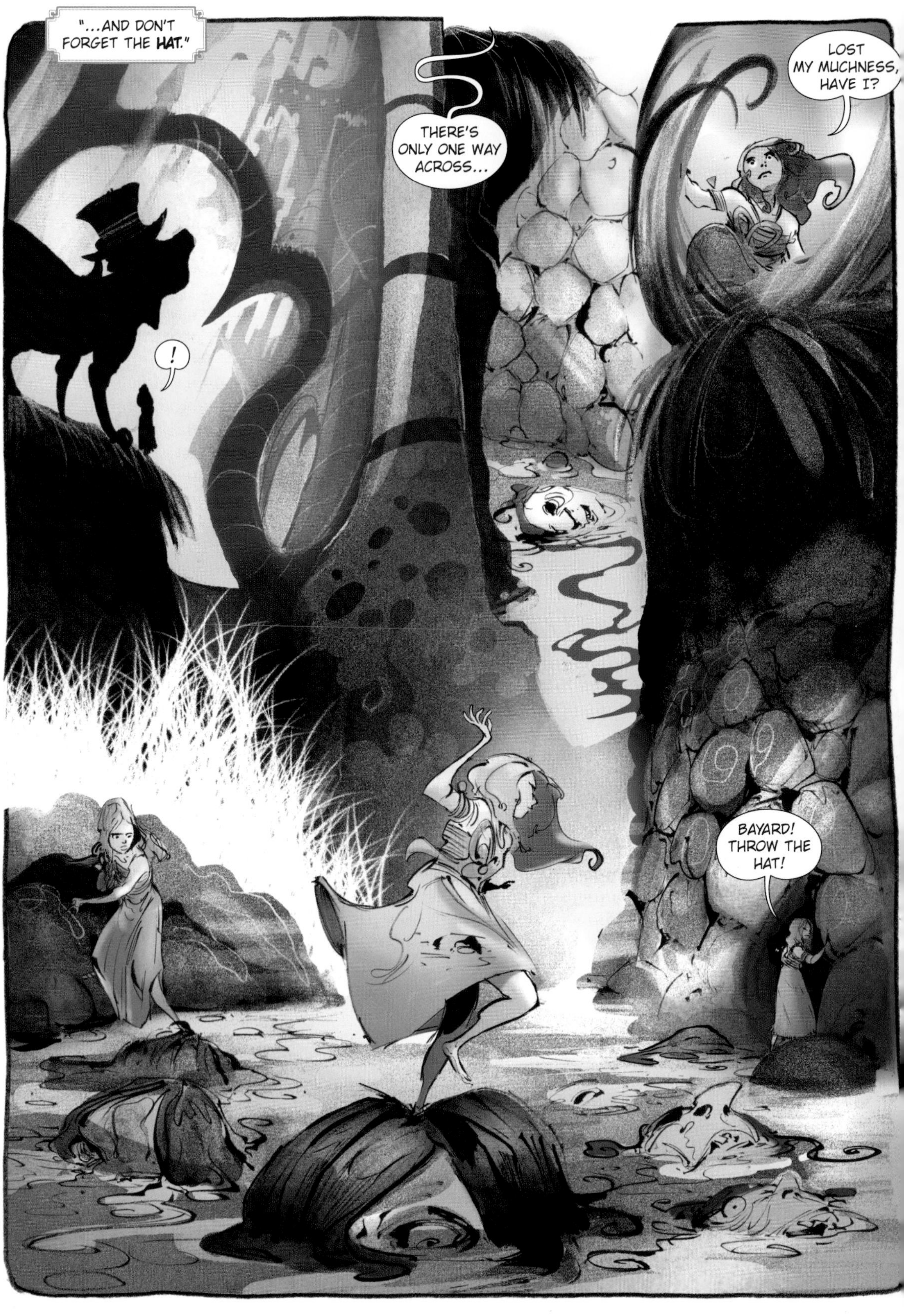
"...AND DON'T FORGET THE HAT."
THERE'S ONLY ONE WAY ACROSS...
LOST MY MUCHNESS, HAVE I?
!
BAYARD! THROW THE HAT!

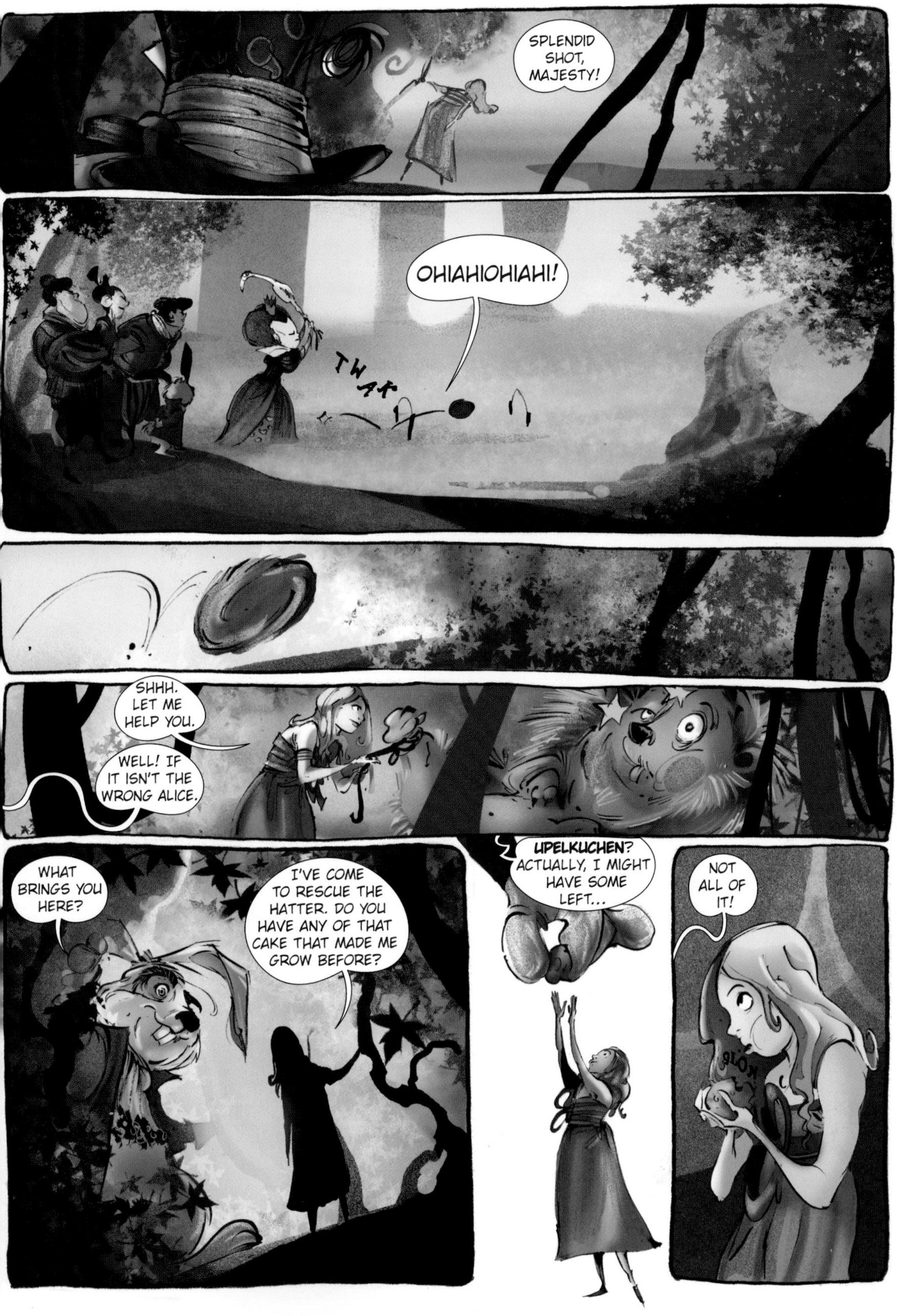

SPLENDID SHOT, MAJESTY!
OHIAHIOHIAHI!
TWAK
SHHH. LET ME HELP YOU.
WELL! IF IT ISN'T THE WRONG ALICE.
WHAT BRINGS YOU HERE?
I'VE COME TO RESCUE THE HATTER. DO YOU HAVE ANY OF THAT CAKE THAT MADE ME GROW BEFORE?
UPELKUCHEN? ACTUALLY, I MIGHT HAVE SOME LEFT...
NOT ALL OF IT!

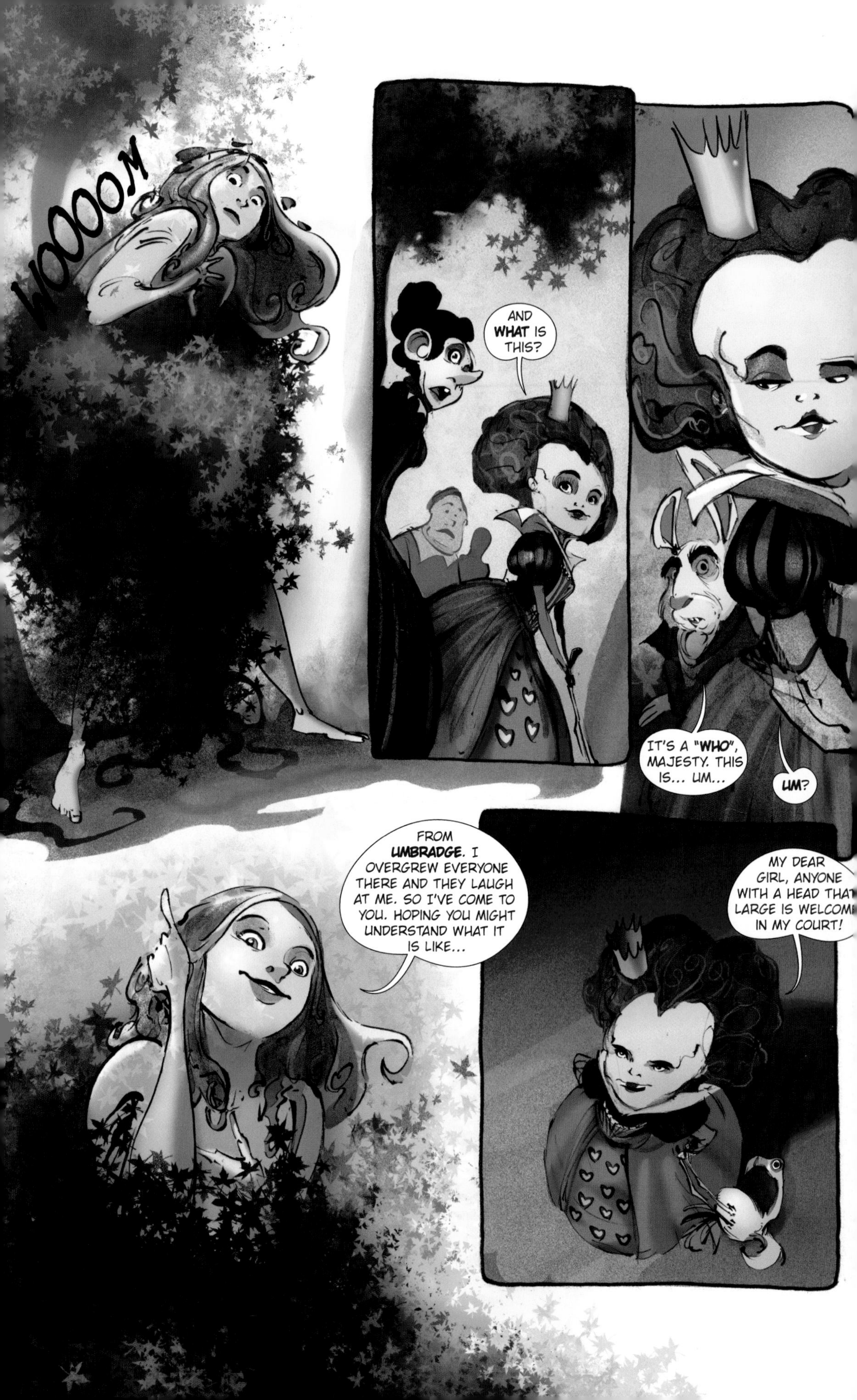
WOOOOM
AND WHAT IS THIS?
IT'S A "WHO", MAJESTY. THIS IS... UM...
UM?
FROM UMBRADGE. I OVERGREW EVERYONE THERE AND THEY LAUGH AT ME. SO I'VE COME TO YOU. HOPING YOU MIGHT UNDERSTAND WHAT IT IS LIKE...
MY DEAR GIRL, ANYONE WITH A HEAD THAT LARGE IS WELCOME IN MY COURT!

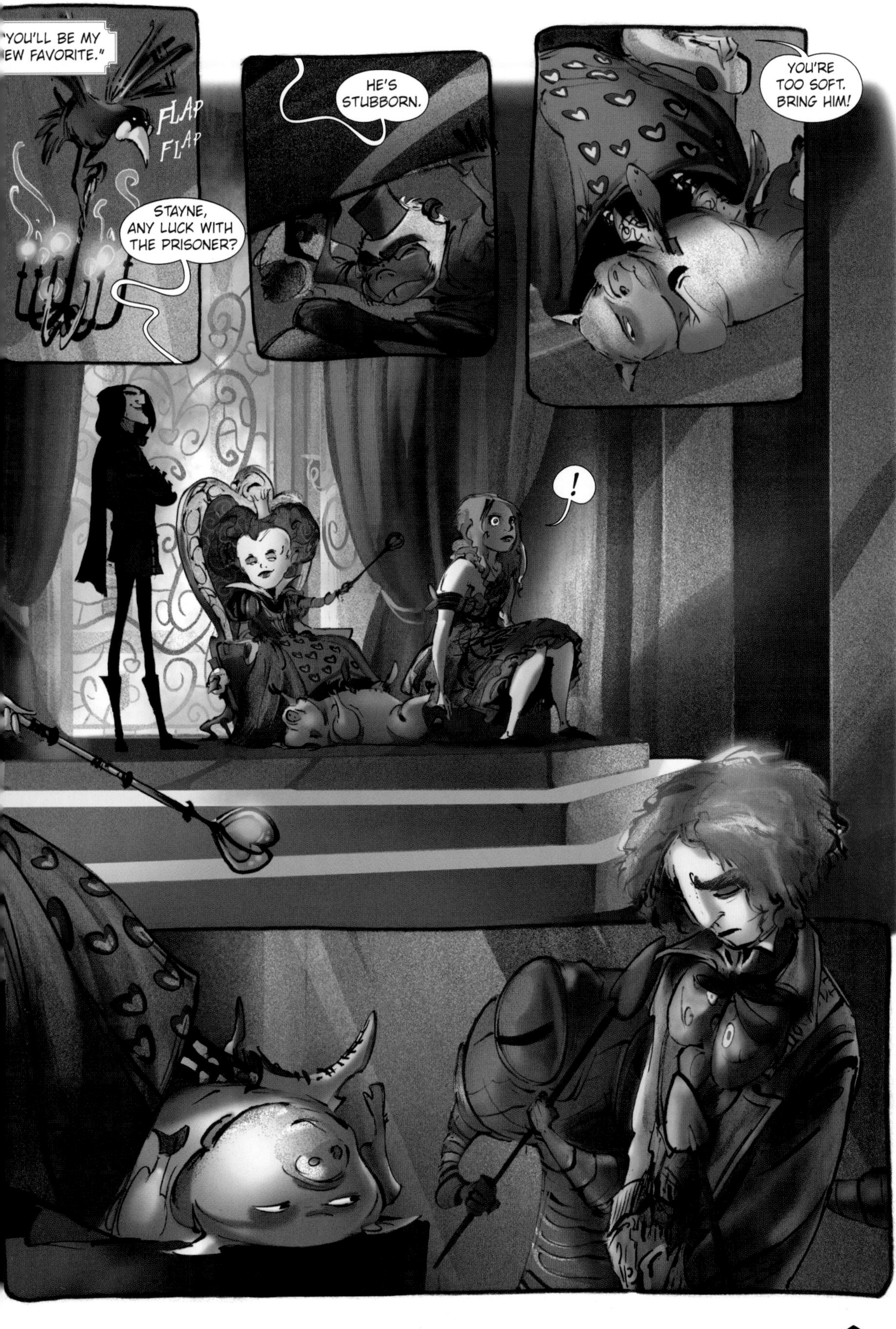
"YOU'LL BE MY
EW FAVORITE."
FLAP
FLAP
STAYNE,
ANY LUCK WITH
THE PRISONER?
HE'S
STUBBORN.
YOU'RE
TOO SOFT.
BRING HIM!
!

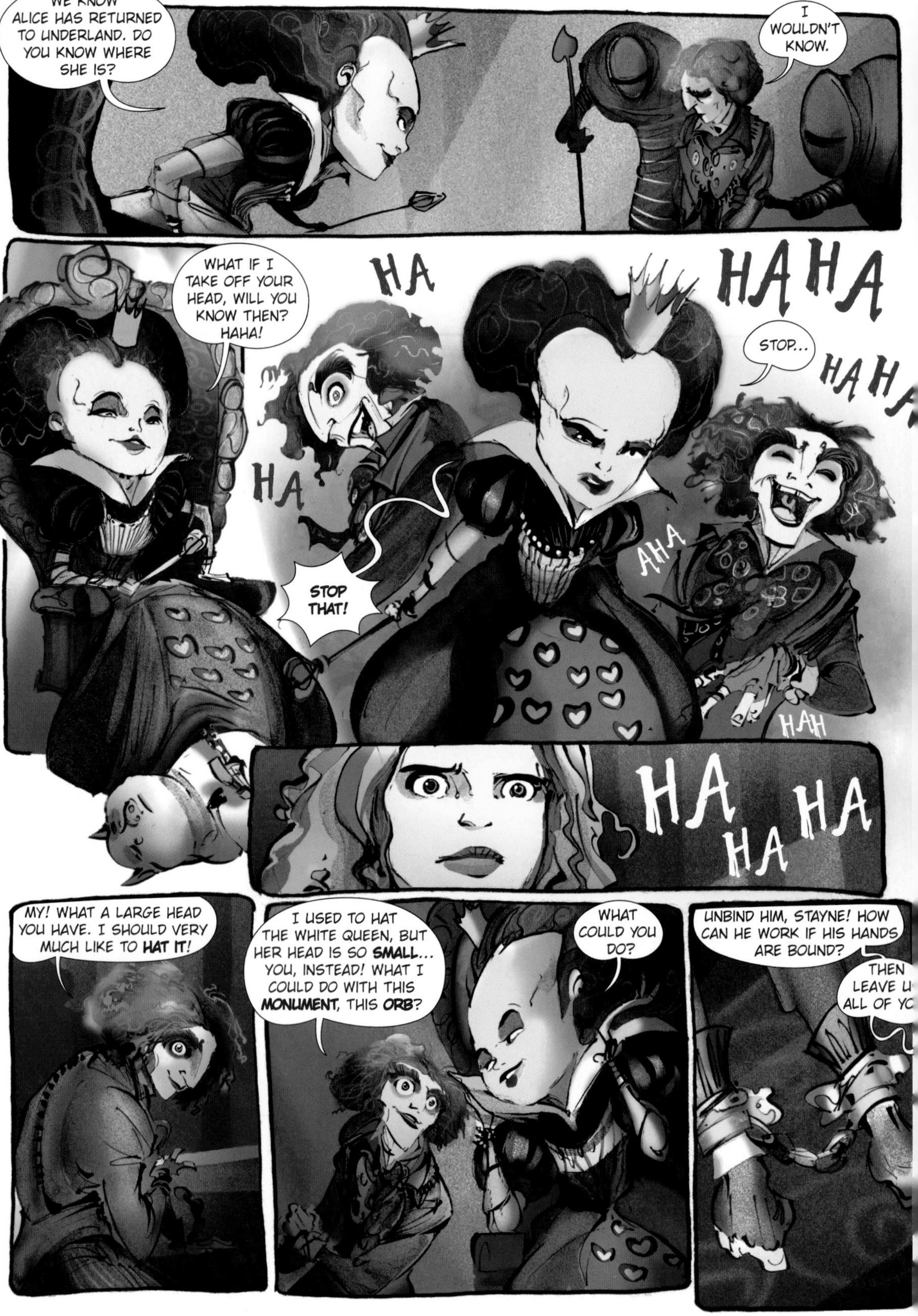
WE KNOW ALICE HAS RETURNED TO UNDERLAND. DO YOU KNOW WHERE SHE IS?
I WOULDN'T KNOW.
WHAT IF I TAKE OFF YOUR HEAD, WILL YOU KNOW THEN? HAHA!
HA
HA
HAHA
STOP...
HAHA
STOP THAT!
AHA
HAH
HA HA HA
MY! WHAT A LARGE HEAD YOU HAVE. I SHOULD VERY MUCH LIKE TO **HAT IT**!
I USED TO HAT THE WHITE QUEEN, BUT HER HEAD IS SO **SMALL**... YOU, INSTEAD! WHAT I COULD DO WITH THIS **MONUMENT**, THIS **ORB**?
WHAT COULD YOU DO?
UNBIND HIM, STAYNE! HOW CAN HE WORK IF HIS HANDS ARE BOUND?
THEN LEAVE U
ALL OF YO

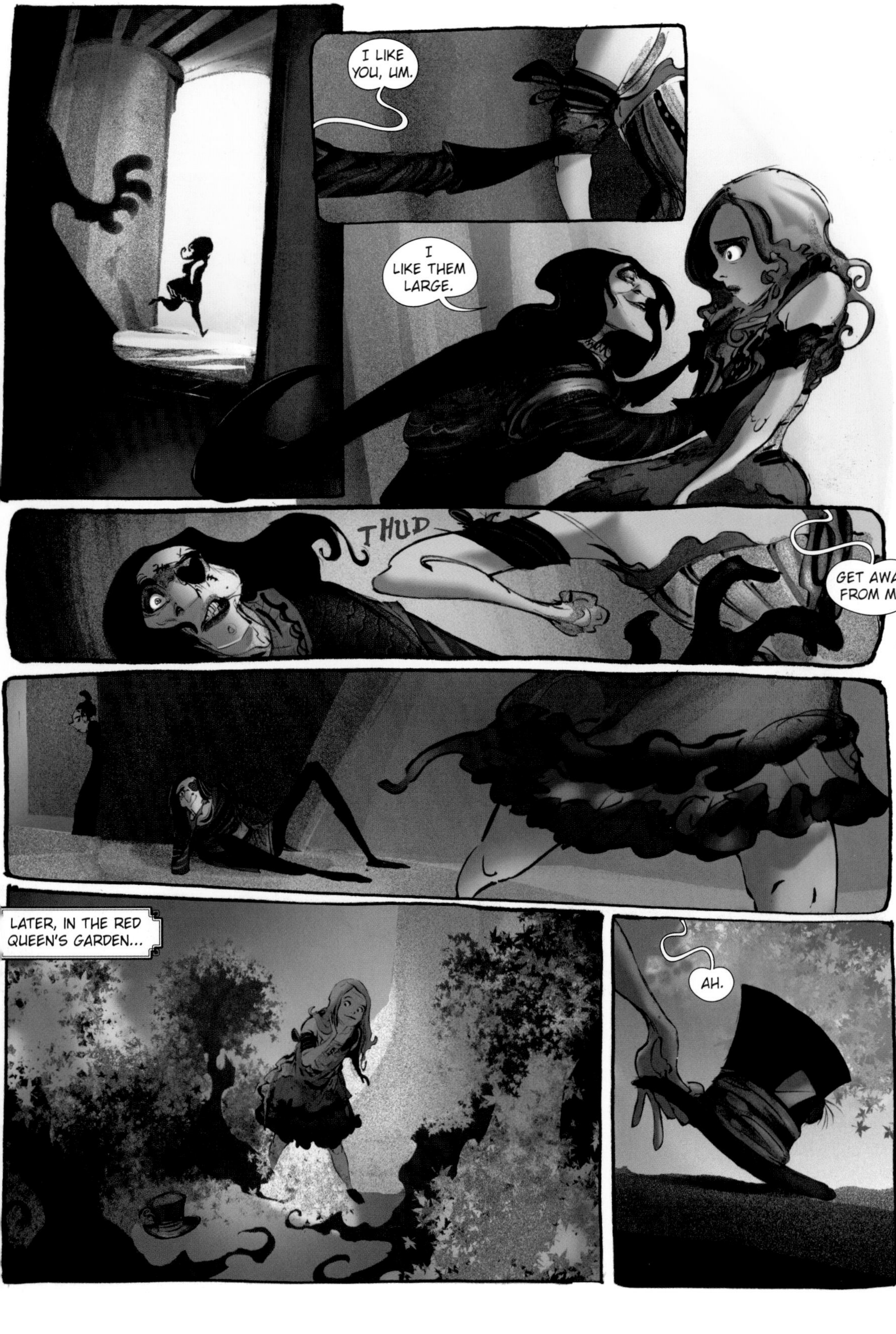
I LIKE YOU, UM.
I LIKE THEM LARGE.
THUD
GET AWAY FROM ME!
LATER, IN THE RED QUEEN'S GARDEN...
AH.

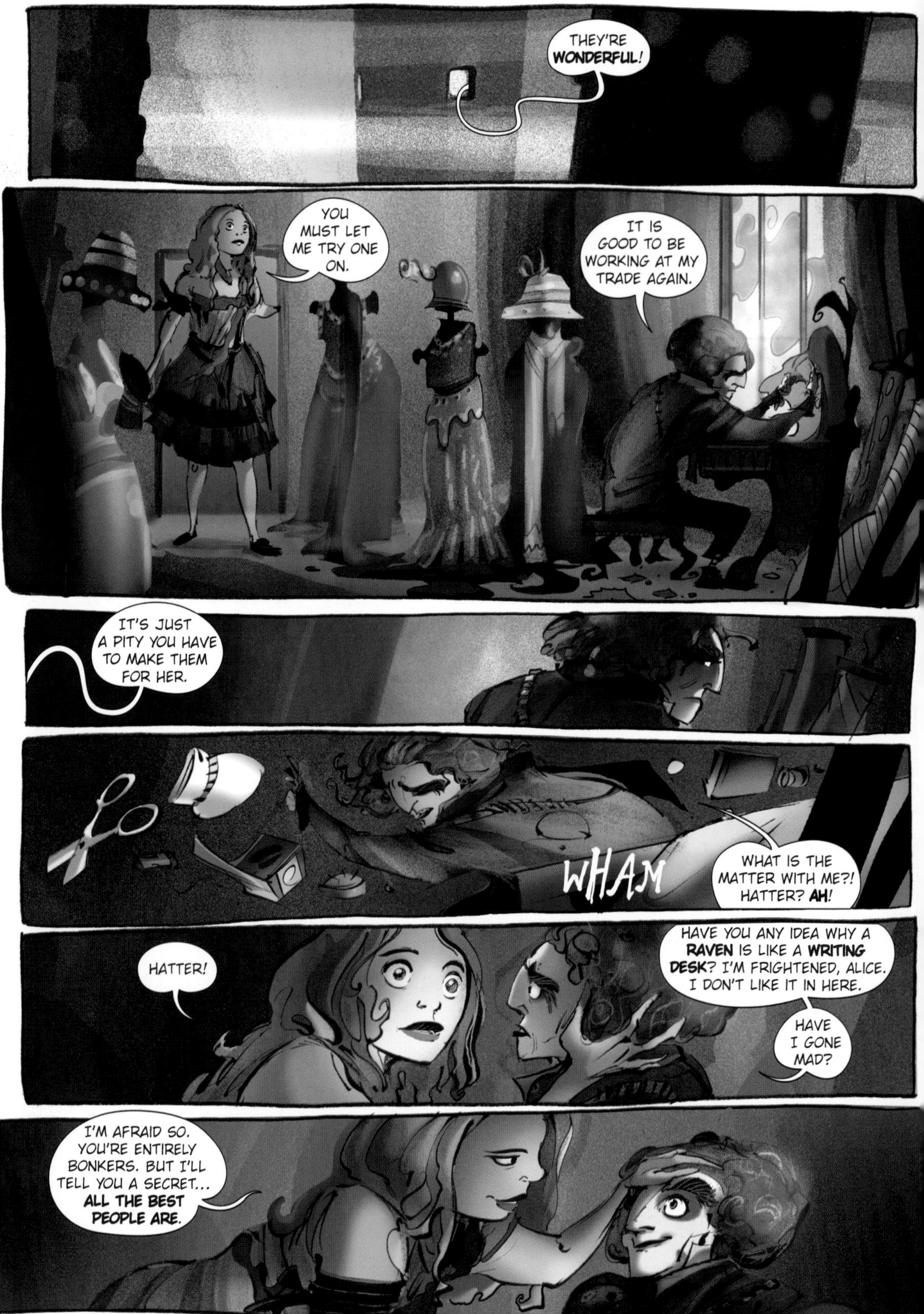
THEY'RE **WONDERFUL**!
YOU MUST LET ME TRY ONE ON.
IT IS GOOD TO BE WORKING AT MY TRADE AGAIN.
IT'S JUST A PITY YOU HAVE TO MAKE THEM FOR HER.
WHAM
WHAT IS THE MATTER WITH ME?! HATTER? **AH**!
HATTER!
HAVE YOU ANY IDEA WHY A **RAVEN** IS LIKE A **WRITING DESK**? I'M FRIGHTENED, ALICE. I DON'T LIKE IT IN HERE.
HAVE I GONE MAD?
I'M AFRAID SO. YOU'RE ENTIRELY BONKERS. BUT I'LL TELL YOU A SECRET... **ALL THE BEST PEOPLE ARE**.

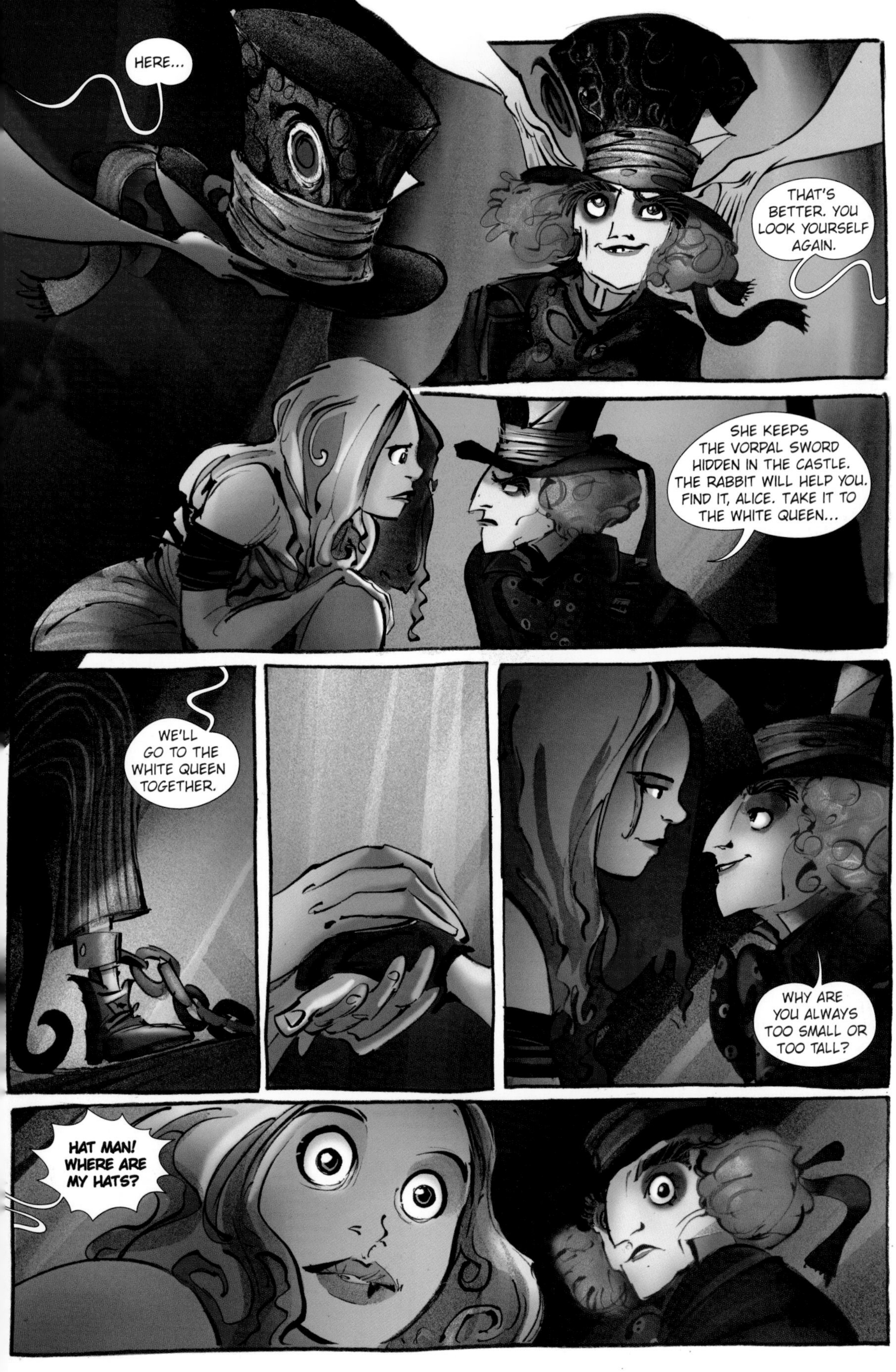
HERE...
THAT'S BETTER. YOU LOOK YOURSELF AGAIN.
SHE KEEPS THE VORPAL SWORD HIDDEN IN THE CASTLE. THE RABBIT WILL HELP YOU. FIND IT, ALICE. TAKE IT TO THE WHITE QUEEN...
WE'LL GO TO THE WHITE QUEEN TOGETHER.
WHY ARE YOU ALWAYS TOO SMALL OR TOO TALL?
HAT MAN! WHERE ARE MY HATS?

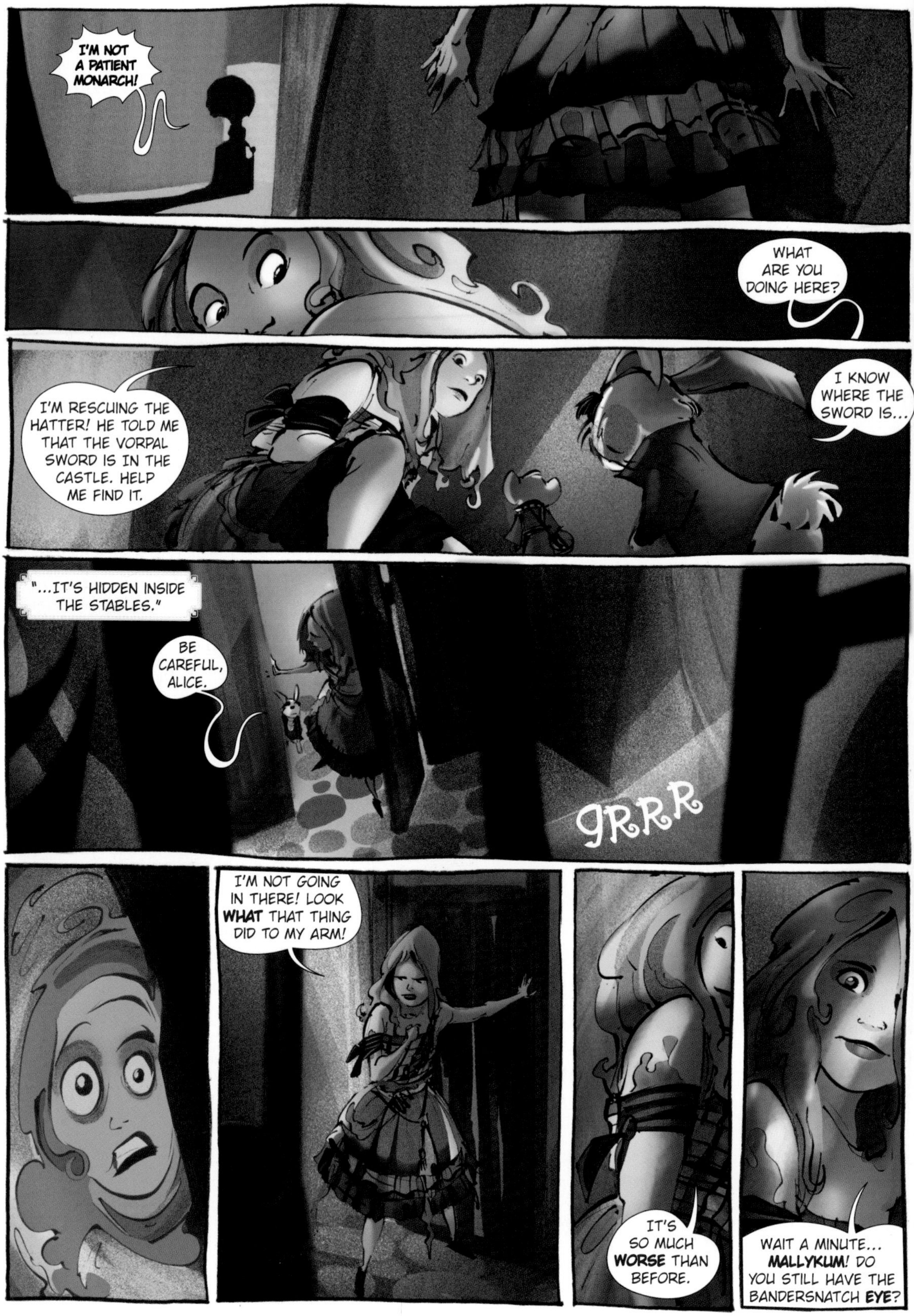
I'M NOT A PATIENT MONARCH!
WHAT ARE YOU DOING HERE?
I'M RESCUING THE HATTER! HE TOLD ME THAT THE VORPAL SWORD IS IN THE CASTLE. HELP ME FIND IT.
I KNOW WHERE THE SWORD IS...
"...IT'S HIDDEN INSIDE THE STABLES."
BE CAREFUL, ALICE.
GRRR
I'M NOT GOING IN THERE! LOOK WHAT THAT THING DID TO MY ARM!
IT'S SO MUCH WORSE THAN BEFORE.
WAIT A MINUTE... MALLYKUM! DO YOU STILL HAVE THE BANDERSNATCH EYE?

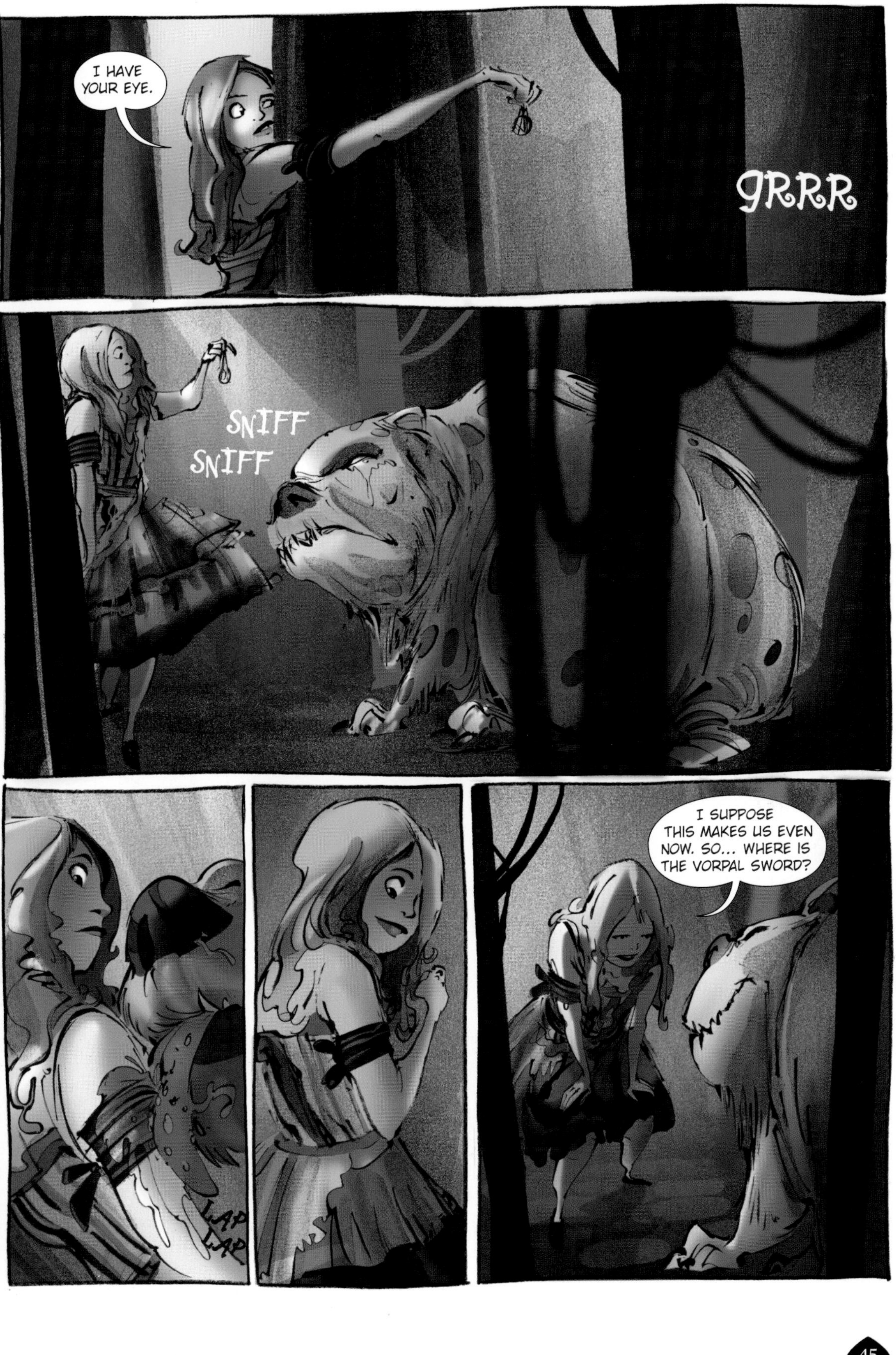
I HAVE YOUR EYE.
GRRR
SNIFF SNIFF
I SUPPOSE THIS MAKES US EVEN NOW. SO... WHERE IS THE VORPAL SWORD?

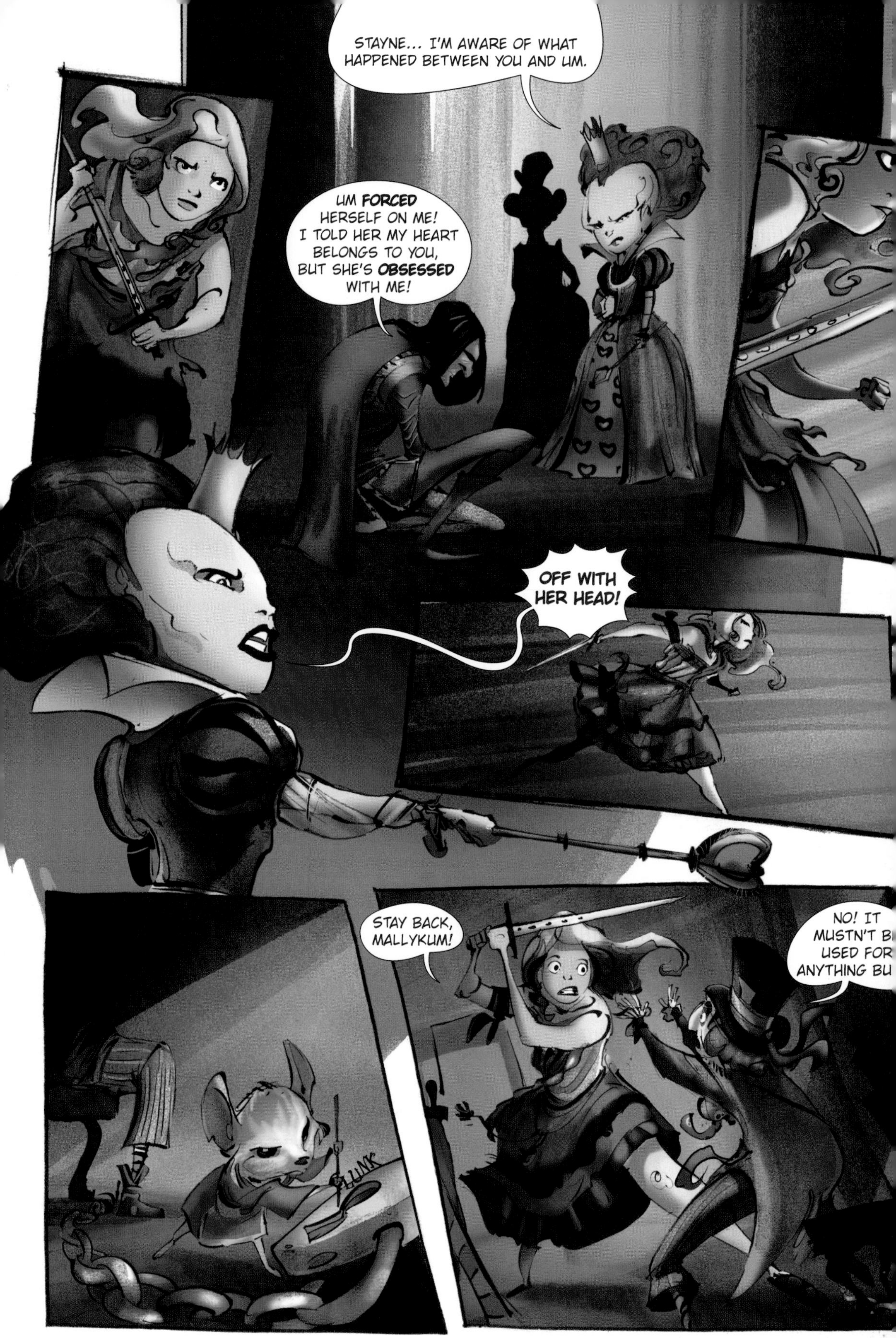
STAYNE... I'M AWARE OF WHAT HAPPENED BETWEEN YOU AND UM.
UM **FORCED** HERSELF ON ME! I TOLD HER MY HEART BELONGS TO YOU, BUT SHE'S **OBSESSED** WITH ME!
OFF WITH HER HEAD!
STAY BACK, MALLYKUM!
NO! IT MUSTN'T B USED FOR ANYTHING BU
LUNK

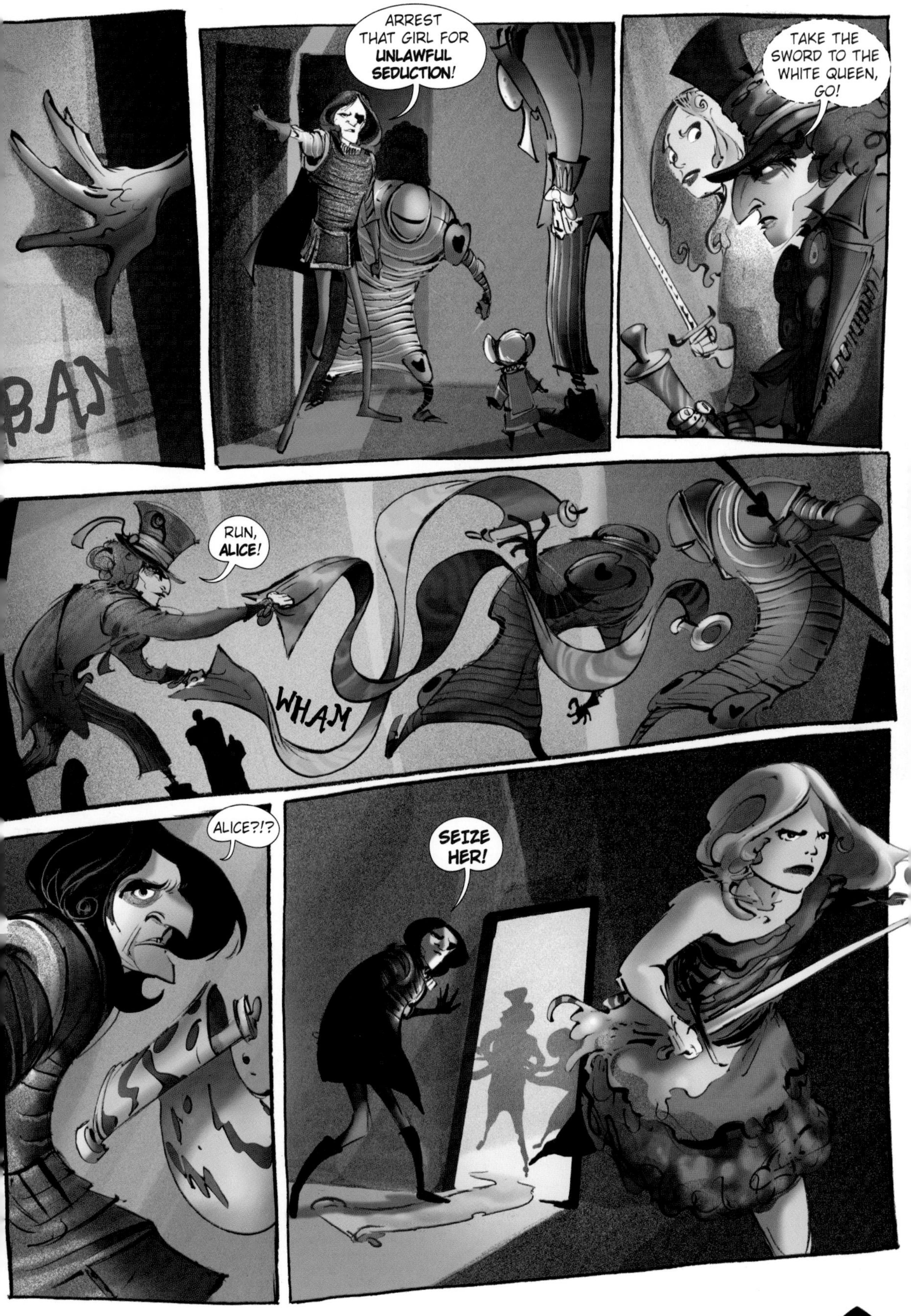
BAN
ARREST THAT GIRL FOR UNLAWFUL SEDUCTION!
TAKE THE SWORD TO THE WHITE QUEEN, GO!
RUN, ALICE!
WHAM
ALICE?!?
SEIZE HER!

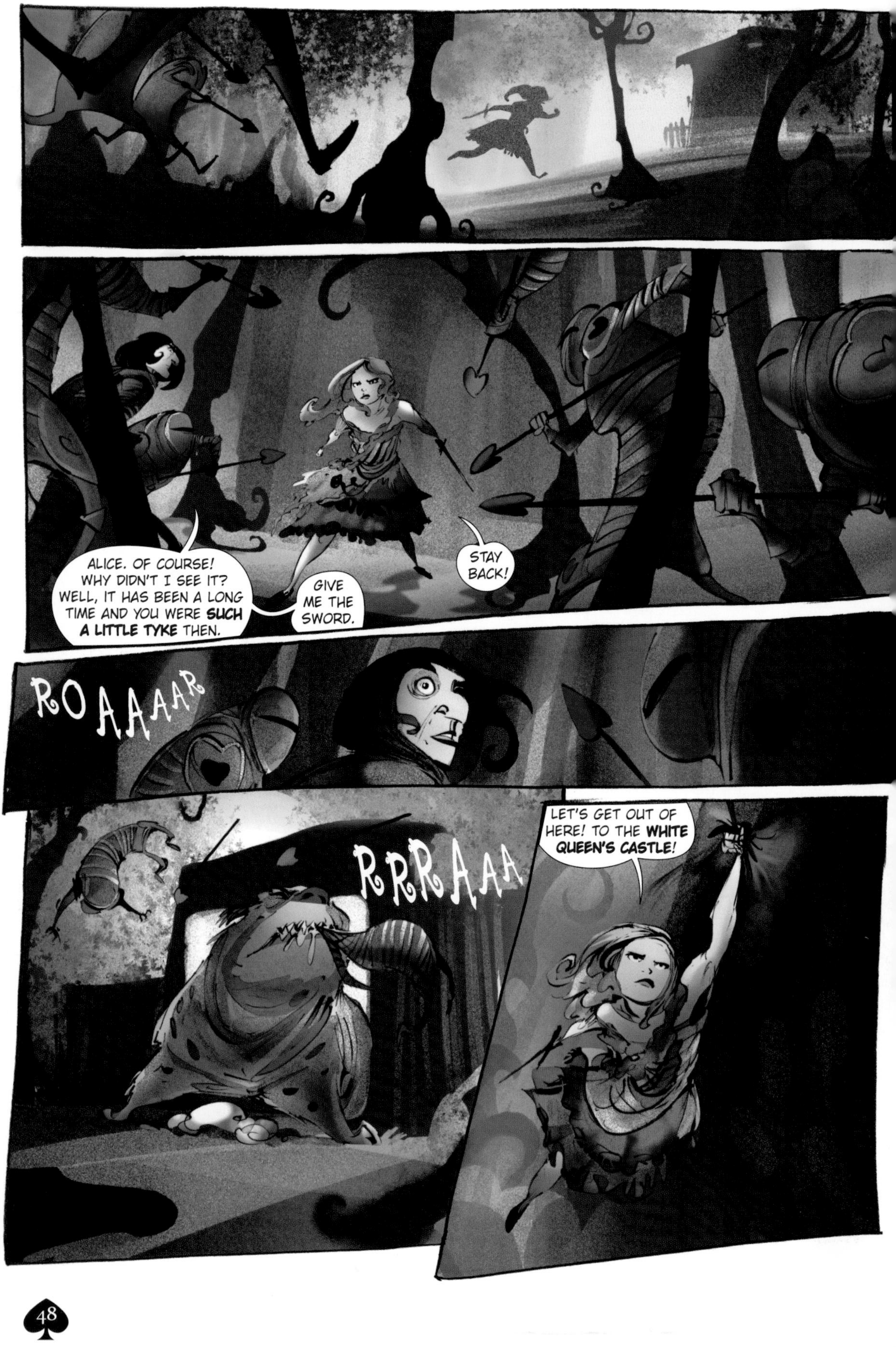
ALICE. OF COURSE! WHY DIDN'T I SEE IT? WELL, IT HAS BEEN A LONG TIME AND YOU WERE **SUCH A LITTLE TYKE** THEN.
GIVE ME THE SWORD.
STAY BACK!
ROAAAAR
RRRAAA
LET'S GET OUT OF HERE! TO THE **WHITE QUEEN'S CASTLE**!

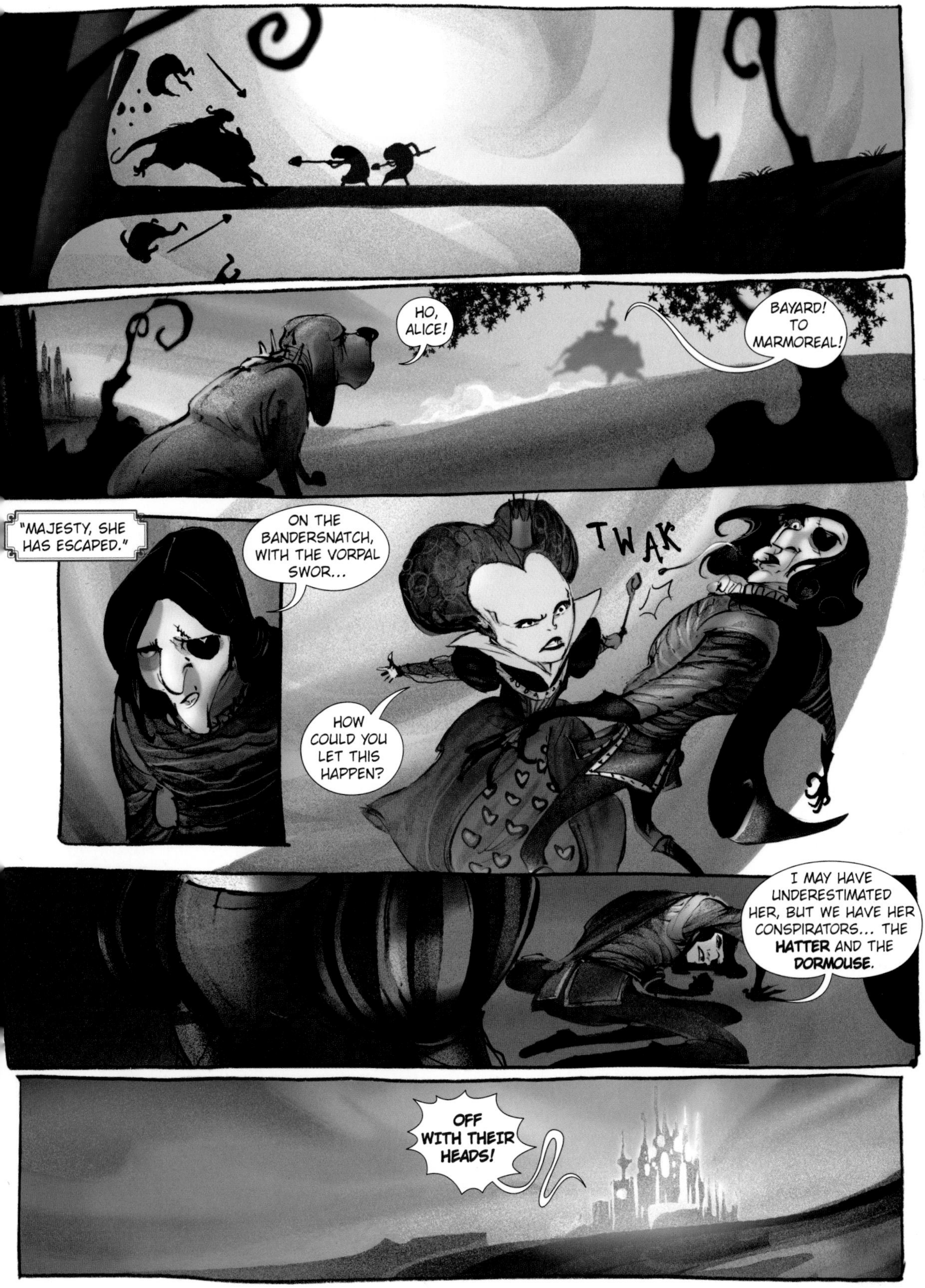
HO, ALICE!
BAYARD! TO MARMOREAL!
"MAJESTY, SHE HAS ESCAPED."
ON THE BANDERSNATCH, WITH THE VORPAL SWOR...
TWAK
HOW COULD YOU LET THIS HAPPEN?
I MAY HAVE UNDERESTIMATED HER, BUT WE HAVE HER CONSPIRATORS... THE **HATTER** AND THE **DORMOUSE**.
OFF WITH THEIR HEADS!

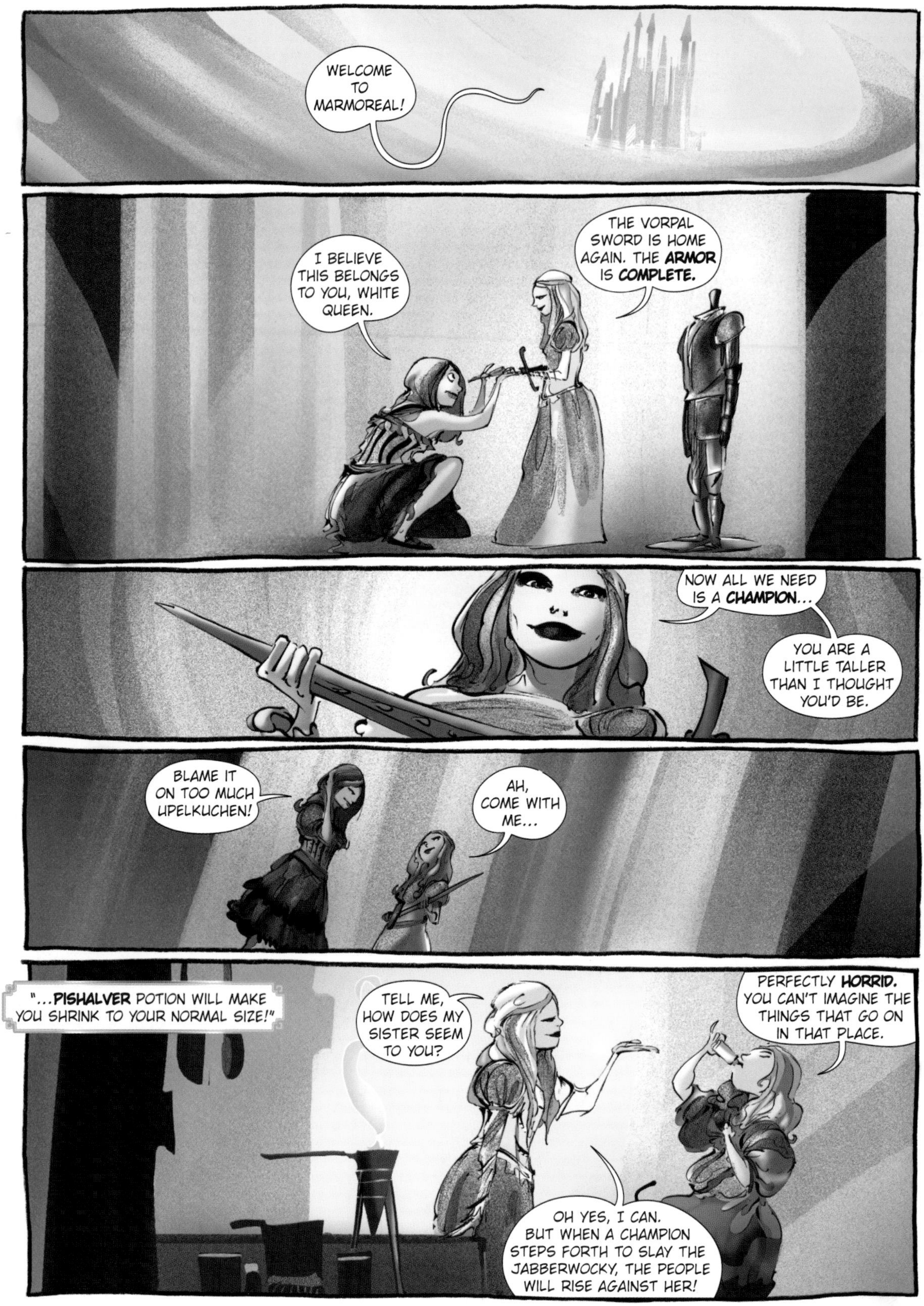
WELCOME TO MARMOREAL!
I BELIEVE THIS BELONGS TO YOU, WHITE QUEEN.
THE VORPAL SWORD IS HOME AGAIN. THE ARMOR IS COMPLETE.
NOW ALL WE NEED IS A CHAMPION...
YOU ARE A LITTLE TALLER THAN I THOUGHT YOU'D BE.
BLAME IT ON TOO MUCH UPELKUCHEN!
AH, COME WITH ME...
"...PISHALVER POTION WILL MAKE YOU SHRINK TO YOUR NORMAL SIZE!"
TELL ME, HOW DOES MY SISTER SEEM TO YOU?
PERFECTLY HORRID. YOU CAN'T IMAGINE THE THINGS THAT GO ON IN THAT PLACE.
OH YES, I CAN. BUT WHEN A CHAMPION STEPS FORTH TO SLAY THE JABBERWOCKY, THE PEOPLE WILL RISE AGAINST HER!

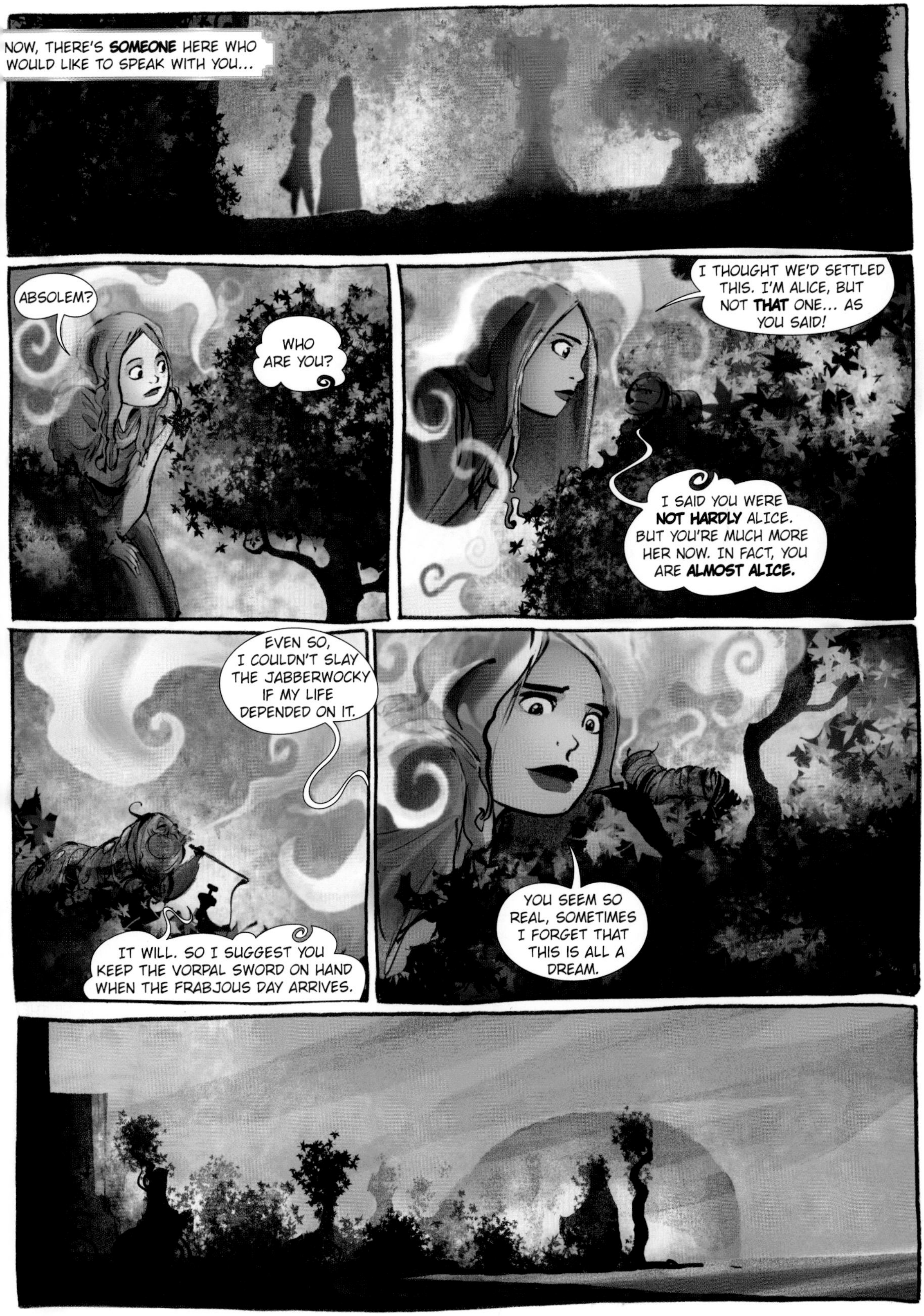
NOW, THERE'S **SOMEONE** HERE WHO WOULD LIKE TO SPEAK WITH YOU...
ABSOLEM?
WHO ARE YOU?
I THOUGHT WE'D SETTLED THIS. I'M ALICE, BUT NOT **THAT** ONE... AS YOU SAID!
I SAID YOU WERE **NOT HARDLY** ALICE. BUT YOU'RE MUCH MORE HER NOW. IN FACT, YOU ARE **ALMOST ALICE.**
EVEN SO, I COULDN'T SLAY THE JABBERWOCKY IF MY LIFE DEPENDED ON IT.
IT WILL. SO I SUGGEST YOU KEEP THE VORPAL SWORD ON HAND WHEN THE FRABJOUS DAY ARRIVES.
YOU SEEM SO REAL, SOMETIMES I FORGET THAT THIS IS ALL A DREAM.

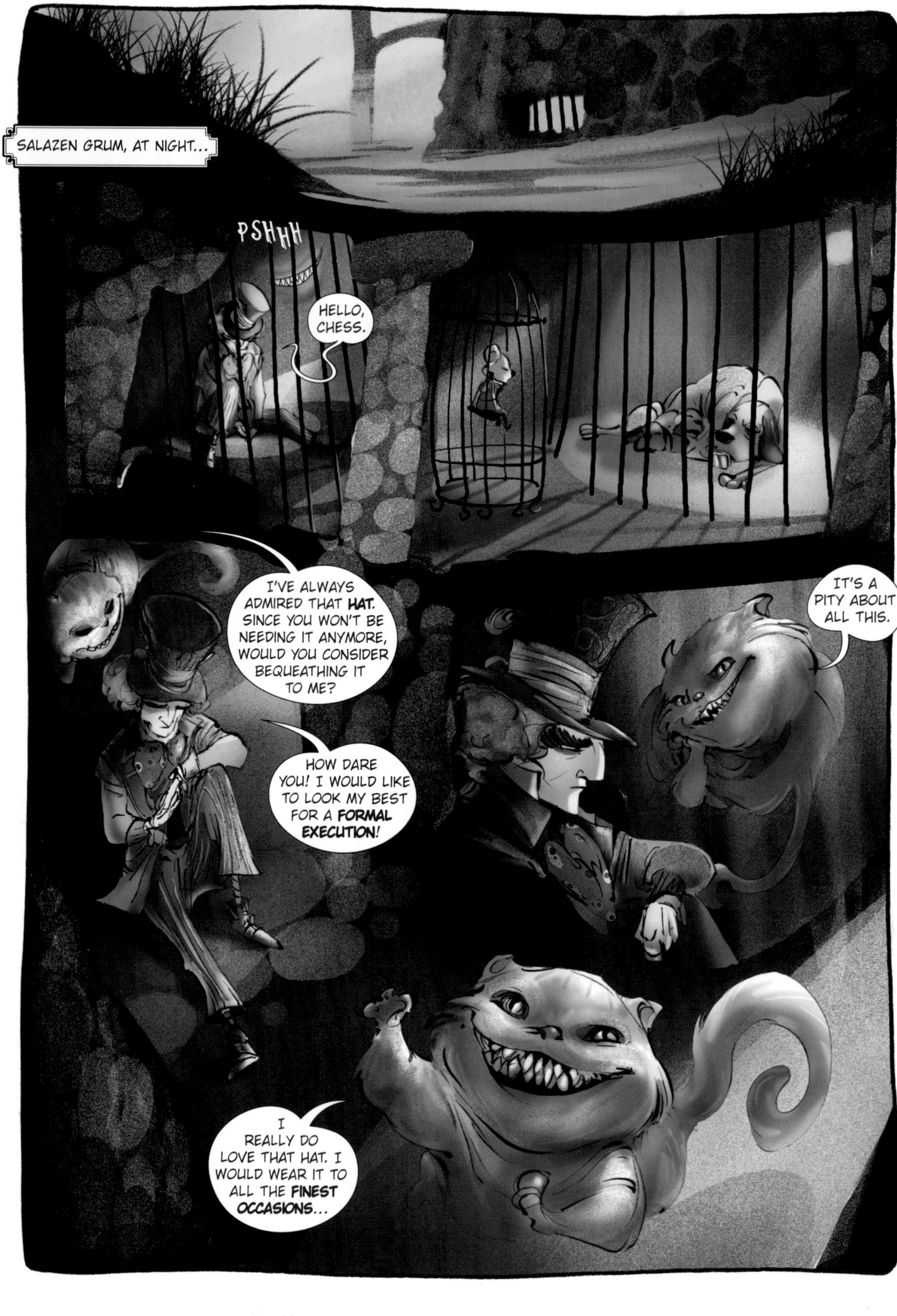
SALAZEN GRUM, AT NIGHT...
PSHHH
HELLO, CHESS.
I'VE ALWAYS ADMIRED THAT HAT. SINCE YOU WON'T BE NEEDING IT ANYMORE, WOULD YOU CONSIDER BEQUEATHING IT TO ME?
HOW DARE YOU! I WOULD LIKE TO LOOK MY BEST FOR A FORMAL EXECUTION!
IT'S A PITY ABOUT ALL THIS.
I REALLY DO LOVE THAT HAT. I WOULD WEAR IT TO ALL THE FINEST OCCASIONS...

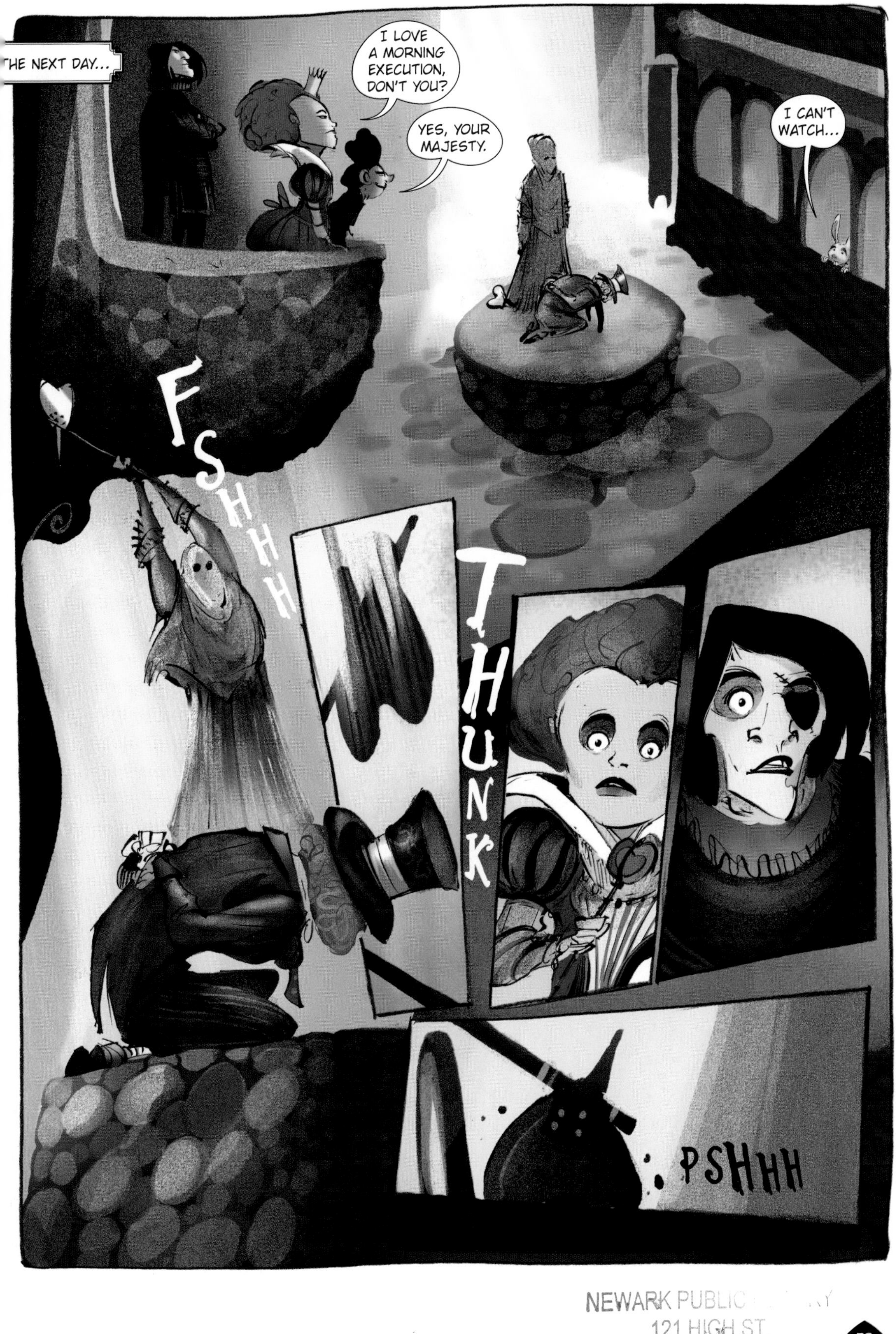

THE NEXT DAY...
I LOVE A MORNING EXECUTION, DON'T YOU?
YES, YOUR MAJESTY.
I CAN'T WATCH...
FSHHH
THUNK
PSHHH

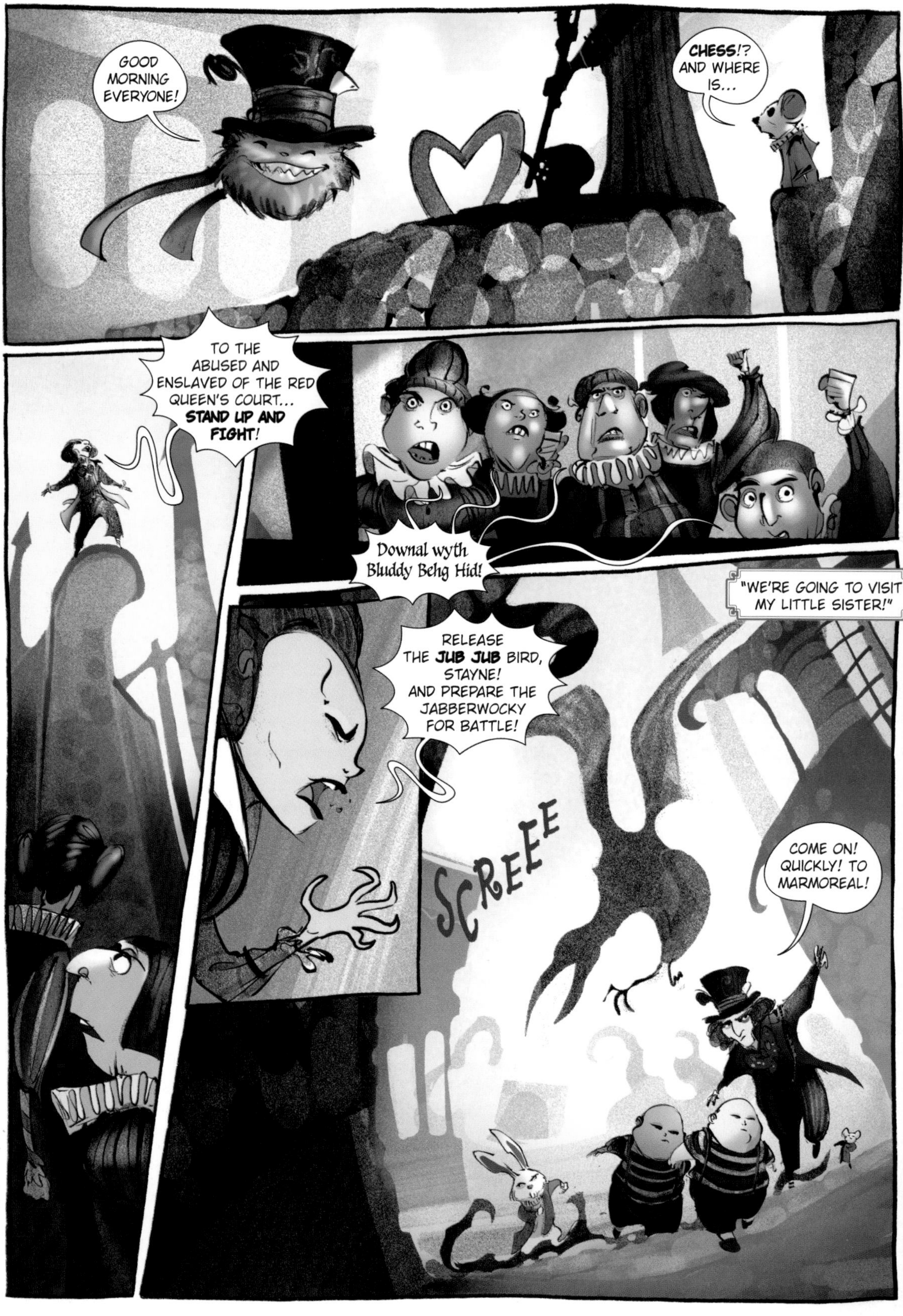
GOOD MORNING EVERYONE!
CHESS!? AND WHERE IS...
TO THE ABUSED AND ENSLAVED OF THE RED QUEEN'S COURT... STAND UP AND FIGHT!
Downal wyth Bluddy Behg Hid!
RELEASE THE JUB JUB BIRD, STAYNE! AND PREPARE THE JABBERWOCKY FOR BATTLE!
"WE'RE GOING TO VISIT MY LITTLE SISTER!"
SCREEE
COME ON! QUICKLY! TO MARMOREAL!

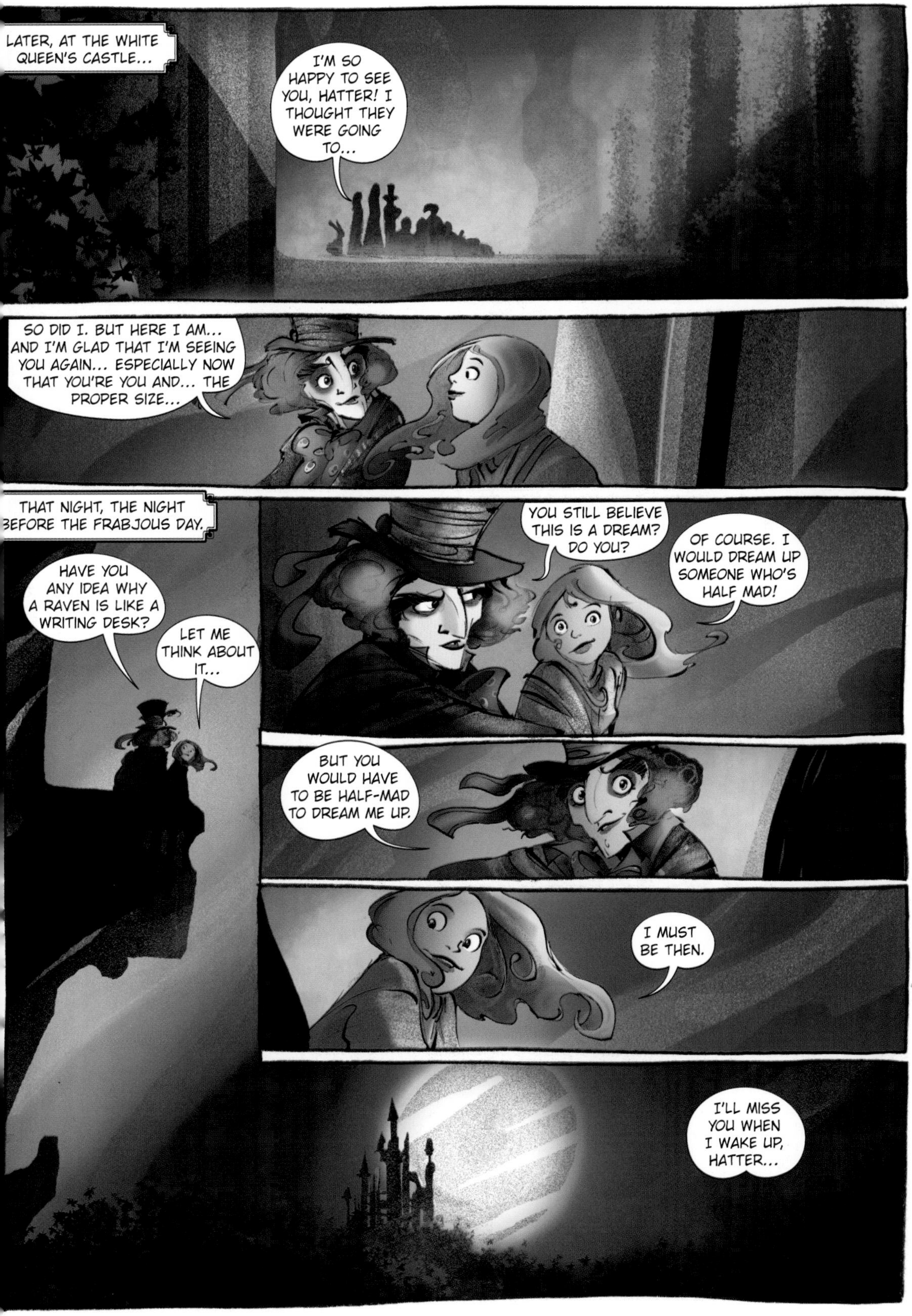
LATER, AT THE WHITE QUEEN'S CASTLE...
I'M SO HAPPY TO SEE YOU, HATTER! I THOUGHT THEY WERE GOING TO...
SO DID I. BUT HERE I AM... AND I'M GLAD THAT I'M SEEING YOU AGAIN... ESPECIALLY NOW THAT YOU'RE YOU AND... THE PROPER SIZE...
THAT NIGHT, THE NIGHT BEFORE THE FRABJOUS DAY.
HAVE YOU ANY IDEA WHY A RAVEN IS LIKE A WRITING DESK?
LET ME THINK ABOUT IT...
YOU STILL BELIEVE THIS IS A DREAM? DO YOU?
OF COURSE. I WOULD DREAM UP SOMEONE WHO'S HALF MAD!
BUT YOU WOULD HAVE TO BE HALF-MAD TO DREAM ME UP.
I MUST BE THEN.
I'LL MISS YOU WHEN I WAKE UP, HATTER...

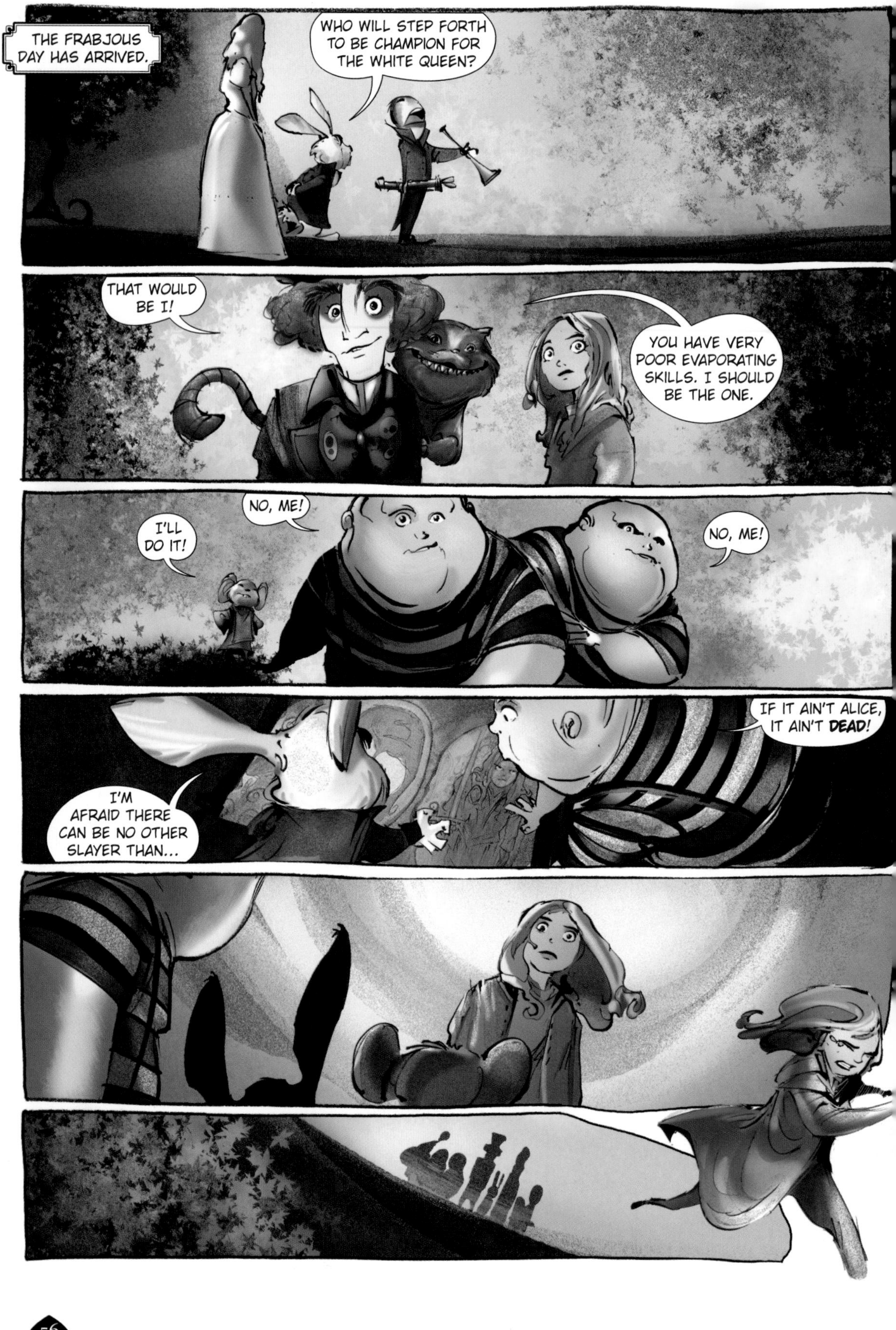
THE FRABJOUS DAY HAS ARRIVED.
WHO WILL STEP FORTH TO BE CHAMPION FOR THE WHITE QUEEN?
THAT WOULD BE I!
YOU HAVE VERY POOR EVAPORATING SKILLS. I SHOULD BE THE ONE.
I'LL DO IT!
NO, ME!
NO, ME!
IF IT AIN'T ALICE, IT AIN'T **DEAD**!
I'M AFRAID THERE CAN BE NO OTHER SLAYER THAN...

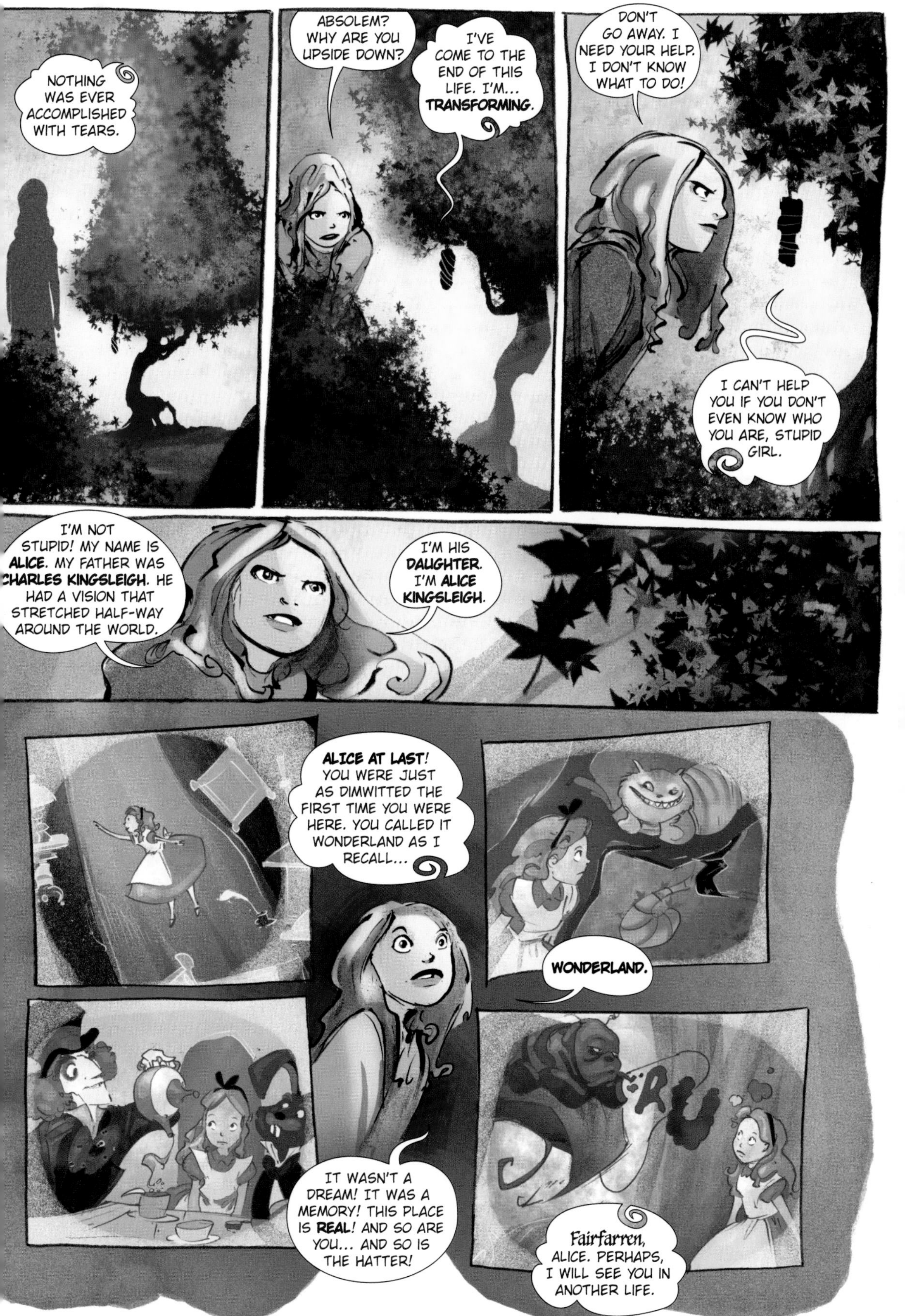
NOTHING WAS EVER ACCOMPLISHED WITH TEARS.
ABSOLEM? WHY ARE YOU UPSIDE DOWN?
I'VE COME TO THE END OF THIS LIFE. I'M... TRANSFORMING.
DON'T GO AWAY. I NEED YOUR HELP. I DON'T KNOW WHAT TO DO!
I CAN'T HELP YOU IF YOU DON'T EVEN KNOW WHO YOU ARE, STUPID GIRL.
I'M NOT STUPID! MY NAME IS ALICE. MY FATHER WAS CHARLES KINGSLEIGH. HE HAD A VISION THAT STRETCHED HALF-WAY AROUND THE WORLD.
I'M HIS DAUGHTER. I'M ALICE KINGSLEIGH.
ALICE AT LAST! YOU WERE JUST AS DIMWITTED THE FIRST TIME YOU WERE HERE. YOU CALLED IT WONDERLAND AS I RECALL...
WONDERLAND.
IT WASN'T A DREAM! IT WAS A MEMORY! THIS PLACE IS REAL! AND SO ARE YOU... AND SO IS THE HATTER!
Fairfarren, ALICE. PERHAPS, I WILL SEE YOU IN ANOTHER LIFE.

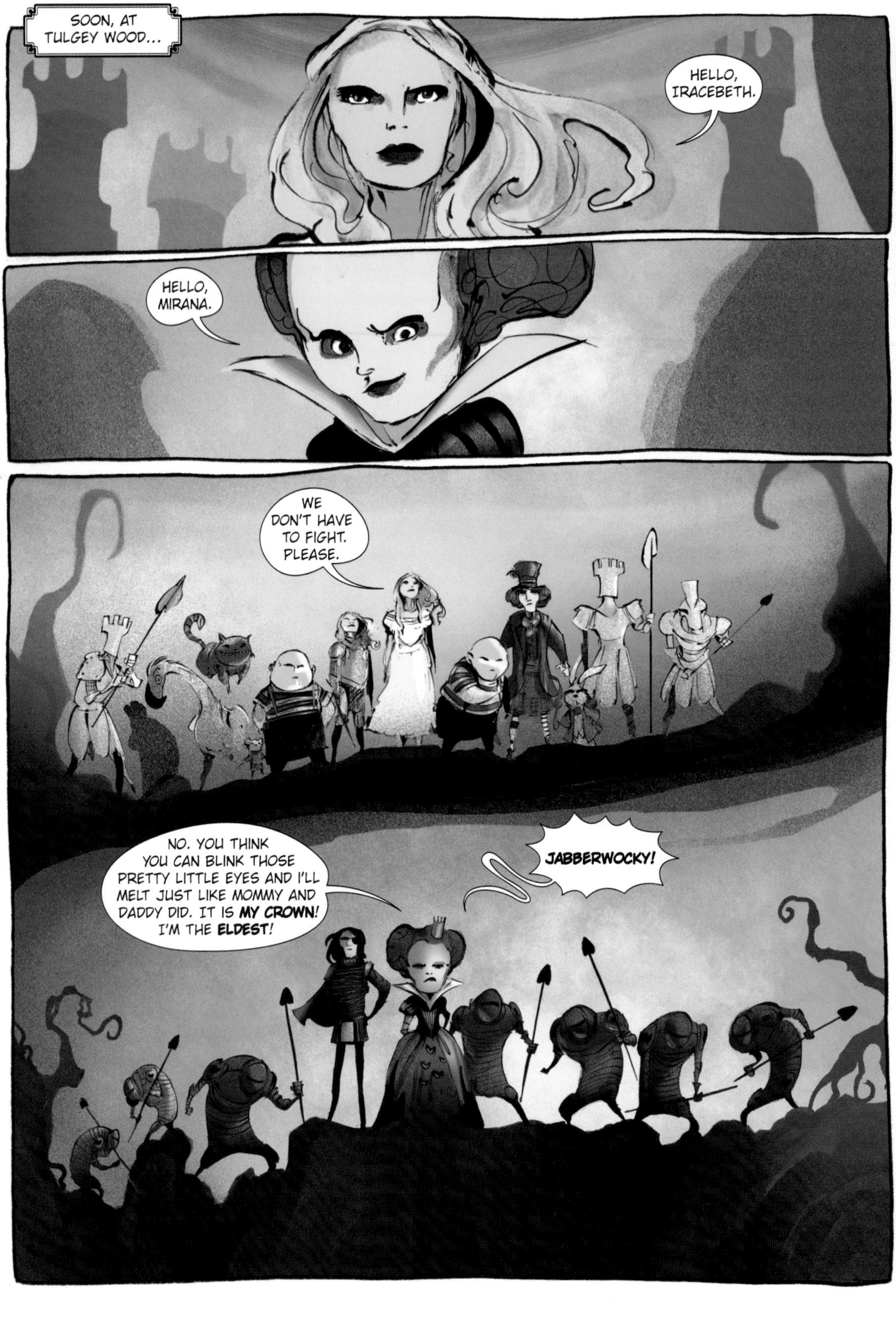
SOON, AT TULGEY WOOD...
HELLO, IRACEBETH.
HELLO, MIRANA.
WE DON'T HAVE TO FIGHT. PLEASE.
NO. YOU THINK YOU CAN BLINK THOSE PRETTY LITTLE EYES AND I'LL MELT JUST LIKE MOMMY AND DADDY DID. IT IS **MY CROWN**! I'M THE **ELDEST**!
JABBERWOCKY!

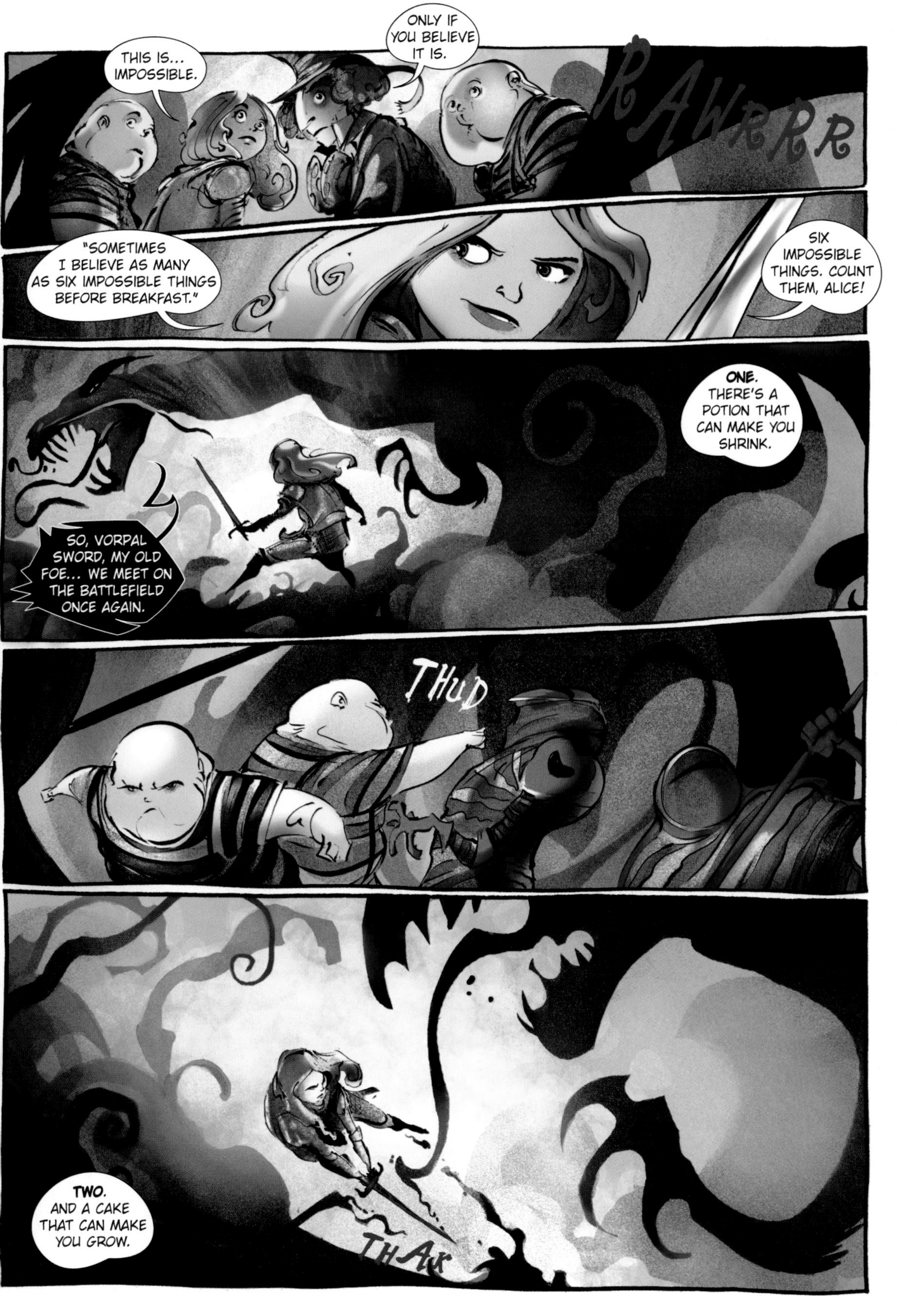
THIS IS... IMPOSSIBLE.
ONLY IF YOU BELIEVE IT IS.
RAWRRR
"SOMETIMES I BELIEVE AS MANY AS SIX IMPOSSIBLE THINGS BEFORE BREAKFAST."
SIX IMPOSSIBLE THINGS. COUNT THEM, ALICE!
ONE. THERE'S A POTION THAT CAN MAKE YOU SHRINK.
SO, VORPAL SWORD, MY OLD FOE... WE MEET ON THE BATTLEFIELD ONCE AGAIN.
THUD
TWO. AND A CAKE THAT CAN MAKE YOU GROW.
THAK

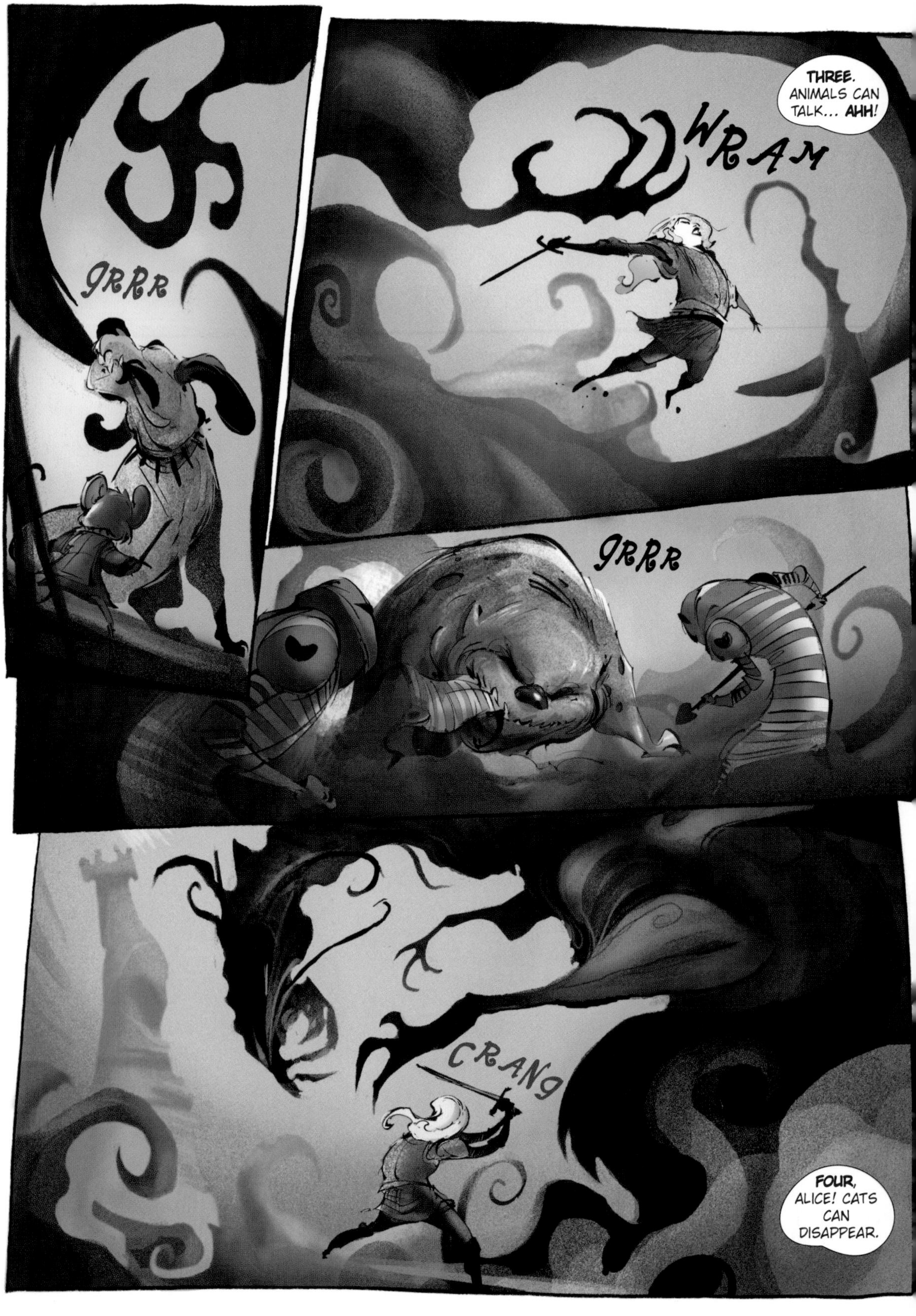
GRRR
THREE. ANIMALS CAN TALK... AHH!
WRAM
GRRR
CRANG
FOUR, ALICE! CATS CAN DISAPPEAR.

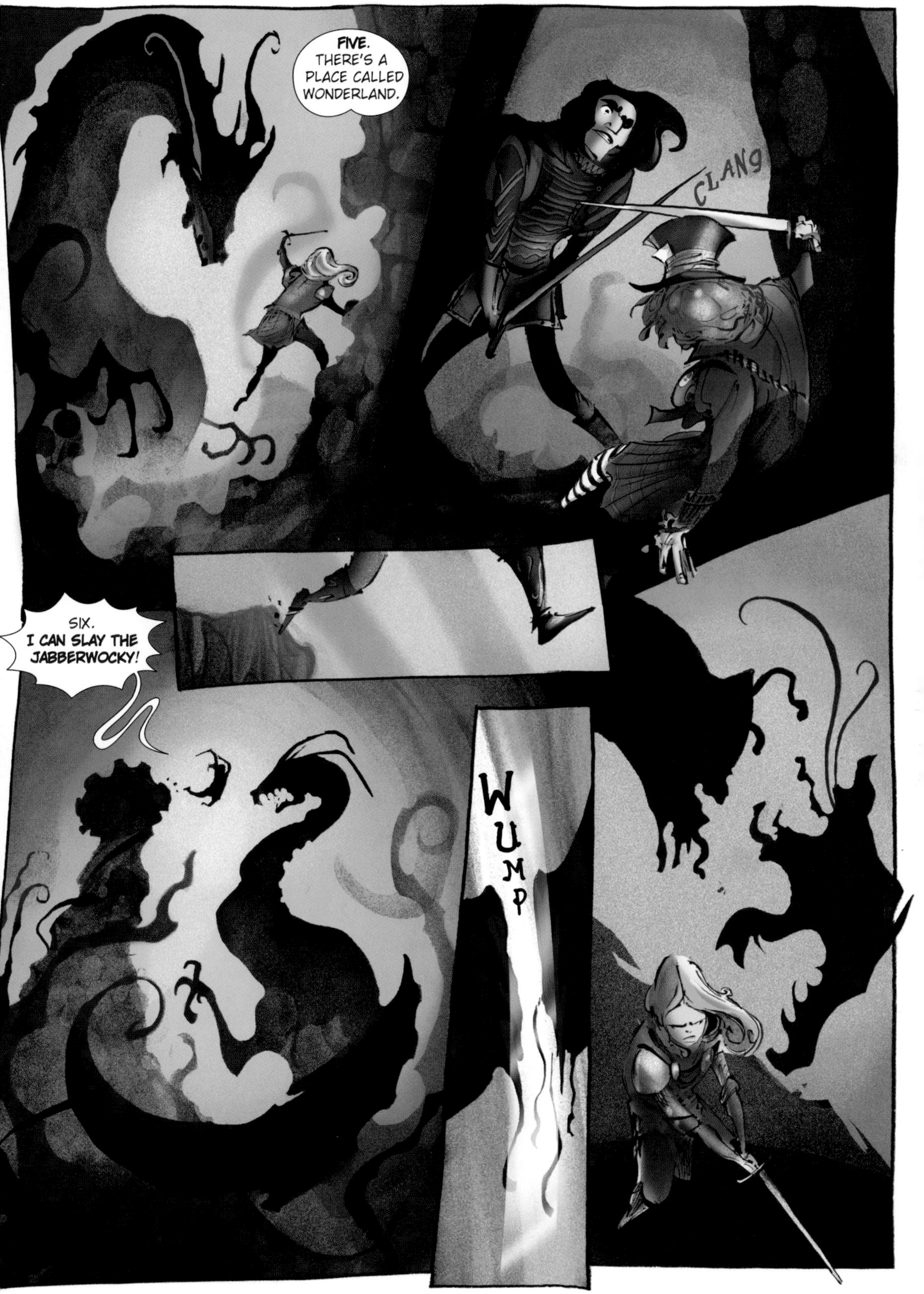
FIVE.
THERE'S A PLACE CALLED WONDERLAND.
CLANG
SIX.
I CAN SLAY THE JABBERWOCKY!
WUMP

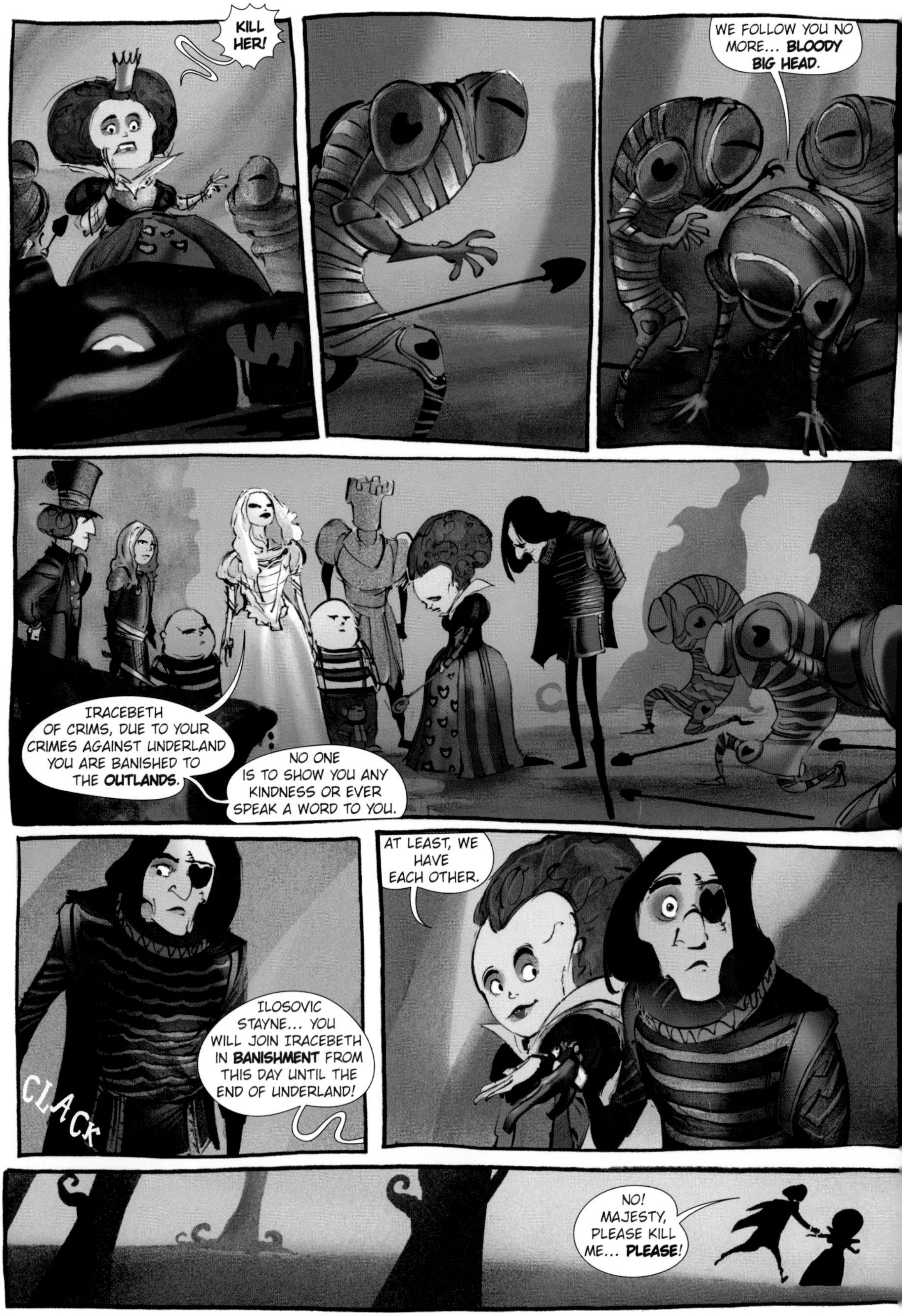
KILL HER!
WE FOLLOW YOU NO MORE... **BLOODY BIG HEAD**.
IRACEBETH OF CRIMS, DUE TO YOUR CRIMES AGAINST UNDERLAND YOU ARE BANISHED TO THE **OUTLANDS**.
NO ONE IS TO SHOW YOU ANY KINDNESS OR EVER SPEAK A WORD TO YOU.
ILOSOVIC STAYNE... YOU WILL JOIN IRACEBETH IN **BANISHMENT** FROM THIS DAY UNTIL THE END OF UNDERLAND!
CLACK
AT LEAST, WE HAVE EACH OTHER.
NO! MAJESTY, PLEASE KILL ME... **PLEASE**!

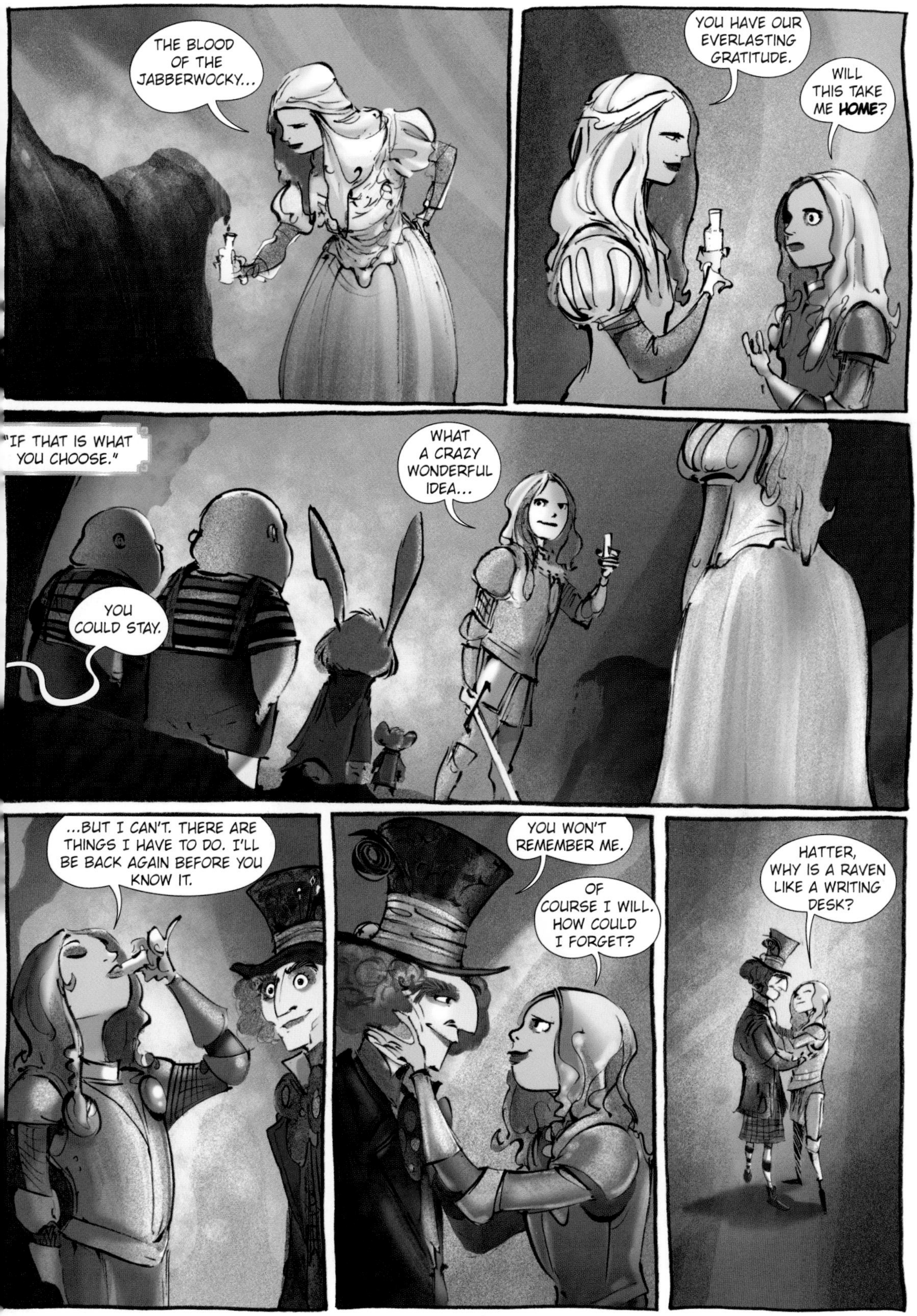
THE BLOOD OF THE JABBERWOCKY...
YOU HAVE OUR EVERLASTING GRATITUDE.
WILL THIS TAKE ME **HOME**?
"IF THAT IS WHAT YOU CHOOSE."
WHAT A CRAZY WONDERFUL IDEA...
YOU COULD STAY.
...BUT I CAN'T. THERE ARE THINGS I HAVE TO DO. I'LL BE BACK AGAIN BEFORE YOU KNOW IT.
YOU WON'T REMEMBER ME.
OF COURSE I WILL. HOW COULD I FORGET?
HATTER, WHY IS A RAVEN LIKE A WRITING DESK?

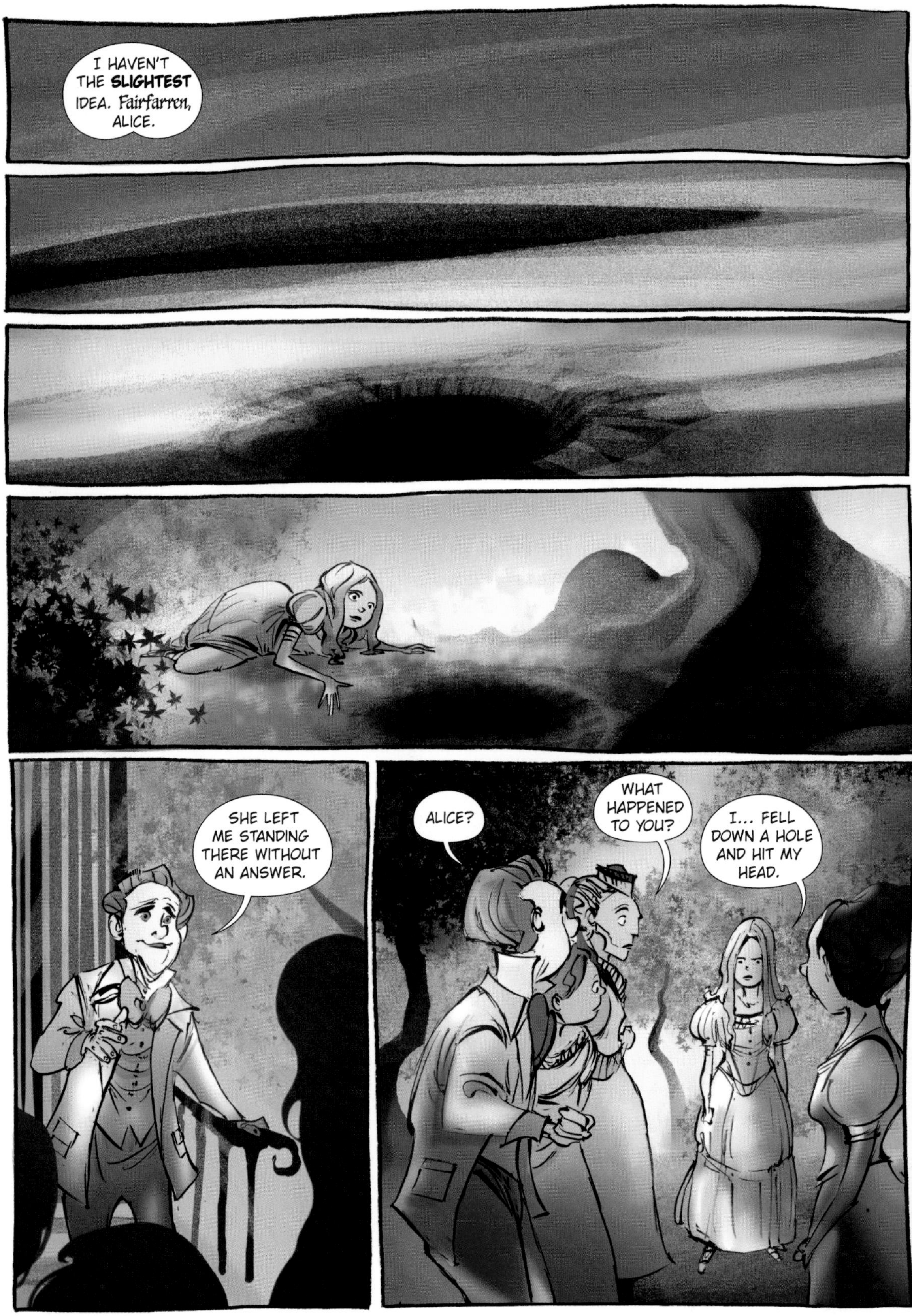
I HAVEN'T THE SLIGHTEST IDEA. Fairfarren, ALICE.
SHE LEFT ME STANDING THERE WITHOUT AN ANSWER.
ALICE?
WHAT HAPPENED TO YOU?
I... FELL DOWN A HOLE AND HIT MY HEAD.

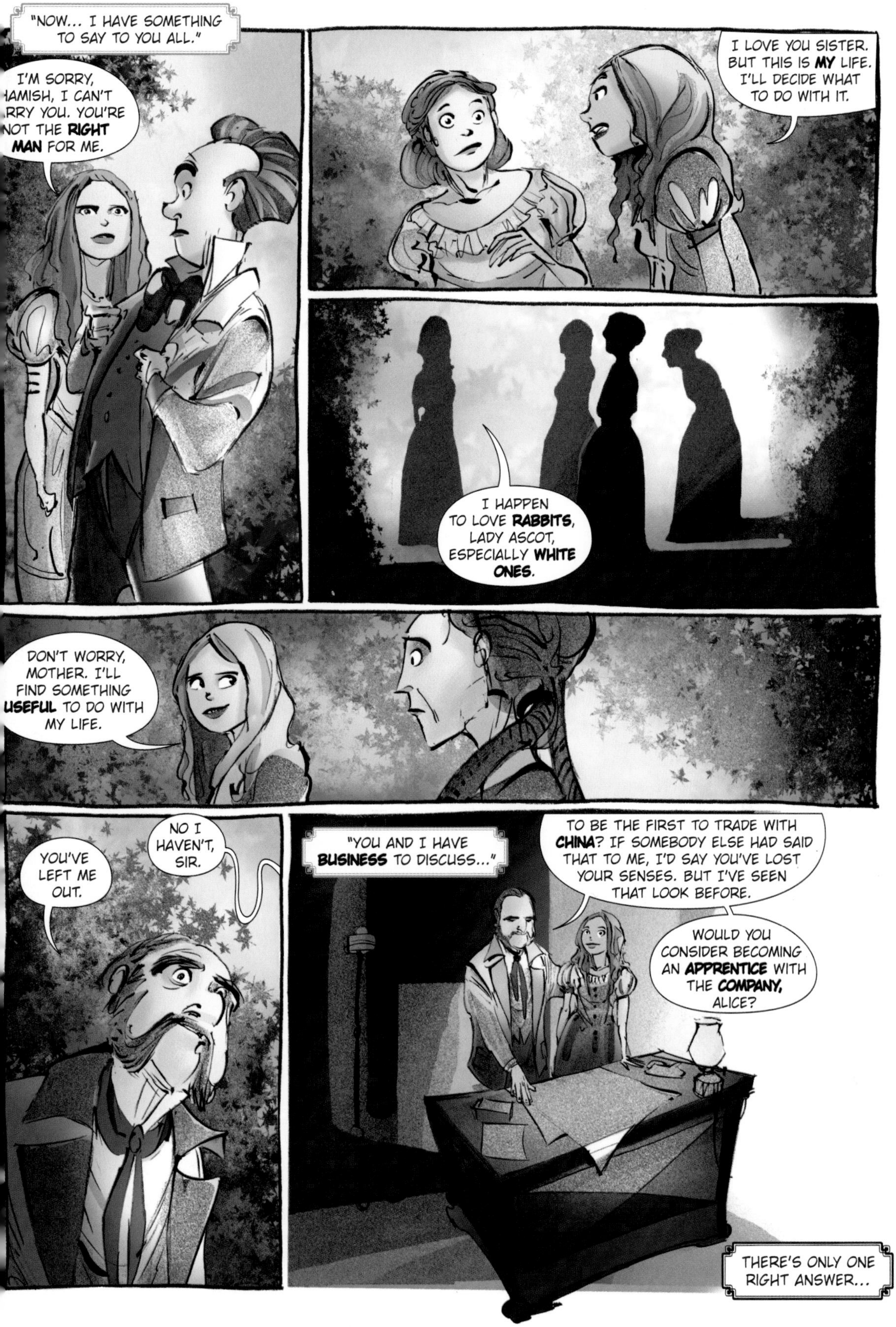
"NOW... I HAVE SOMETHING TO SAY TO YOU ALL."
I'M SORRY, HAMISH, I CAN'T MARRY YOU. YOU'RE NOT THE **RIGHT MAN** FOR ME.
I LOVE YOU SISTER. BUT THIS IS **MY** LIFE. I'LL DECIDE WHAT TO DO WITH IT.
I HAPPEN TO LOVE **RABBITS**, LADY ASCOT, ESPECIALLY **WHITE ONES**.
DON'T WORRY, MOTHER. I'LL FIND SOMETHING **USEFUL** TO DO WITH MY LIFE.
YOU'VE LEFT ME OUT.
NO I HAVEN'T, SIR.
"YOU AND I HAVE **BUSINESS** TO DISCUSS..."
TO BE THE FIRST TO TRADE WITH **CHINA**? IF SOMEBODY ELSE HAD SAID THAT TO ME, I'D SAY YOU'VE LOST YOUR SENSES. BUT I'VE SEEN THAT LOOK BEFORE.
WOULD YOU CONSIDER BECOMING AN **APPRENTICE** WITH THE **COMPANY,** ALICE?
THERE'S ONLY ONE RIGHT ANSWER...

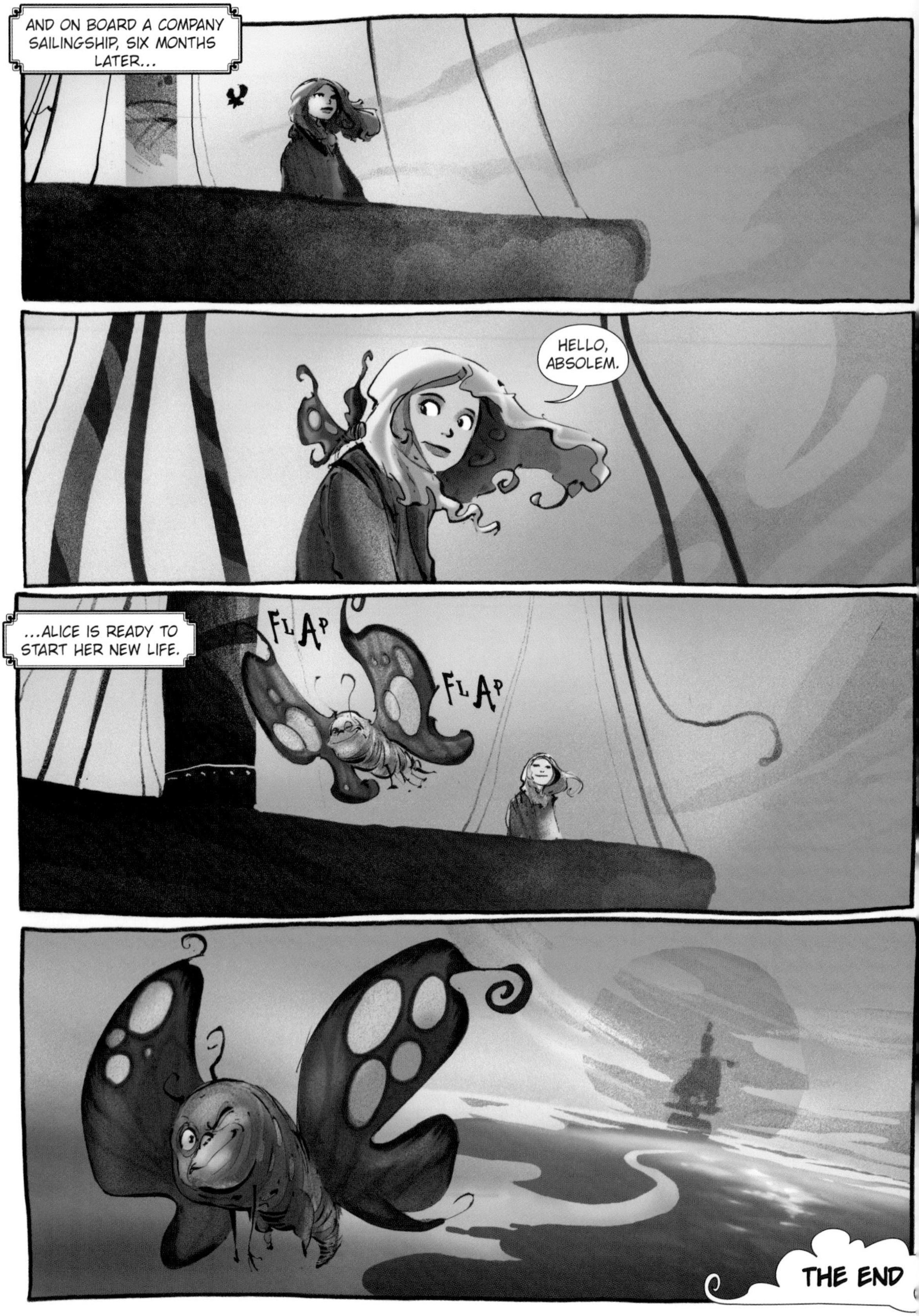
AND ON BOARD A COMPANY SAILINGSHIP, SIX MONTHS LATER...
HELLO, ABSOLEM.
...ALICE IS READY TO START HER NEW LIFE.
FLAP
FLAP
THE END

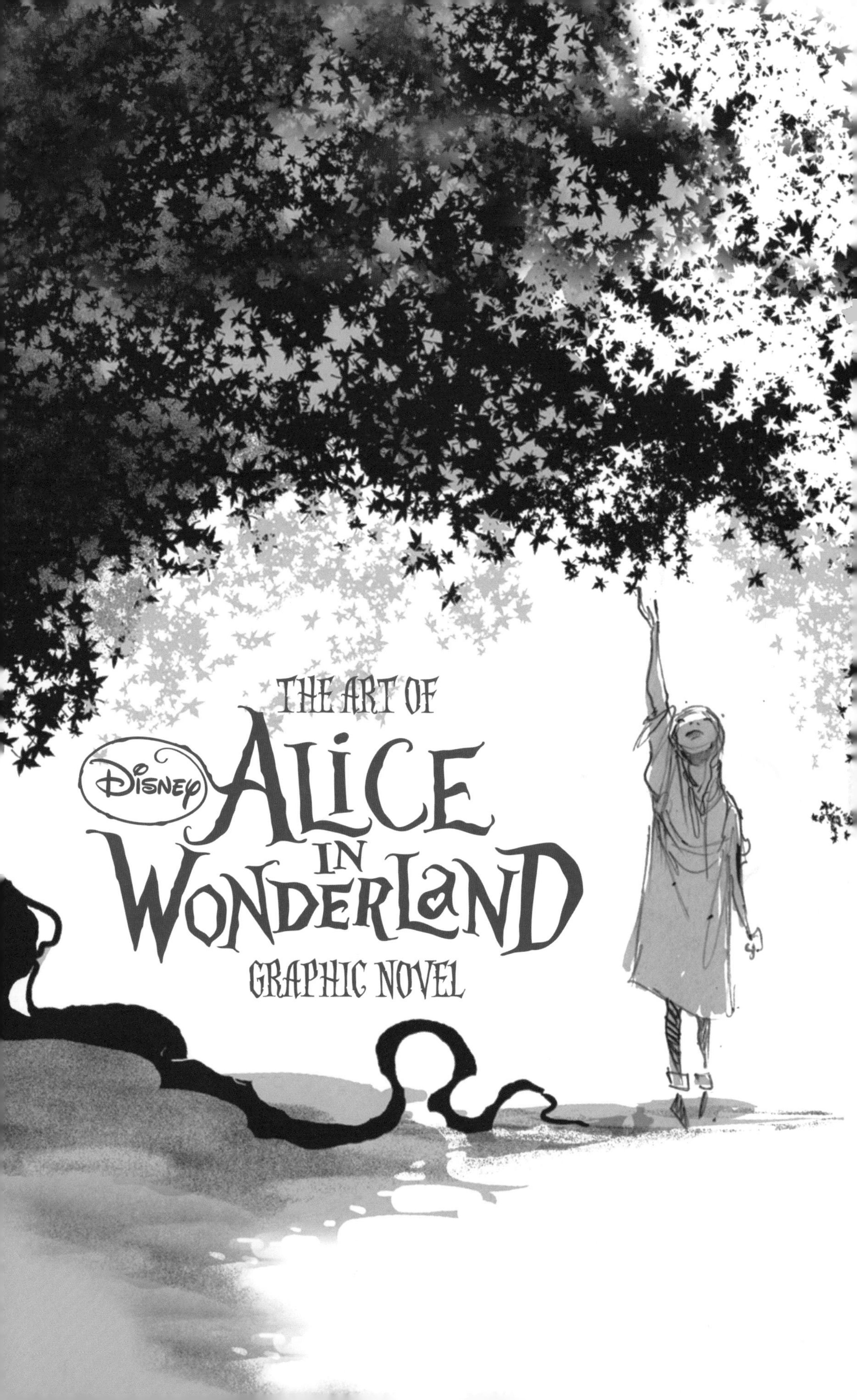
THE ART OF
DISNEY
ALICE IN WONDERLAND
GRAPHIC NOVEL

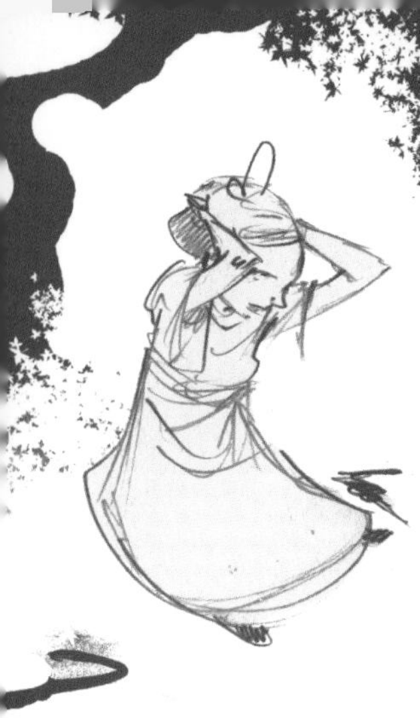

INTRODUCTION

July 4, 1862. During a trip down the Thames with Reverend **Robinson Duckworth** and math teacher Mr. **Charles Lutwidge Dodgson**, **Alice Liddell** and her sisters insist on hearing a story. So Dodgson invents one about a girl named Alice who falls down a rabbit hole and embarks on an amazing adventure. Little Alice is thrilled with the story and asks Dodgson to write it down in a book.

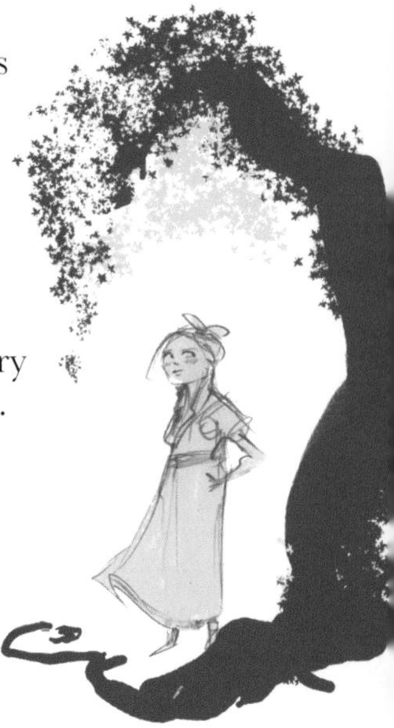

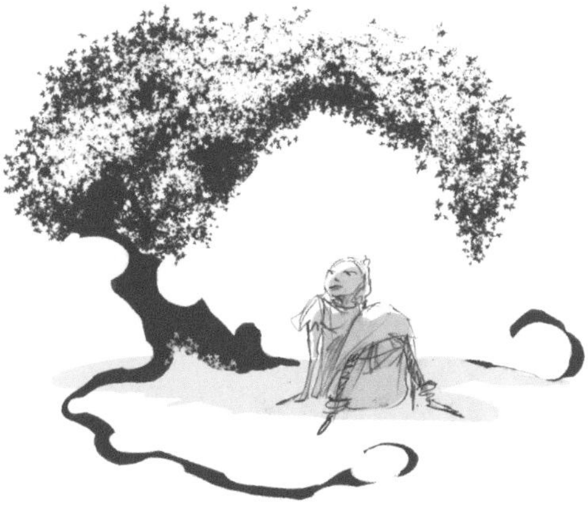

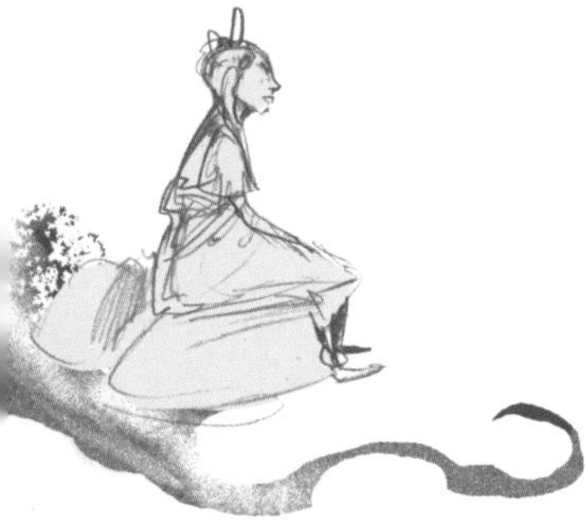

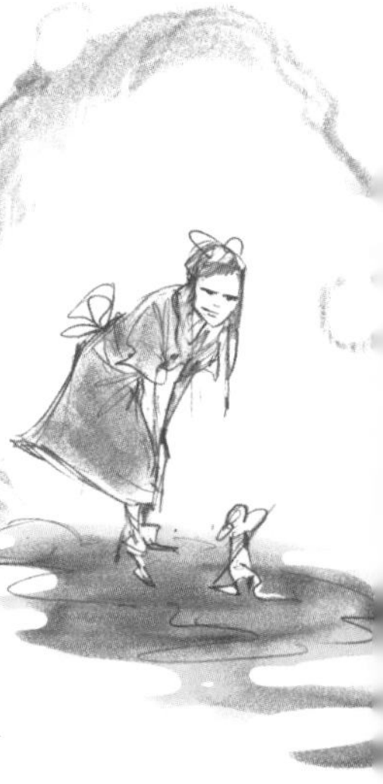

It takes him two years, but Dodgson finally hands the manuscript over to Alice. It's titled *Alice's Adventures Underground*, and it tells of an incredible journey through forests filled with talking mushrooms and flowers while in the company of the **Mad Hatter**, the **Cheshire Cat** and the **Queen of Hearts**.

In 1865, the book is published by **MacMillan** and achieves enormous success. The title has changed – it's now *Alice's Adventures in Wonderland* – and the author, Dodgson, uses the pen name **Lewis Carroll**. But the story remains the same. It's an incredible adventure that will change children's literature forever, because this time the story is written from a child's point of view.

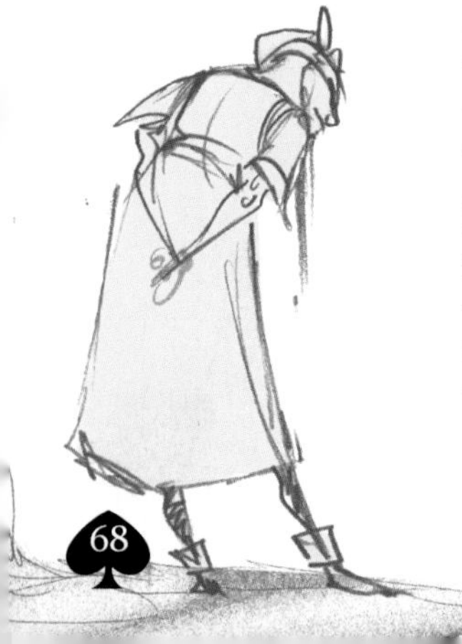

Another book is published in 1871: *Through the Looking Glass and What Alice Found There.* Even more popular than its predecessor, Carroll's second book introduces characters like **Tweedle Dee** and **Tweedle Dum**, the **White Queen**, the **Red Queen**, and **Humpty Dumpty**.

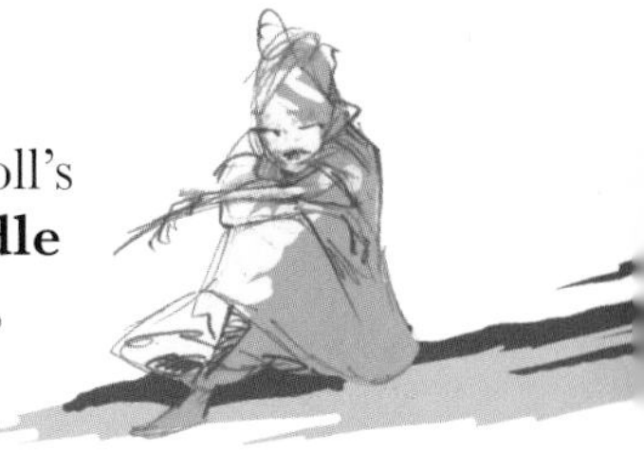

Lewis Carroll doesn't write any other stories about Alice, but her adventures continue as adaptations are made of Carroll's books: movies, cartoons, musicals, plays, television series, songs, videogames…and comic strips.

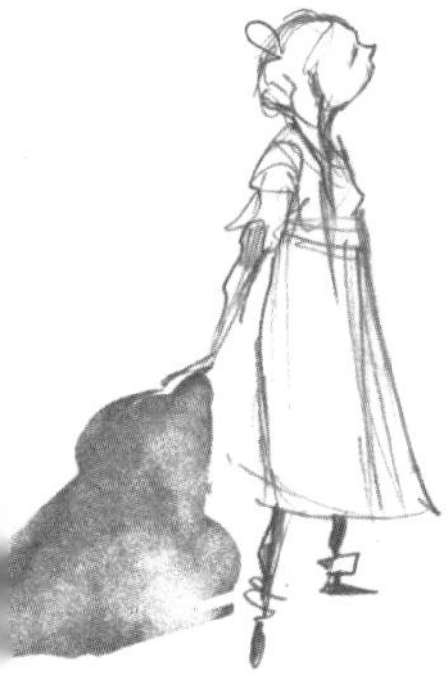

In 2007, the Walt Disney Studios start working on a new movie inspired by Alice's adventures. This time, though, it's not an adaptation. The story starts many years later, when Alice is 19 years old and is about to get married. She thinks that Wonderland and all the characters she met there were a dream, the same dream that has been tormenting her since she was a child. But when she tumbles into the rabbit hole again, she finds herself living the dream once more, and she discovers that nothing is like it was before, not even herself.

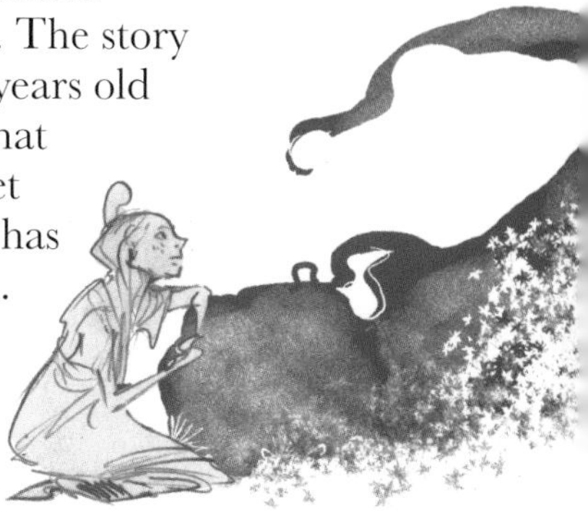

It all begins with **Linda Woolverton** (screenwriter for *Beauty and the Beast* and *The Lion King*), who has an idea for updating the famous and beloved character. Then the director arrives: **Tim Burton**, former in-between artist at Disney and creator of Disney's masterpiece *The Nightmare Before Christmas*. Poet of the diverse throughout his filmography, Burton is the perfect choice to give shape to the story written by Woolverton.

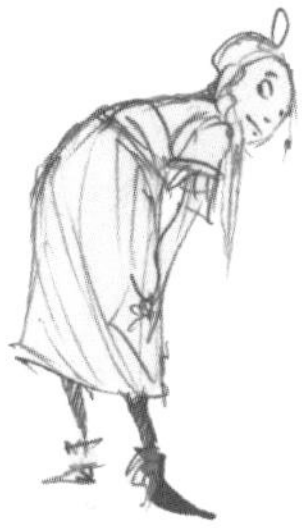

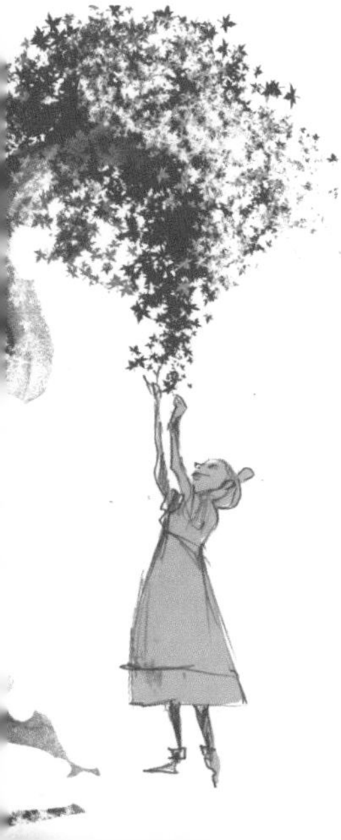

After her father's death, Alice feels nobody understands her. She feels lost. Only Wonderland will be able to show her the way again. It's a perfect story for the cinema, and for a comic strip. That's what they thought at Disney Publishing when they began creating this graphic novel back in 2009. The original script was rewritten using vignettes and balloons instead of actors and sound. And creative research was undertaken to find the style, the character design, and the approach that would best render Alice's new, unforgettable adventure on paper. This is the result…

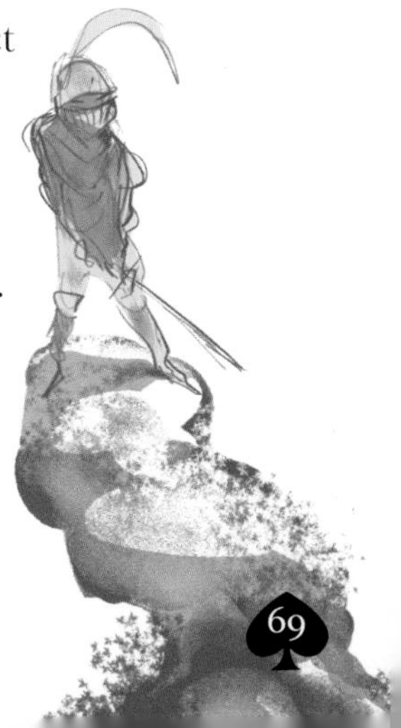

DOWN the RABBIT HOLE:
SKETCHES

*Before work begins on the actual comic pages, it's necessary
to define the style of the drawings, what shape the characters
will have, and which poses best represent their personalities.
For this graphic novel, the illustrators studied the concept art
done for the movie as well as Tim Burton's early drawings,
and artistic notes from the filmmakers. The first sketches
from this creative process are shown here and on
the following pages.*

With Max Narciso

Massimiliano Narciso, one of the artists
involved in the creative research, first tried
to capture the characters' personalities by simply
sketching pencil drawings, then by adding details
on computer with a graphics pad. To best recreate
the atmosphere of the movie, he chose a style using
contrasts and net silhouettes: black on white and
white on black.

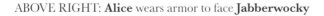

ABOVE: **Alice** meets **Absolem,** the Caterpillar,
in **Narciso's** version

ABOVE RIGHT: **Alice** wears armor to face **Jabberwocky**

RIGHT: **Alice**'s first studies, with striped socks and a ribbon in her hair as in the famous 1951 Disney animated version

BELOW: A roundup of the main characters - Twins **Tweedledee** and **Tweedledum**, the **Cheshire Cat**, the **White Rabbit**, **Alice**, the **Mad Hatter**, **Mally** and an interesting new entry: **Dodo**

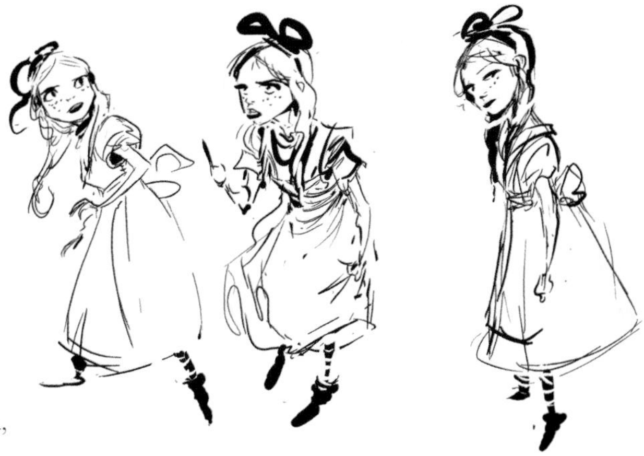

"All I want to do is wake up from this dream!"
ALICE

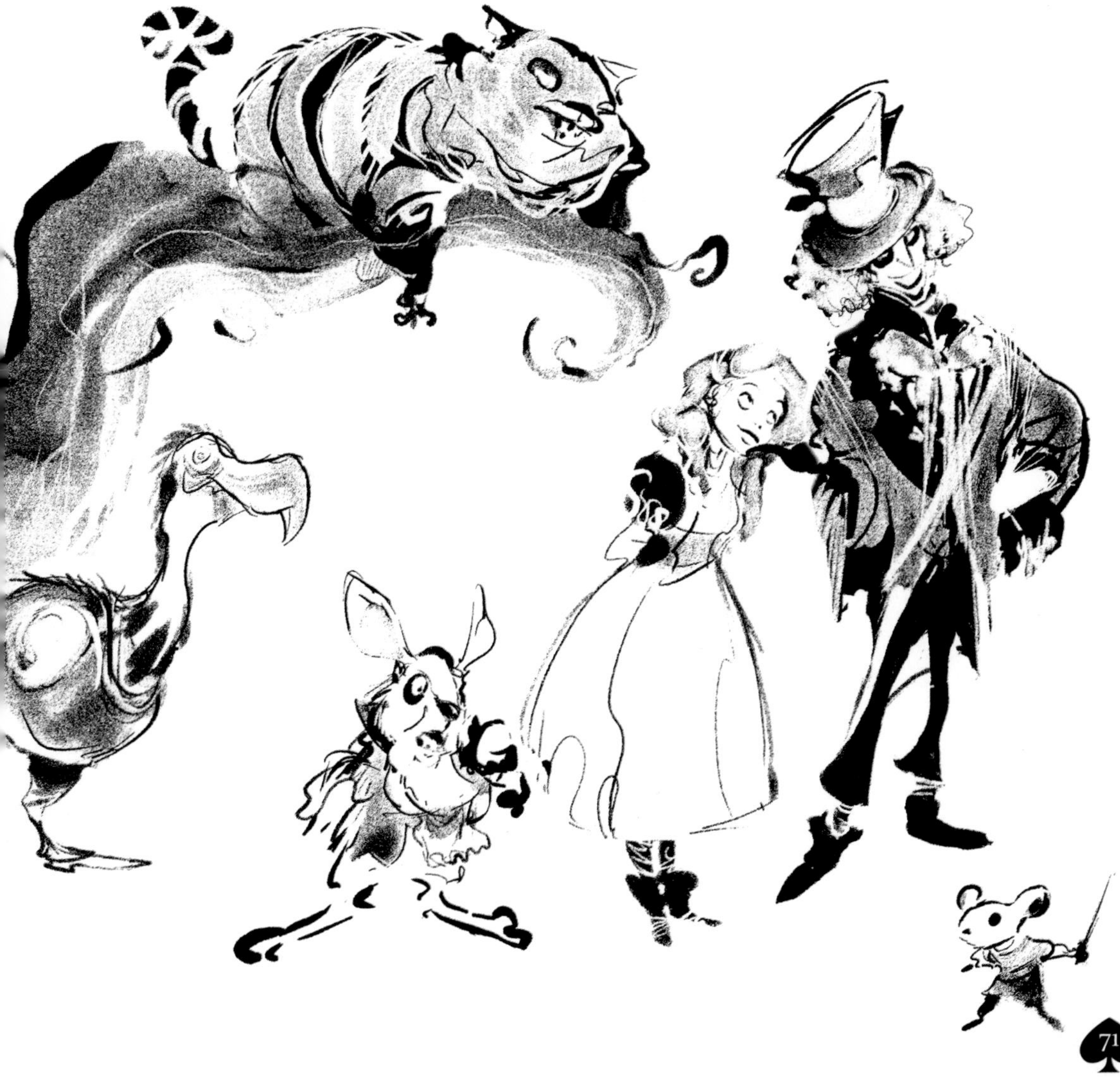

With Anna Merli

Anna Merli's approach differs from Narciso's. She based her work on the same reference material from the movie, but driven by her own personal influences, she pursued a more fairy-tale route, using colored pencils and wax pastels to create illustrations with soft colors and tones.

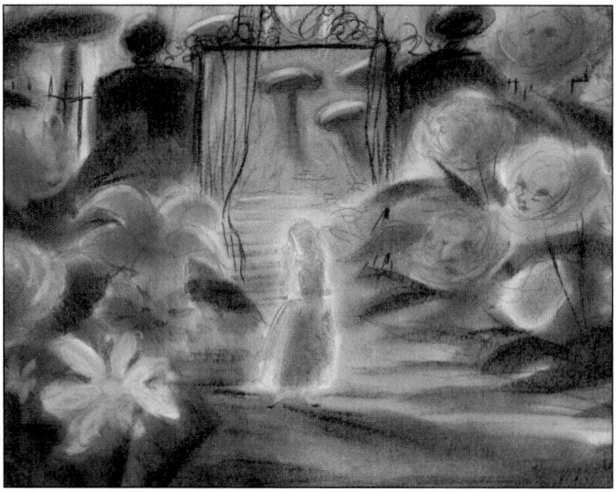

ABOVE: **Alice** enters the garden of talking flowers

LEFT AND RIGHT: The **Mad Hatter**

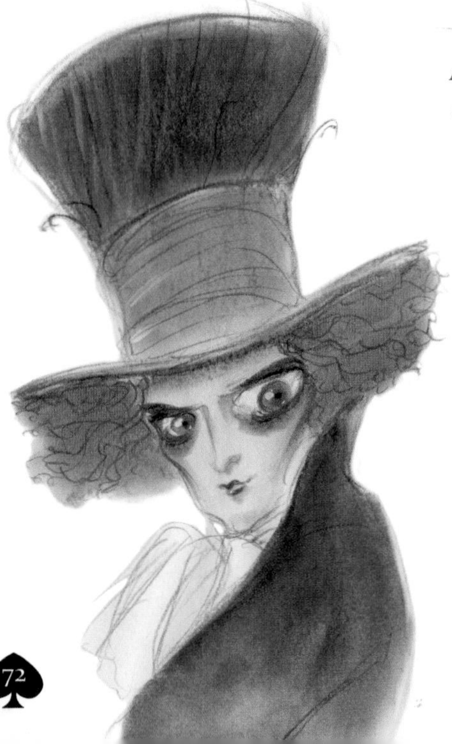

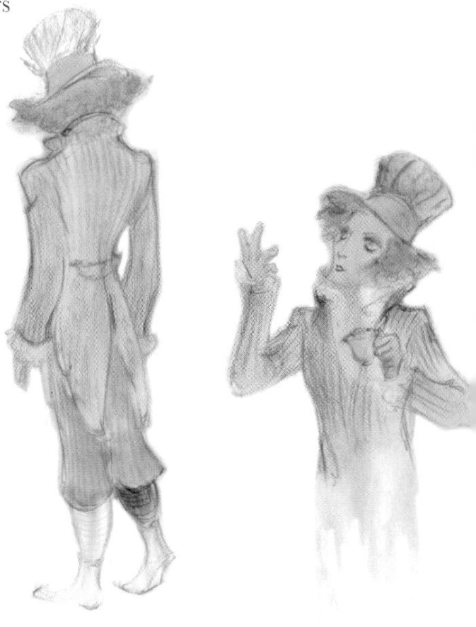

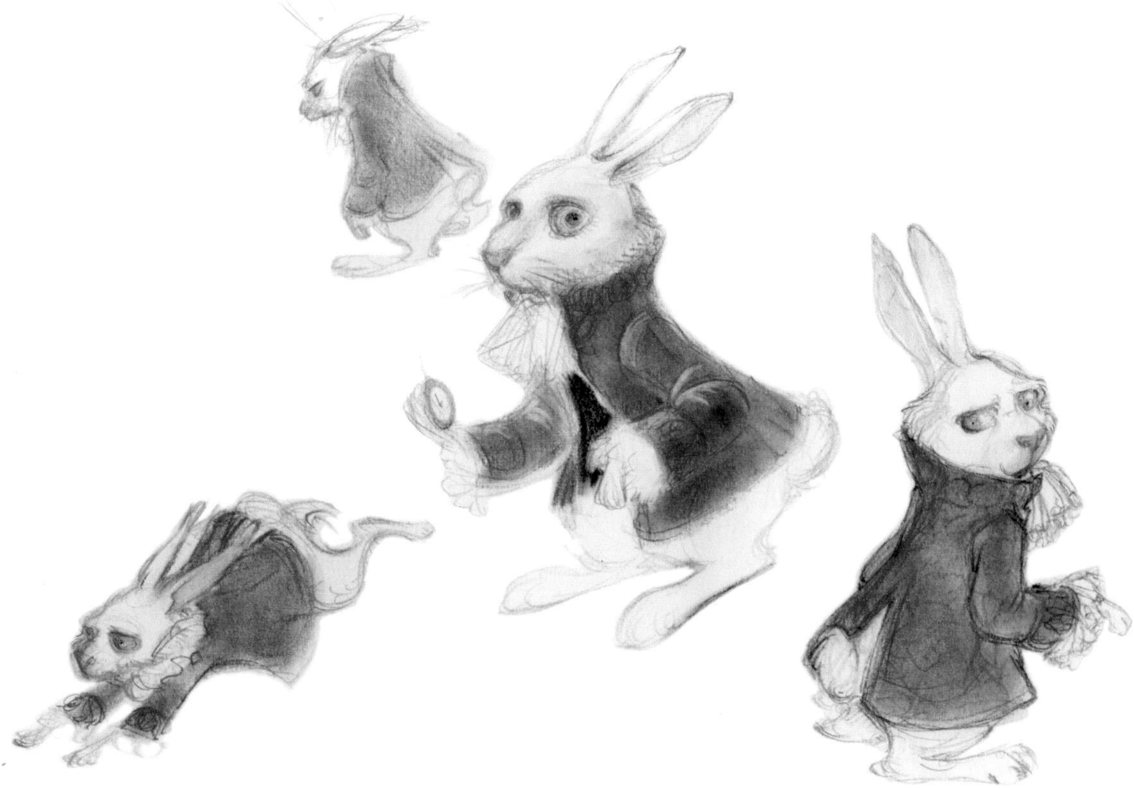

ABOVE: Studies for the character of **McTwisp**, the unmistakable White Rabbit

BELOW: Studies for the character of **Absolem** and his meeting with **Alice**

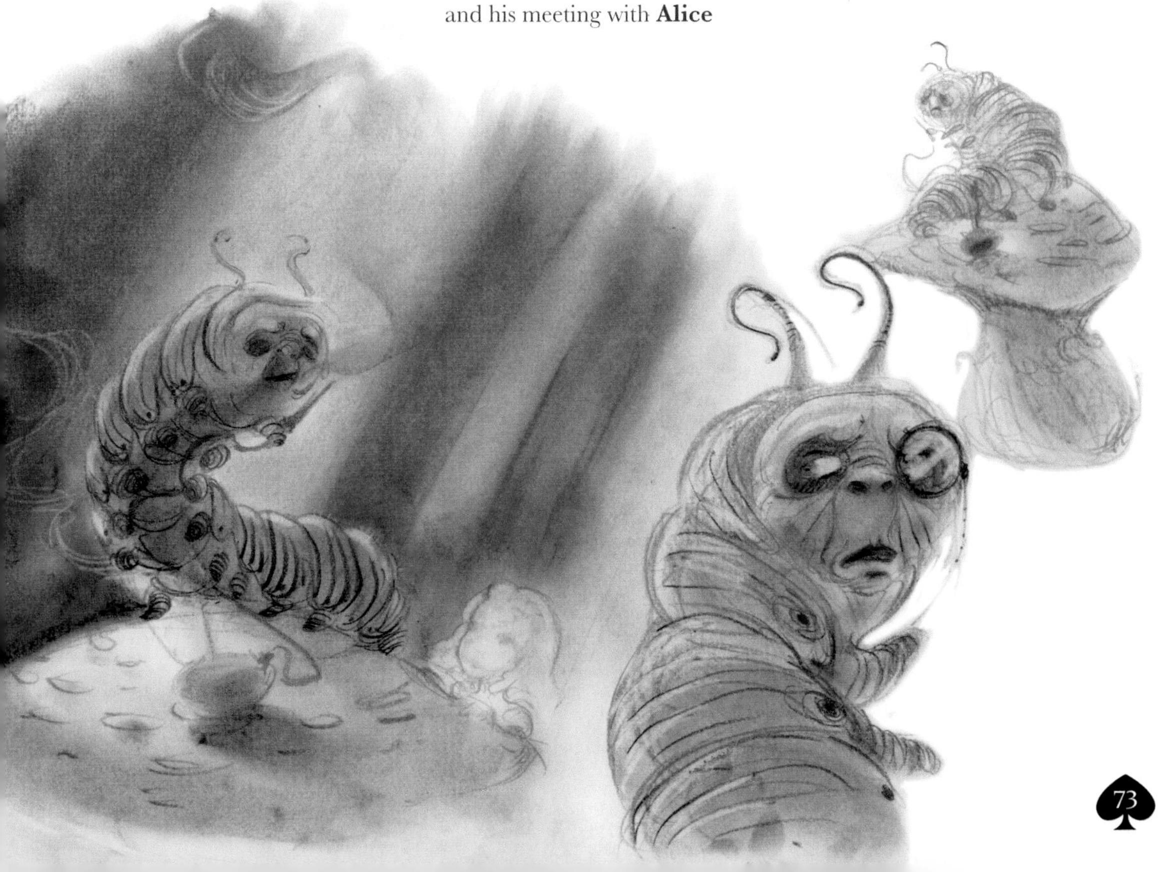

With Giovanni Rigano

A third illustrator, and a third point of view on Alice's world: When asked to draw these characters, **Giovanni Rigano** took a sheet of paper and a felt-tip and let inspiration take the lead. Afterward he colored his sketches on the computer, looking for tones that suggest an 1800s atmosphere, similar to those in Tim Burton's movie.

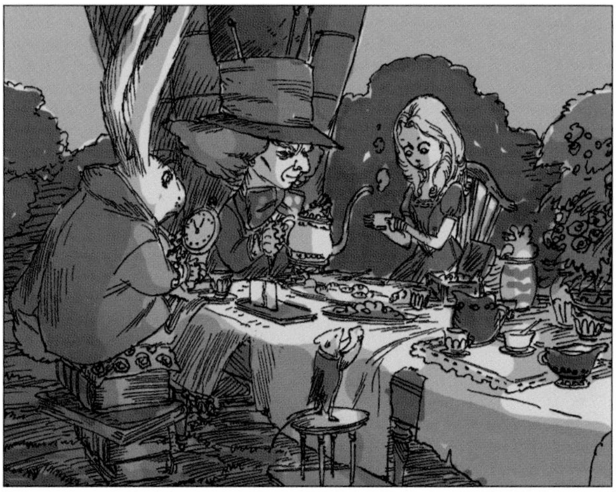

ABOVE: **Alice** drinks tea with the **Mad Hatter**, the **March Hare**, and **Mally**, the dormouse

LEFT: **Alice** has grown after eating a slice of Upelkuchen cake

RIGHT: **Alice** with **Absolem**, the cryptical Caterpillar

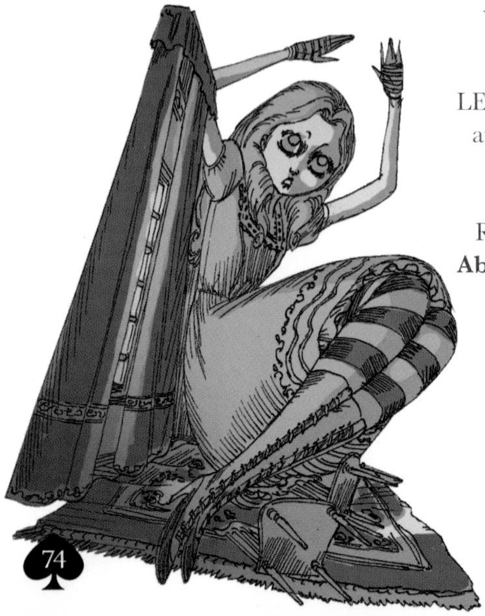

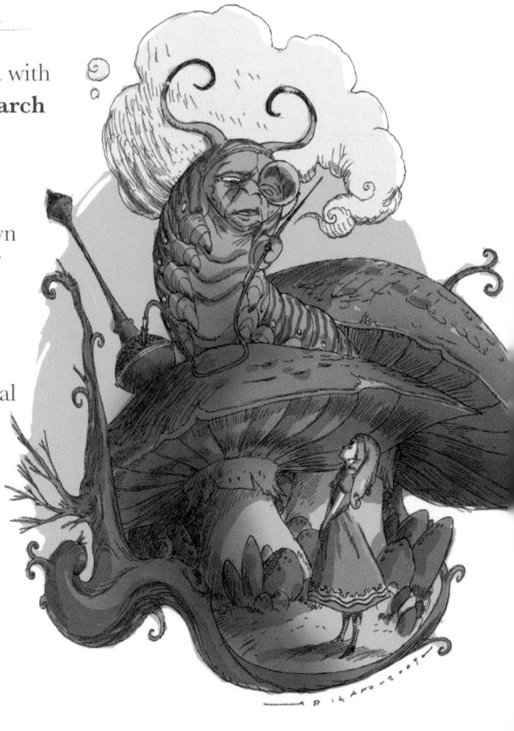

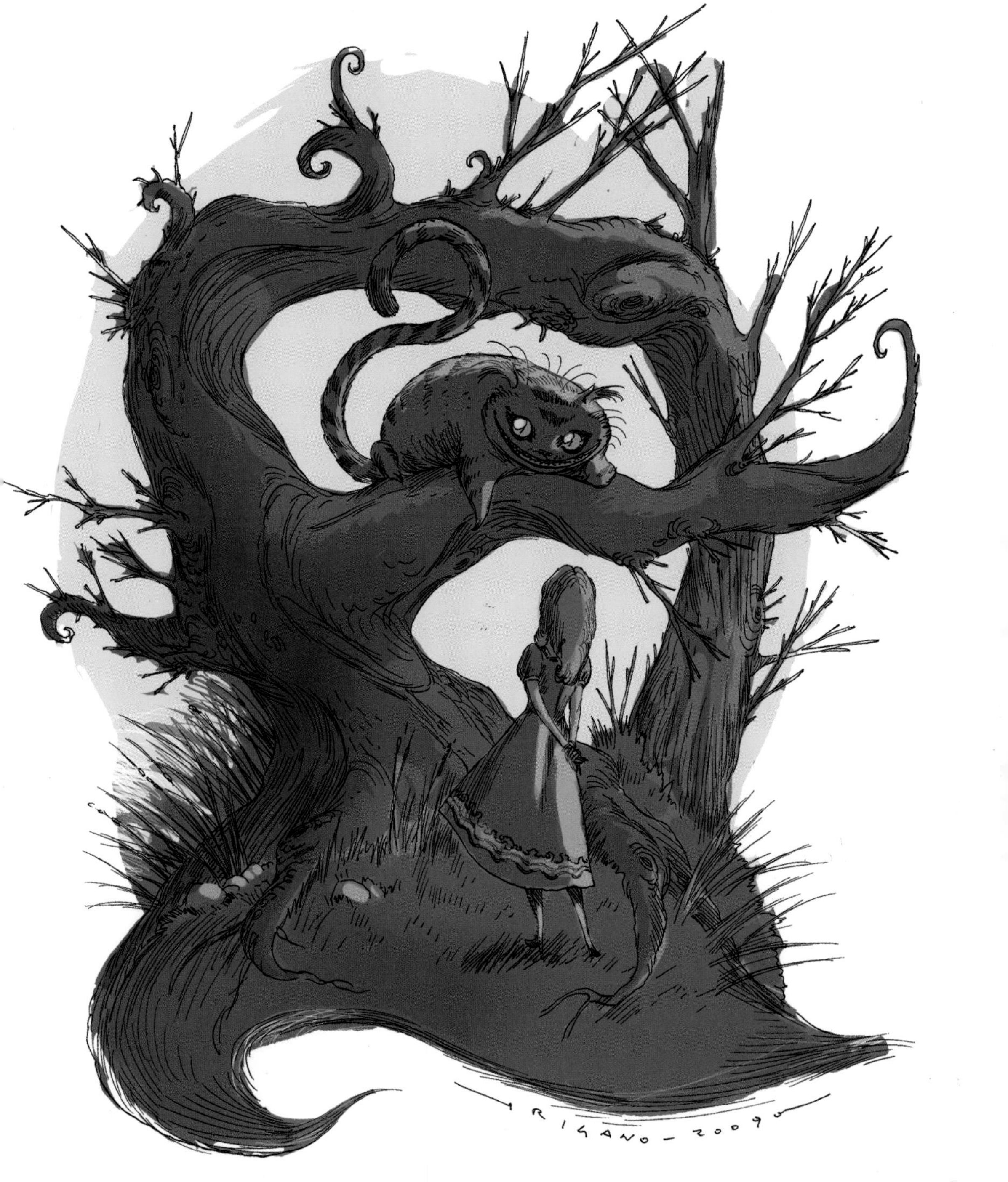
RIGANO - 2009

"And I am still dreaming!"

ALICE

ABOVE: The meeting between **Alice** and the **Cheshire Cat**

The ROUND HALL:

DEVELOPING
THE CHARACTERS

Among the different styles developed during the initial artistic research, Massimiliano Narciso's were seen as the most appropriate to deliver the atmosphere of the movie and characters' personalities. Initial sketches, however, give just a style direction, and an additional step is needed before the character design can be considered fully developed. The artist needs to finalize the main character models, detailing their poses and proper expressions.

Alice

Alice is the first fully-realized model. **Mia Wasikowska**, who plays Alice in the movie, describes her character as very different from the one in Carroll's books.
In the beginning, Alice is insecure and afraid of going mad.
At the end, when she becomes a Wonderland warrior and goes back home, she finds that her father's words were true: the best people are often a little mad.

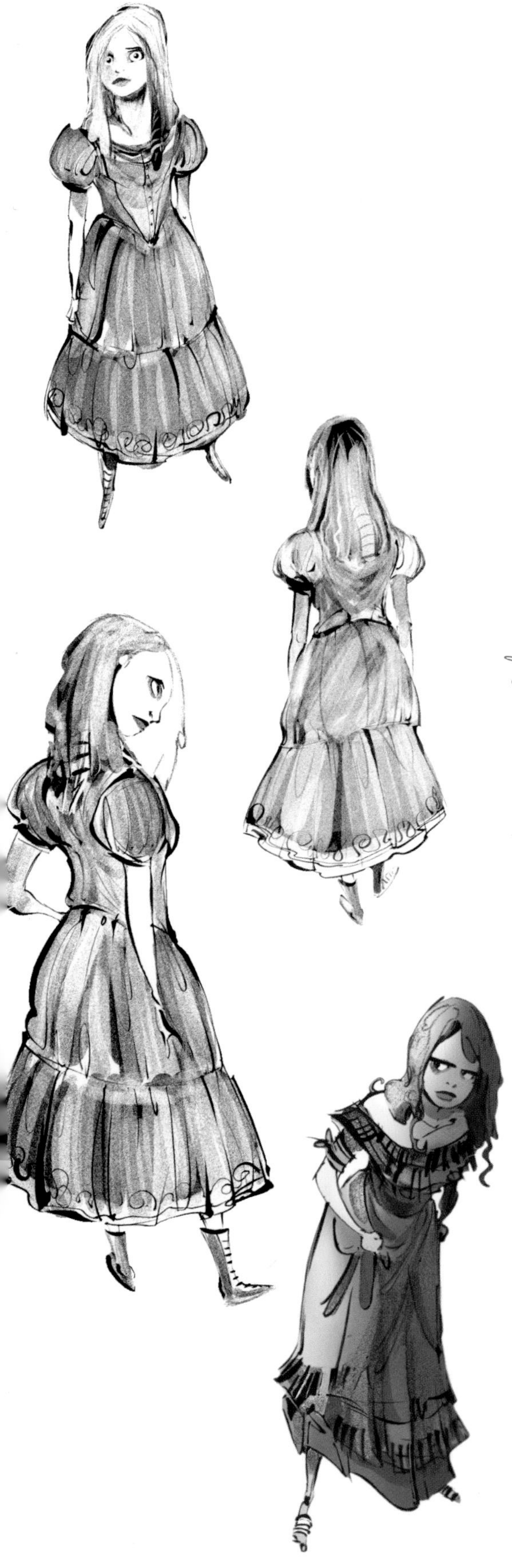

LEFT AND ON THE PREVIOUS PAGE: The studies for the model of **Alice**

BELOW: **Mia Wasikowska** as **Alice**, wearing her blue engagement party dress

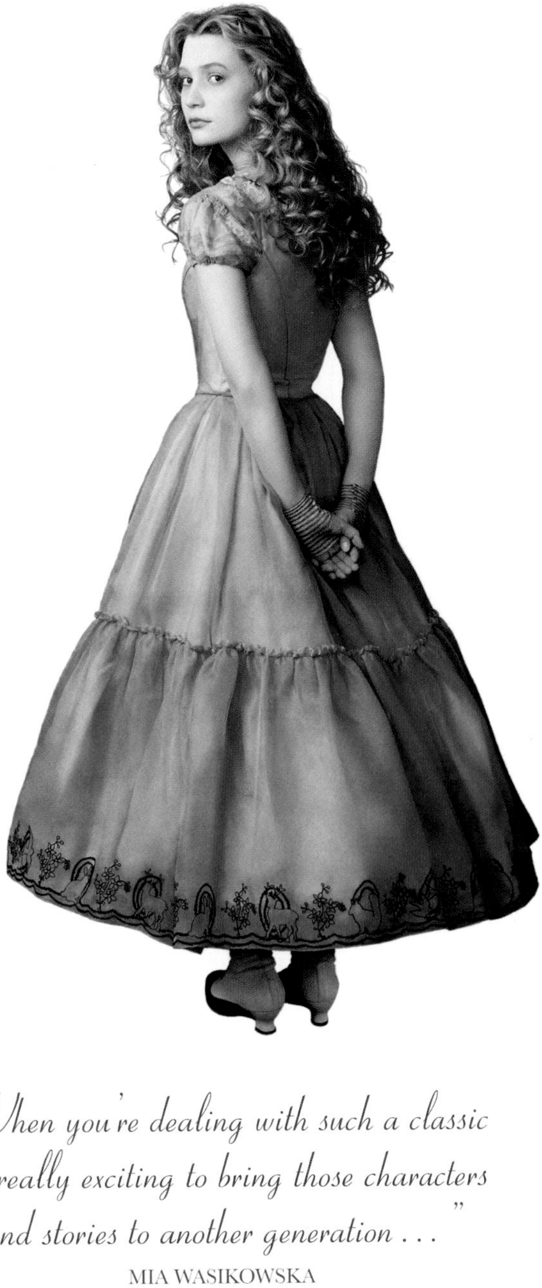

"When you're dealing with such a classic it's really exciting to bring those characters and stories to another generation . . ."

MIA WASIKOWSKA

Mad Hatter

The **Mad Hatter** is a point of reference for Alice in Wonderland. He is the only one who understands her, a little bit like her father. **Johnny Depp** brings him to life in the movie and says the Hatter just seems strange to people because he can't hide his emotions. His feelings, his fears and his happiness are so strong they have no filter. And that's why his clothes change color and shape depending on how he feels.

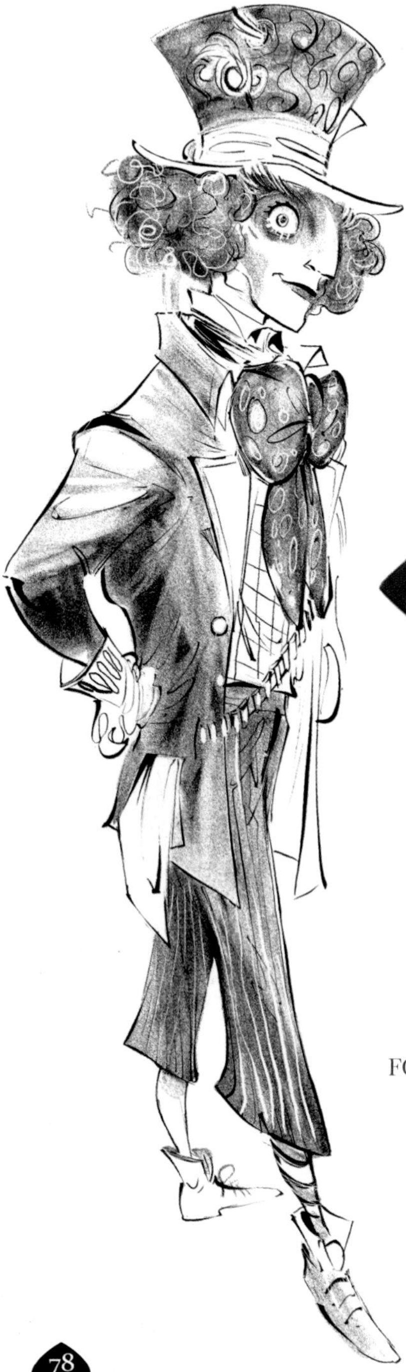

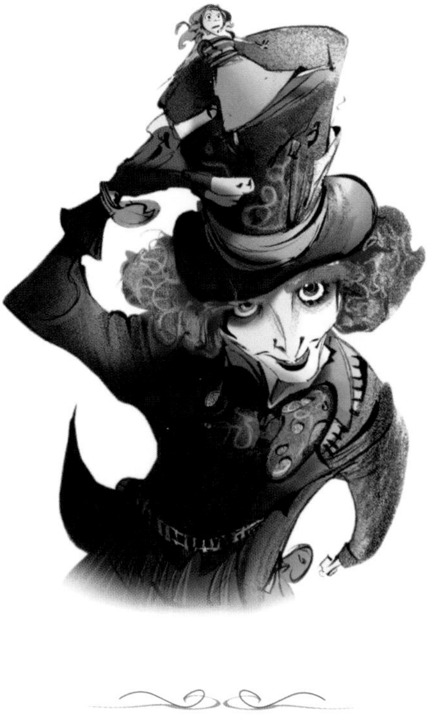

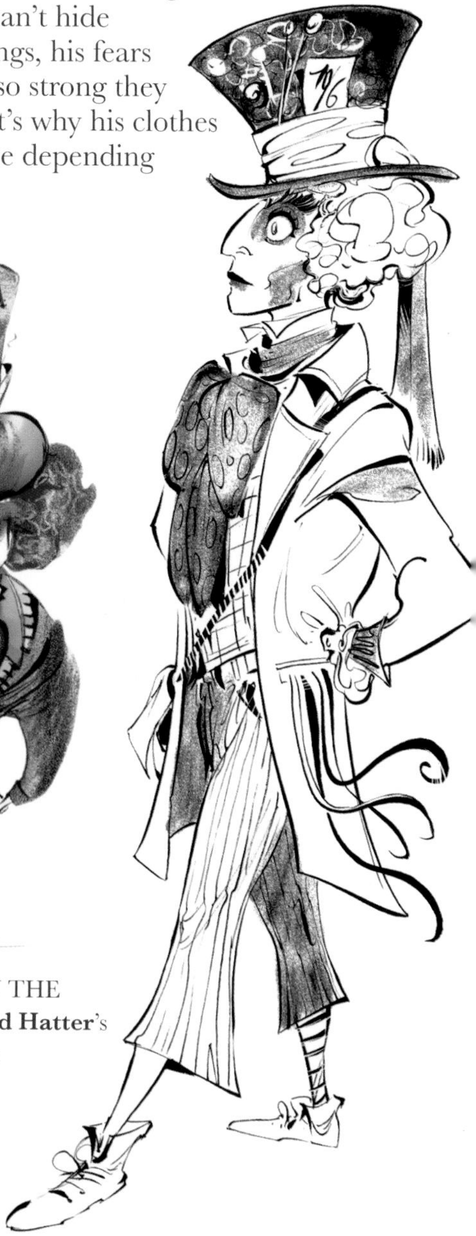
10/6

SHOWN HERE AND ON THE FOLLOWING PAGE: The **Mad Hatter**'s final character design

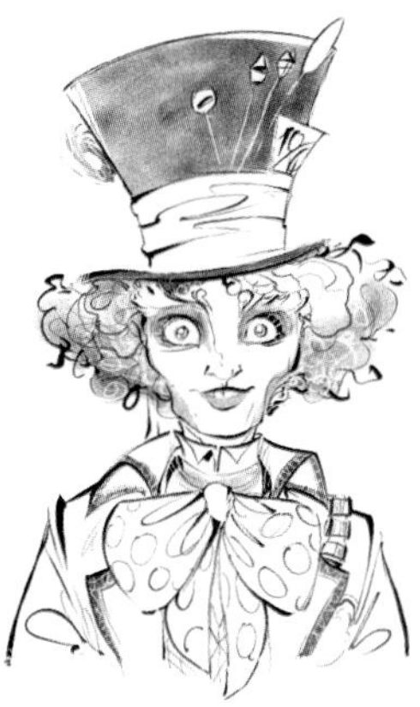

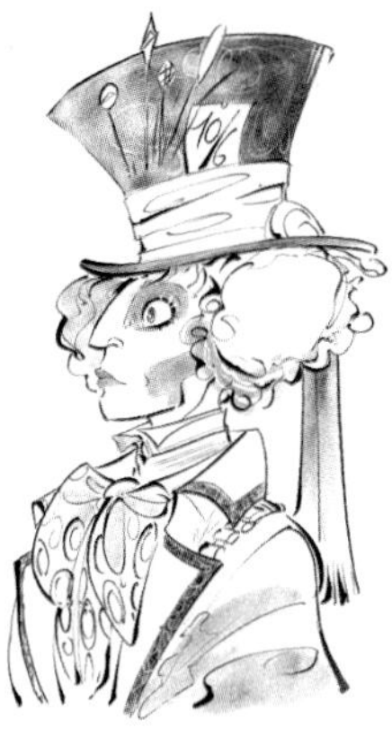

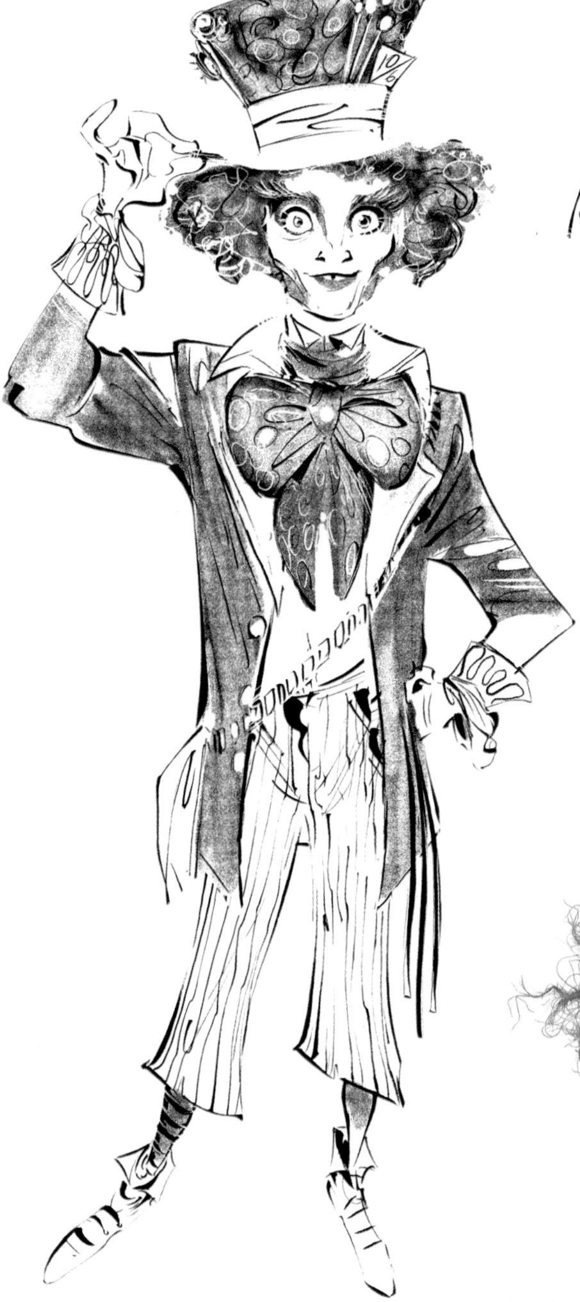

BELOW: **Johnny Depp** as the **Mad Hatter**

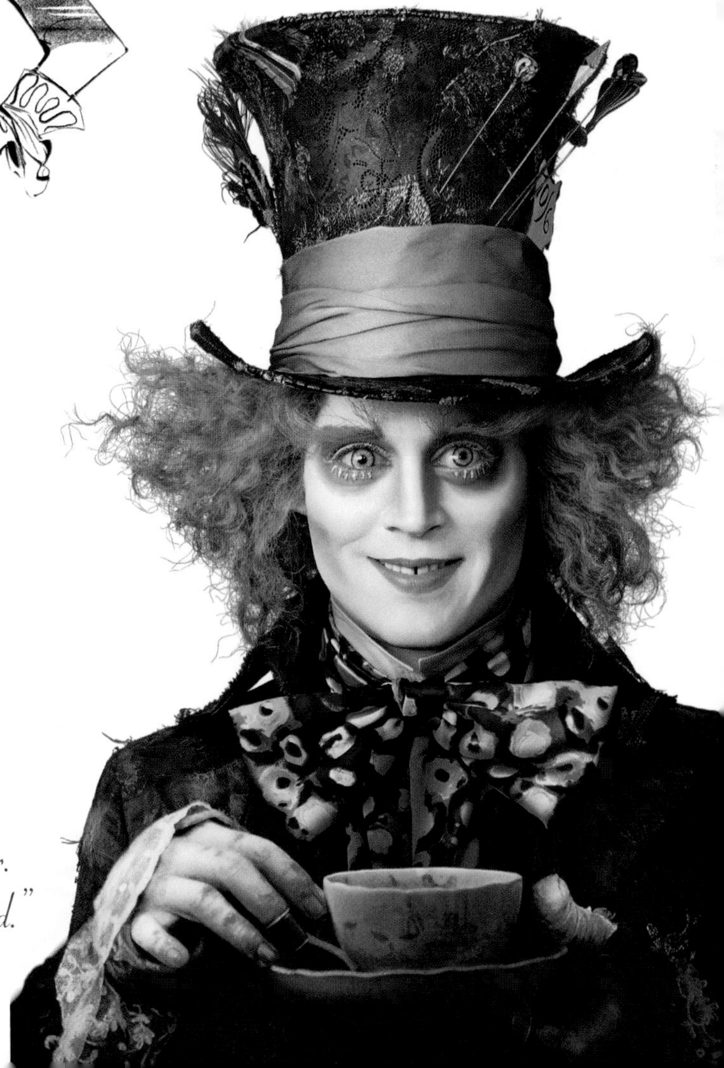

"I play the Mad Hatter. What is he like? He's mad."

JOHNNY DEPP

Red Queen

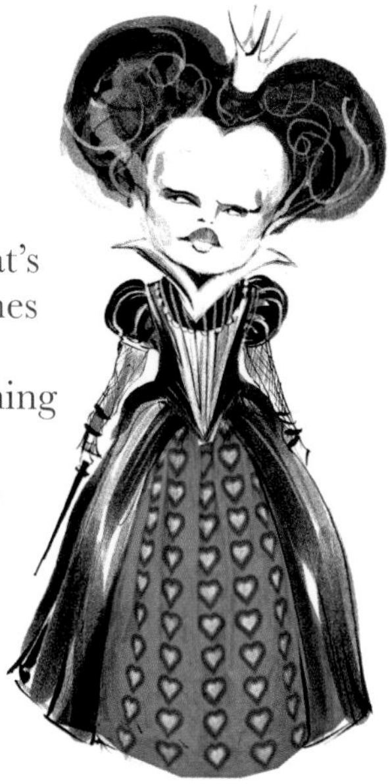

Iracebeth (the Red Queen's real name) is the baddy of the story who adores ordering that heads be cut off. Maybe that's because her own head is at least three times bigger than normal. Screenwriter Linda Woolverton believes there may be something growing inside that misshapen head. **Helena Bonham Carter**, who portrays the Red Queen in the movie, believes her character is just a spoiled girl.

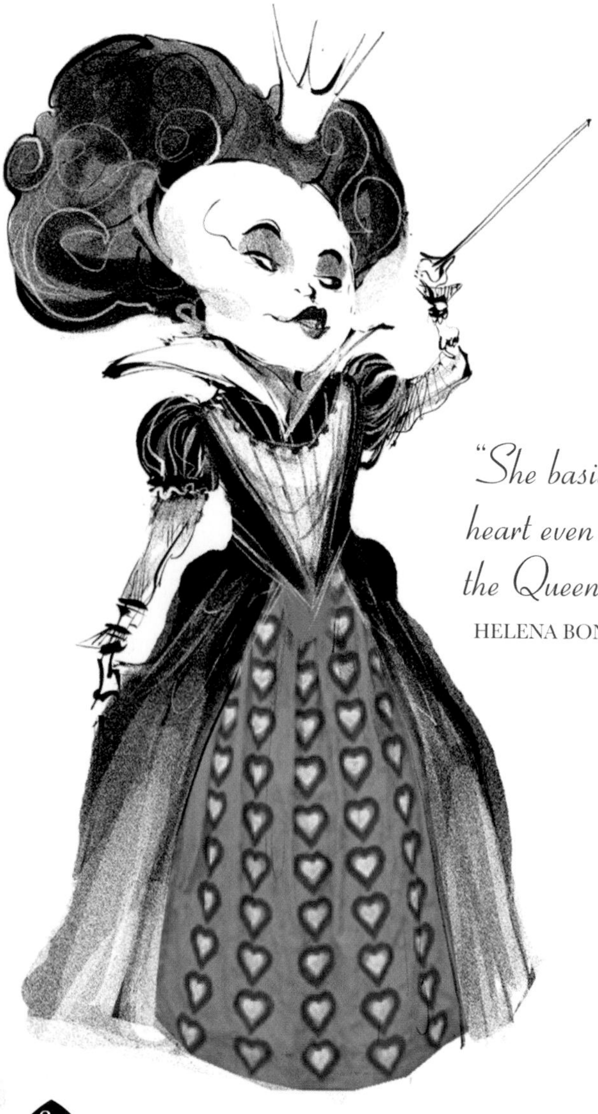

ABOVE AND LEFT: The definitive model. Note the shape of the head: it resembles a heart

BELOW: **Helena Bonham Carter** as the **Red Queen**

"She basically has no heart even though she's the Queen of Hearts."
HELENA BONHAM CARTER

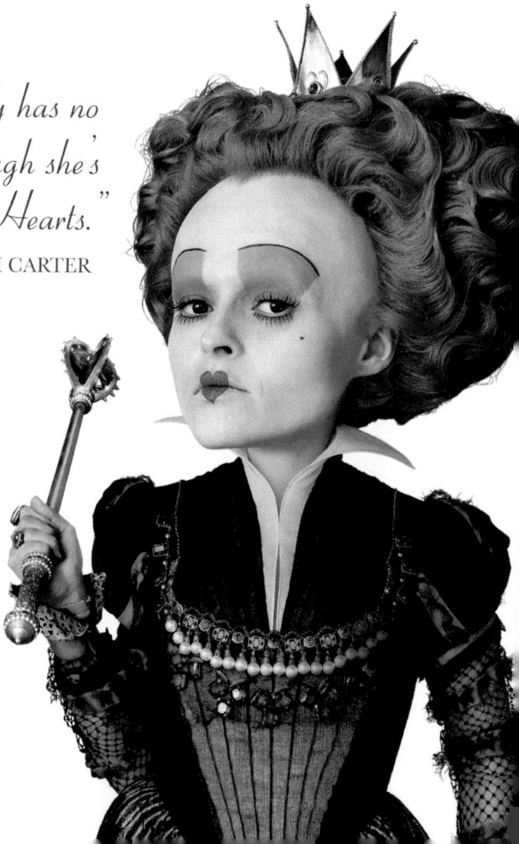

White Queen

Mirana is the Red Queen's sister and her complete opposite: good, kind and loved by her subjects. She awaits the arrival of a knight who can defeat her sister's Jabberwocky monster. Elegant and graceful, she dresses in white, which is also the predominant color in her castle.

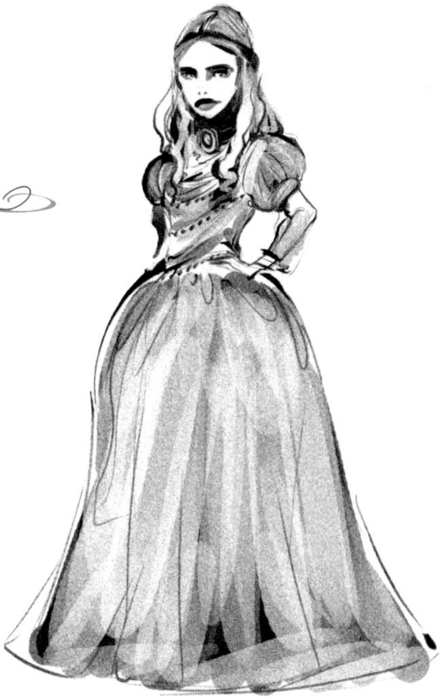

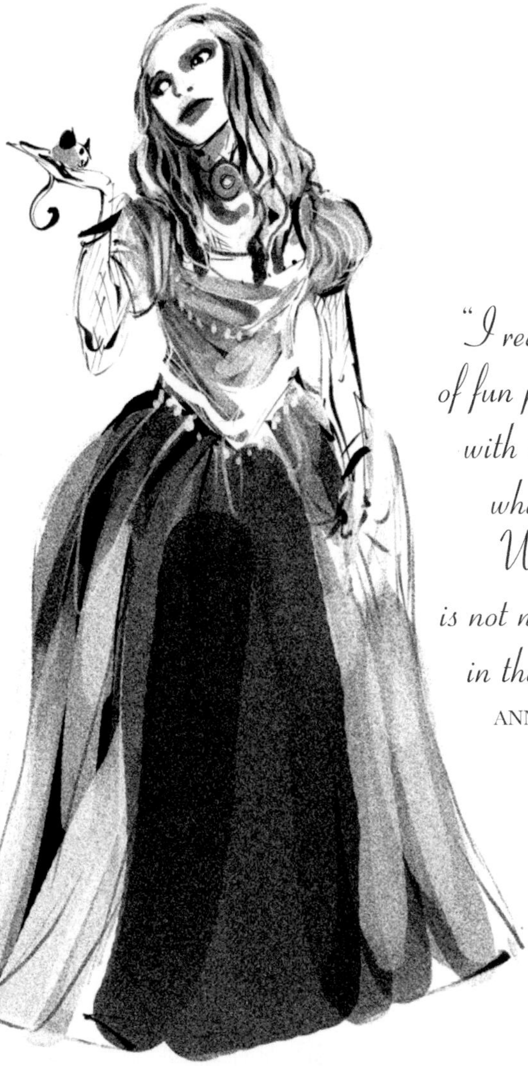

ABOVE AND LEFT: The definitive model for the graphic novel

BELOW: **Anne Hathaway** as the **White Queen**

"I really had a lot of fun playing around with this idea that what's good in Wonderland is not necessarily good in the real world."

ANNE HATHAWAY

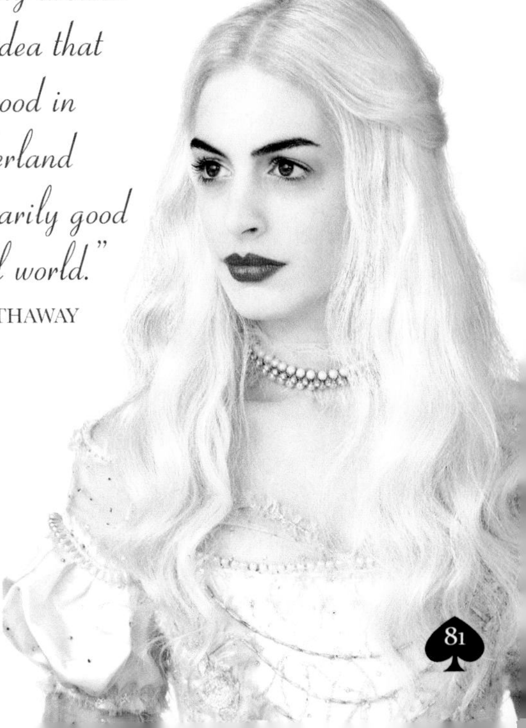

Knave of Hearts

In Lewis Carroll's first book, he was the Queen of Hearts' servant who was falsely accused of stealing a pie and risked losing his head. In actor **Crispin Glover**'s fascinating performance, his name is **Ilosovic Stayne**, and he is a cruel leader: He is the one who cuts off heads by order of his hated mistress, the Red Queen.

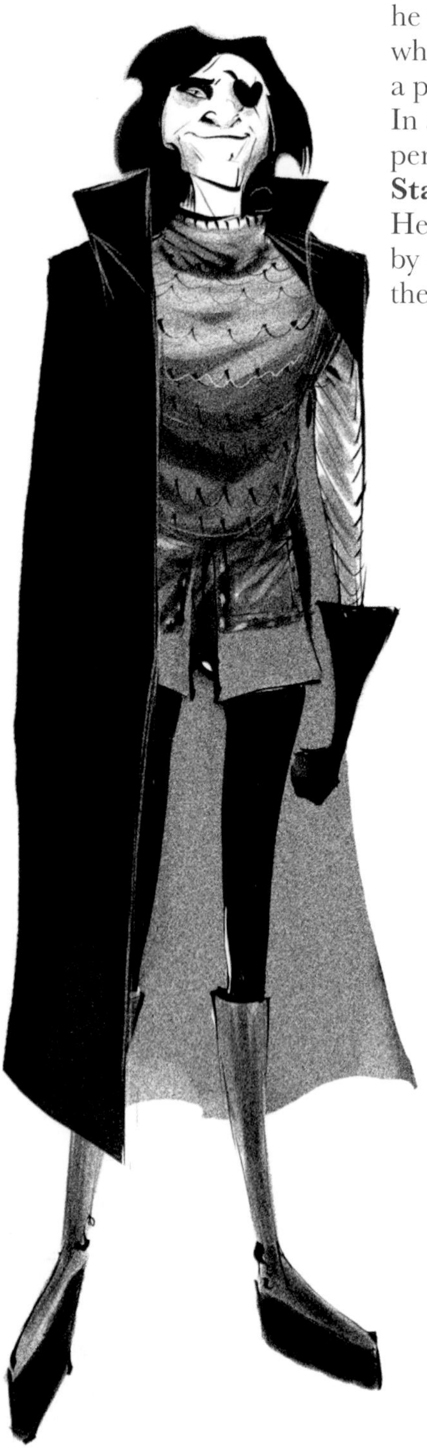

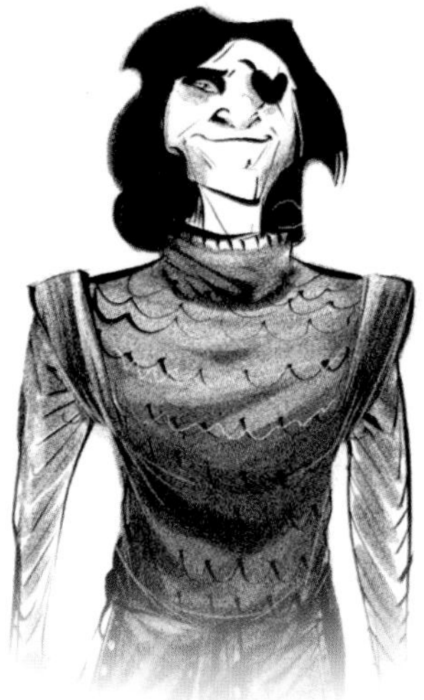

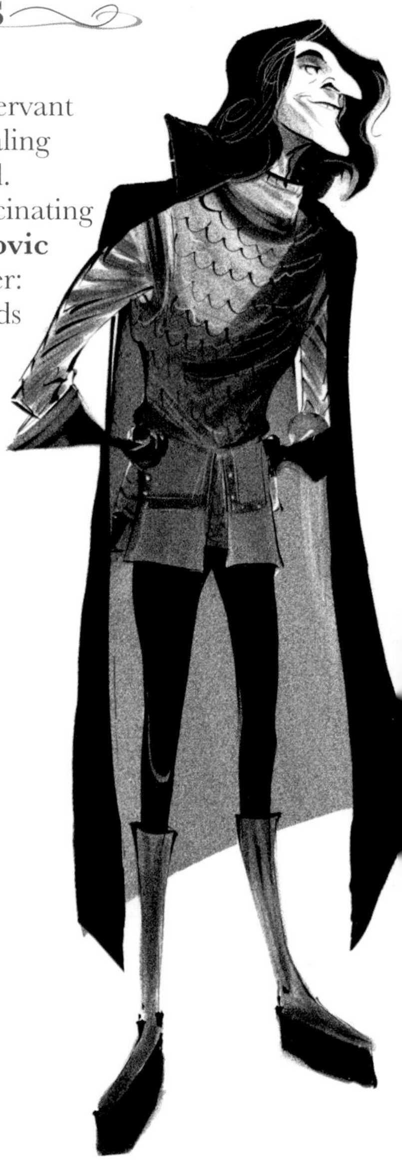

ABOVE:
The character's final look for the graphic novel

BELOW: **Crispin Glover** as the **Knave of Hearts**, looking at the Oraculum

"It does seem that my character is quite . . . diplomatic."

CRISPIN GLOVER

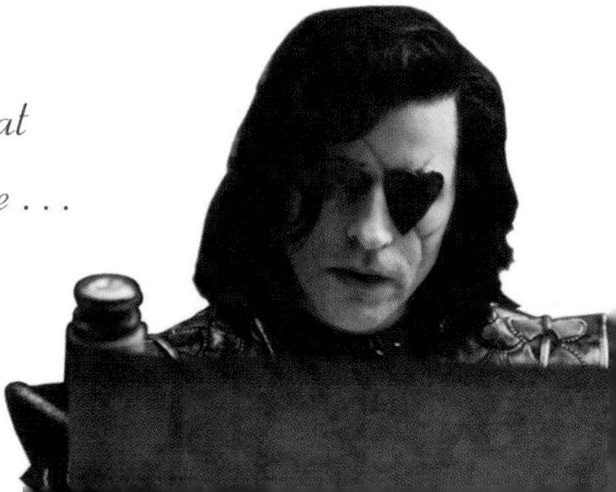

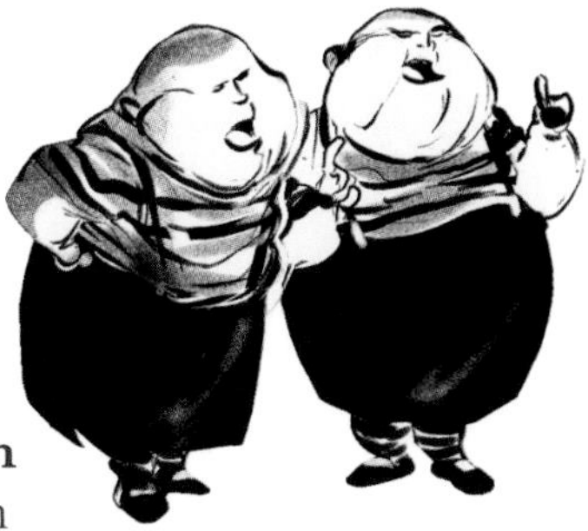

Tweedles

Tweedledee and **Tweedledum** are the twins Alice meets through the looking glass in Carroll's second book. Always quarrelling and complaining, they never agree on anything, continuously contradicting each other. But according to **Matt Lucas**, who plays both twins in the movie, when they need to, the Tweedles can be a very close couple.

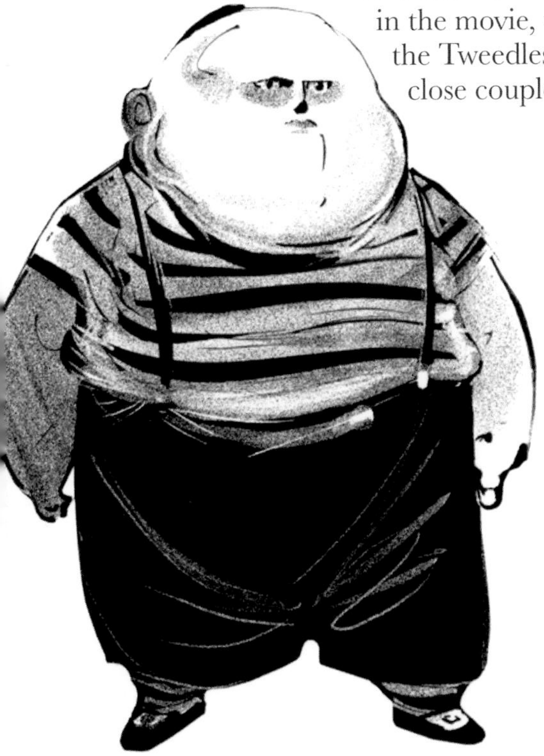

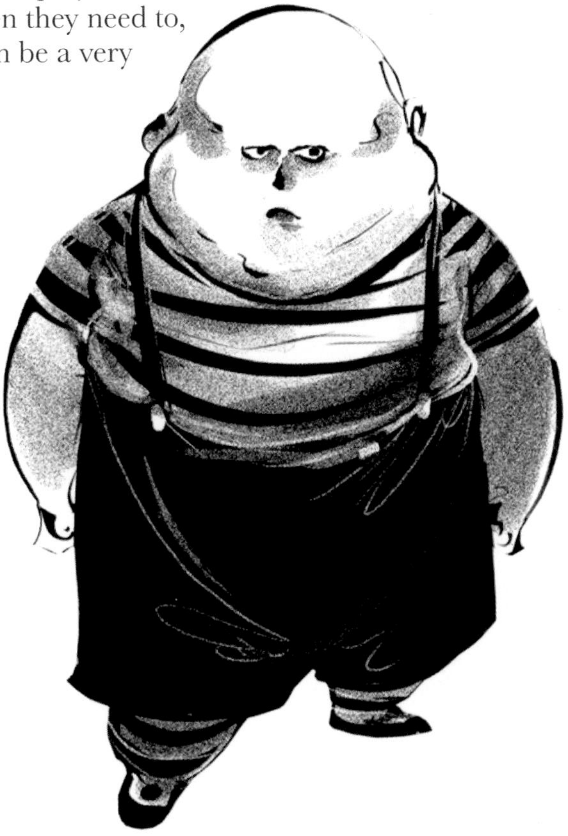

SHOWN HERE: The twins' final models

RIGHT: **Matt Lucas** in the double role of **Dee** and **Dum**

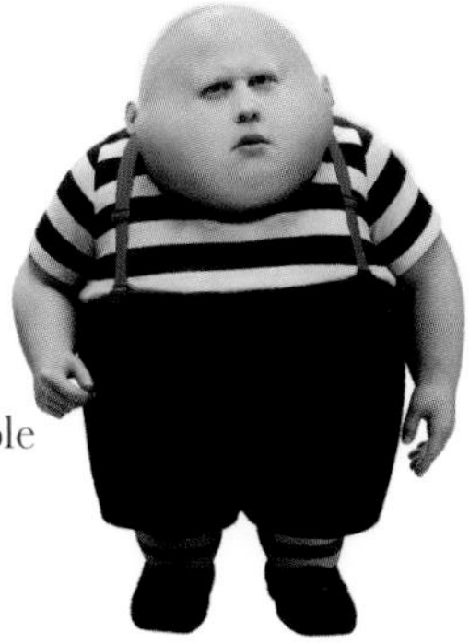

"I could sort of see them with their hand in the honey jar."

MATT LUCAS

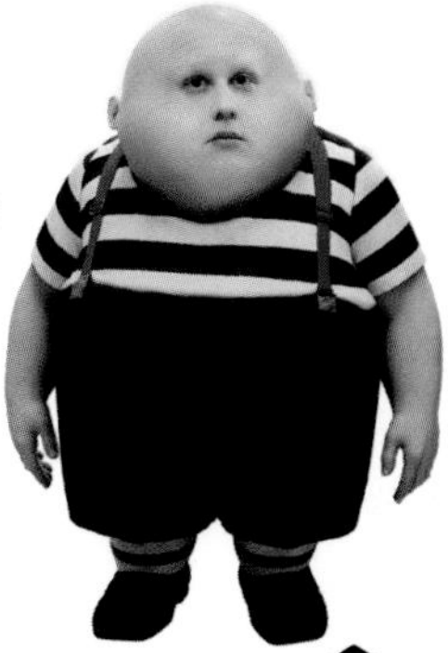

DEVELOPING THE PAGES

After creating the models of the main characters, the creative team – scriptwriter, illustrator, painter, designers and editors – work together to create the actual pages of the graphic novel. Step by step, in perfect assembly-line fashion with a continuous exchange of creative inspiration, they work to achieve the best quality in the final page.

From Film to Paper

A film's original screenplay indicates movements and dialogue for every character, as well as scene and action changes. Directions describe what will be played and recorded, shot and edited.

Starting from there, graphic novel writer **Alessandro Ferrari** wrote a manuscript adaptation that tells the movie story for an illustrated version.

Scenes are divided into pages and panels. Dialogue is adapted for space reasons, and captions are added to indicate time and place changes.

Following the new manuscript directions and using scene snapshots of the movie as additional reference, the illustrator and the painter created the final graphic novel pages.

"Not to create a world that didn't really belong in the world of Lewis Carroll and to keep that feeling of wonder and a little bit of insanity. That was a huge challenge for me."
LINDA WOOLVERTON

ON THE FOLLOWING PAGE: A page of **Linda Woolverton**'s original screenplay and the same scene in a page of **Alessandro Ferrari**'s manuscript. Below, layout and clean-up of the same page

EXT. THE GREAT LAWN - DAY - CONT.

Alice looks down at the Red Queen and her courtiers. The tall bushes hide all but her head and shoulders. Everyone stares.

RED QUEEN
And WHAT is this?

The White Rabbit comes out, improvising like mad.

WHITE RABBIT
It's a "who", Majesty. This is… um

RED QUEEN
Um?

ALICE
From Umbradge.

RED QUEEN
What happened to your clothes?

ALICE
I outgrew them. I've been growing an awful lot lately. I tower over everyone in Umbradge. They laugh at me. So I've come to you, hoping you might understand what it's like.

RED QUEEN
My dear girl. Anyone with a head that large is welcome in my court.

(CONTINUED)

PAGE 36

36.1
Pull back. Blocked out. Alice becomes huge (8'6" according to reference), now taller than the bushes that had previously concealed her. The clothes have burst at the seams and now branches cover her nude body, except for shoulders and face.

SFX: **WOOOOM**

36.2
Cut to Red Queen and her courtiers, a full shot of them all as seen from above, from Alice's point of view. All four are looking toward reader with eyes popped open wide. But the Red Queen is not at all afraid. She is curious, enticed.

RQUEEN: **And WHAT is this?**

36.3
Cut to White Rabbit, seen from above, at the feet of Red Queen trying to rectify the disaster.

RABBIT: **It's a "WHO", Majesty. This is… um…**
RQUEEN: **Um?**

36.4
Reverse angle. Close-up of Alice's large face, seen from below. She tries to come up with an excuse for her appearance, flattering the Red Queen.

ALICE: **From Umbradge. I overgrew everyone there and they laugh at me. So I've come to you. Hoping you might understand what is like…**

36.5
Close-up of Red Queen, from above. She smiles benevolently.

RQUEEN: **My dear girl, anyone with a head that large is welcome in my court!**

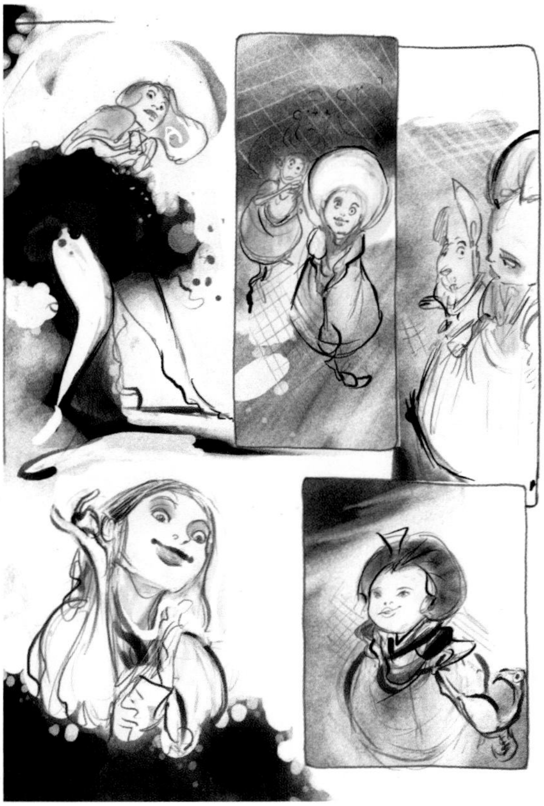

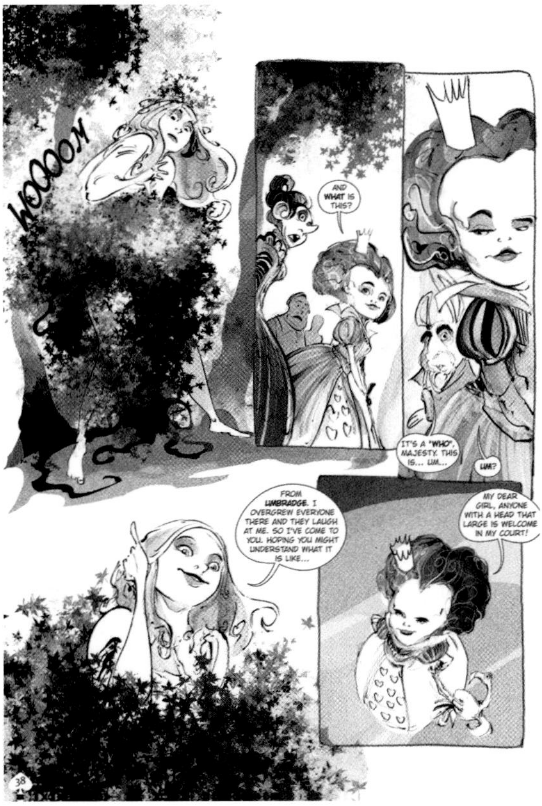
WOOOOM
AND WHAT IS THIS?
IT'S A "WHO", MAJESTY. THIS IS… UM…
UM?
FROM UMBRADGE. I OVERGREW EVERYONE THERE AND THEY LAUGH AT ME. SO I'VE COME TO YOU. HOPING YOU MIGHT UNDERSTAND WHAT IT IS LIKE…
MY DEAR GIRL, ANYONE WITH A HEAD THAT LARGE IS WELCOME IN MY COURT!
38

Falls and Pencils

Everything starts with a **sketch**. Usually it's a set of quickly drawn, rough geometric shapes. But the artist needs it to first understand how to spread the panels on the page. It's like a map of what he will draw later.

From the sketch he goes straight to the **layout**: the page is still in a sketchy version but it already gives a good idea of how big the panels would be, what point of view to use, and how much space must be left to place the balloons with the dialogue. In the layout, the artist makes decisions about action and camera angles, and sets the proportions and expressions of the characters.

All the important elements of the page are put into place, and the editor and the art director are able to check to see that the art matches the manuscript correctly. The story must flow smoothly from panel to panel and the action of the characters must be appropriate for the specific scene.

The page is ready to go to **clean-up**: Literally, the panel is cleaned up, backgrounds and characters are defined in detail. Lines become thinner or thicker to give the characters a full and complete physiognomy, and to give depth to the scene.

It's also at this point that the illustrator shades the page with gradations of grays and blacks, creating what will be the atmosphere of the whole scene, and setting a clear indication for the painter.

ABOVE: In sequence from top layout, clean-up, and color key steps

ON THE FOLLOWING PAGE:
Layout of the complete page

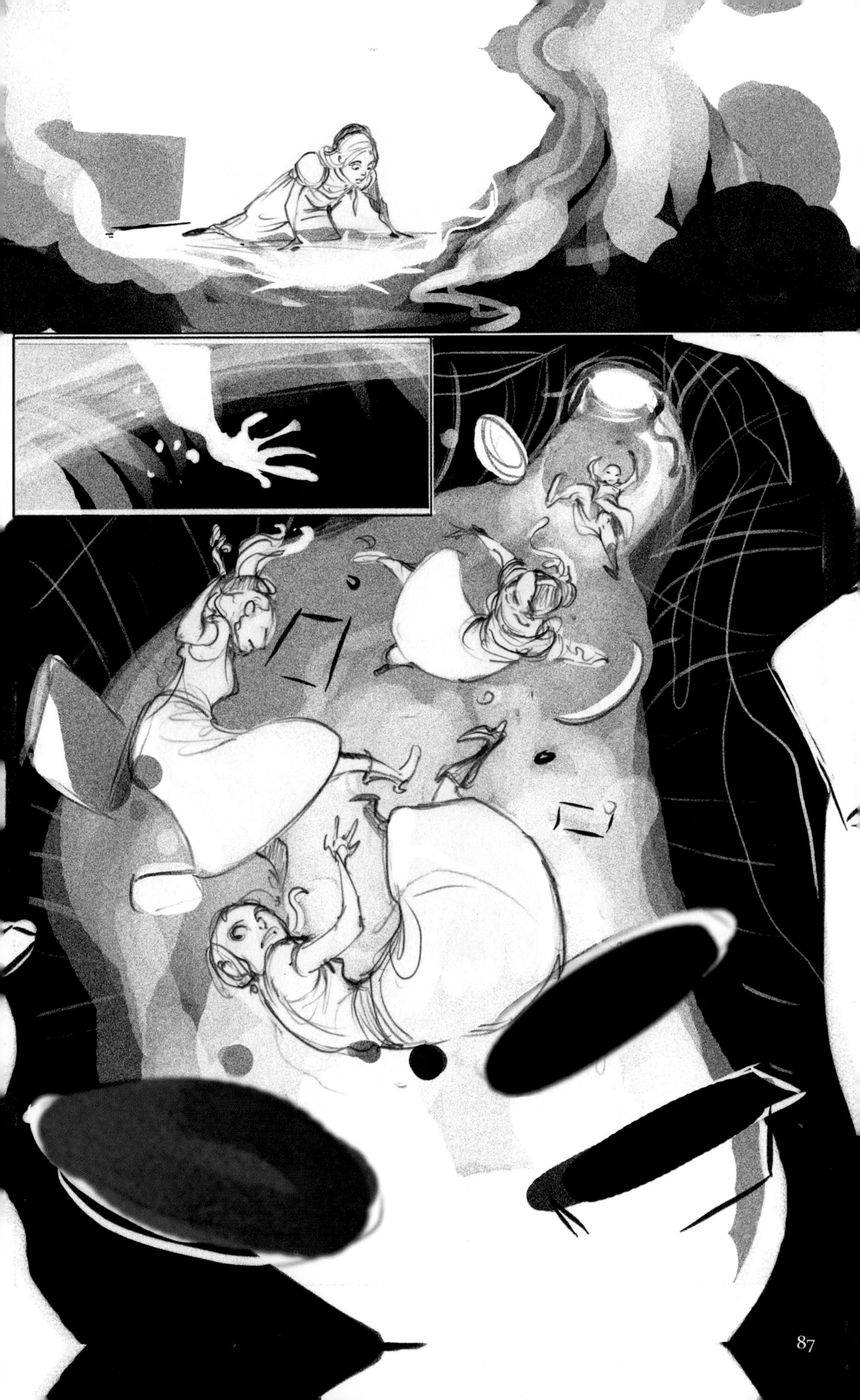

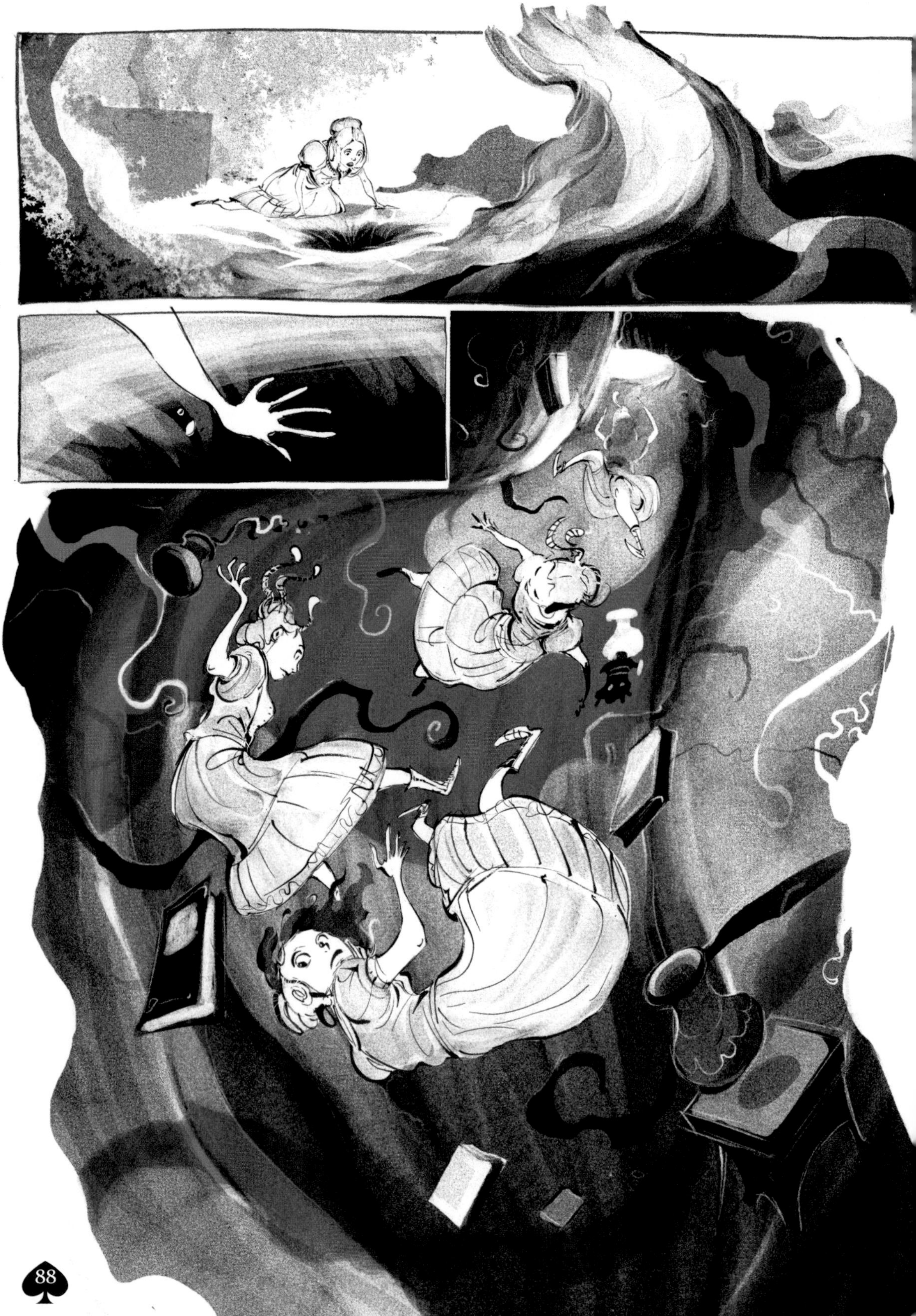

When Alice falls down the rabbit hole, books, tables, paintings and animals pass by, and the fall seems endless. The best way to convey that atmosphere on the graphic novel page was to use an unframed panel and repeat Alice's character in more than one position, from the beginning to the end of the fall.

Interestingly, in the first version of the movie's script, Alice didn't fall alone: McTwisp, the white rabbit, holds her by the ankle to pull her into his hole. The scene was replicated in the graphic novel manuscript, but before the illustrator drew the page, the filmmakers made changes to the script. The scene is now more similar to the first fall, which Alice took as a young girl, seen so many times in so many adaptations.

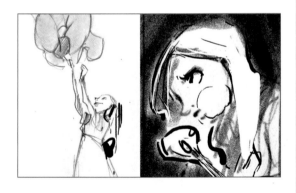

ON THE PREVIOUS PAGE: Clean-up version of the complete page

LEFT AND ABOVE: Details of layout and matching clean-up steps

Colors and Laugh

As with development of the character design, the final painting technique is the result of creative research and a series of tests and color keys – tiny, quick paints to test the overall look of the page. Concept art made for the movie and final frames are precious reference material, helping the painter find the right path. The artist tries to capture the moods and feelings that the filmmakers want to deliver and translates them into colors on the page, keeping in mind how they will turn out in final print.

Marieke Ferrari experimented with various painting approaches before finding the right one. She started with the character of the Mad Hatter, whose bright colors immediately attracted her attention.

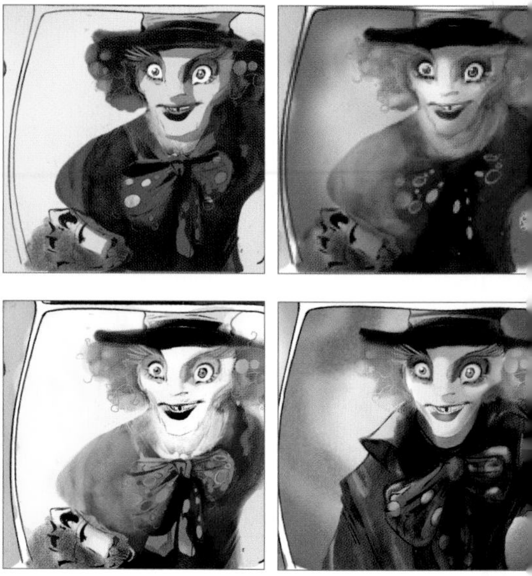

ABOVE: Color tests of the **Mad Hatter**

BELOW: **Alice** enters the Mushroom Forest

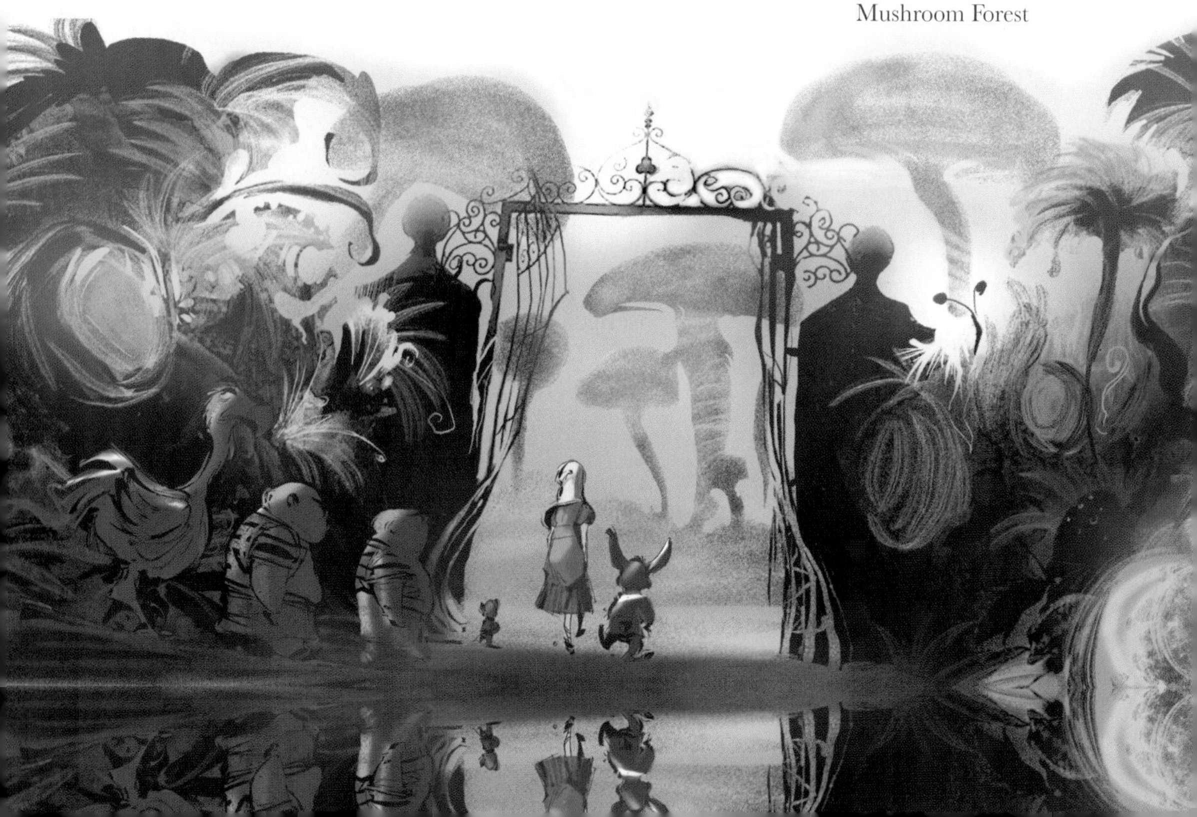

The first step to final paint is a base of **flat colors**. These are usually darker than the final palette because the painter will use them as shadows, while going over with the digital brush to create the lights.

From the masterful use of light and shadows and a precise choice of the color palette, the painter is able to highlight the characters while giving depth to backgrounds, as well as deliver the right mood of the scenes.

Colors are very important in this story and often identify the characters and the environments relating to them.

ABOVE: From flat color to final paint in two details of the **March Hare** and **Mally**

LEFT: Flat color step

A Hat Night

"Anyone can go by horse or rail.
But the best way to travel is by hat!"

That's what the Mad Hatter says to
a minuscule Alice when he offers her
a lift on his head. And everything runs
smoothly until the Red Knights arrive.

So the Mad Hatter throws his hat
far away to save the girl before being
captured himself. Alice stays alone
and waits, spending the whole night
in the hat.

This long scene was given the space
of only one page in the graphic novel.
From manuscript to clean-up to color,
this was the challenge: Time had to be
condensed into a few effective images.
Daytime had to become night in only
three vignettes.

Again the illustrator decided to use
repetition to communicate to the reader
what's happening in the scene, but this
time, instead of movement, what
he wanted to express was the passing
of time.

To achieve the final result, the painter's
contribution was paramount, adding
a soft but effective transition from light
to darkness.

ABOVE: Final paint and detail
of Alice on the hat

ON THE FOLLOWING PAGE: The passage
from daytime to night in the last panel

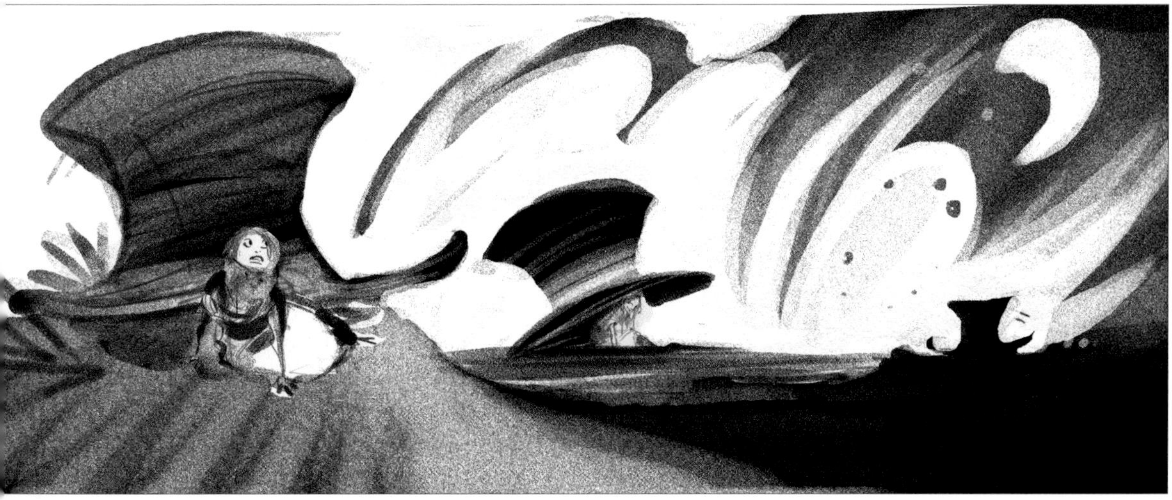

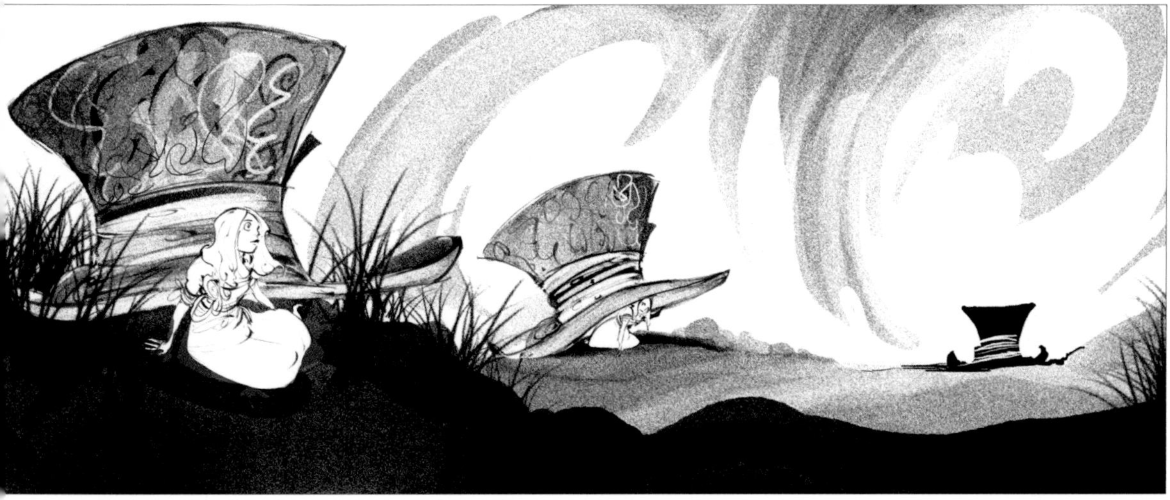

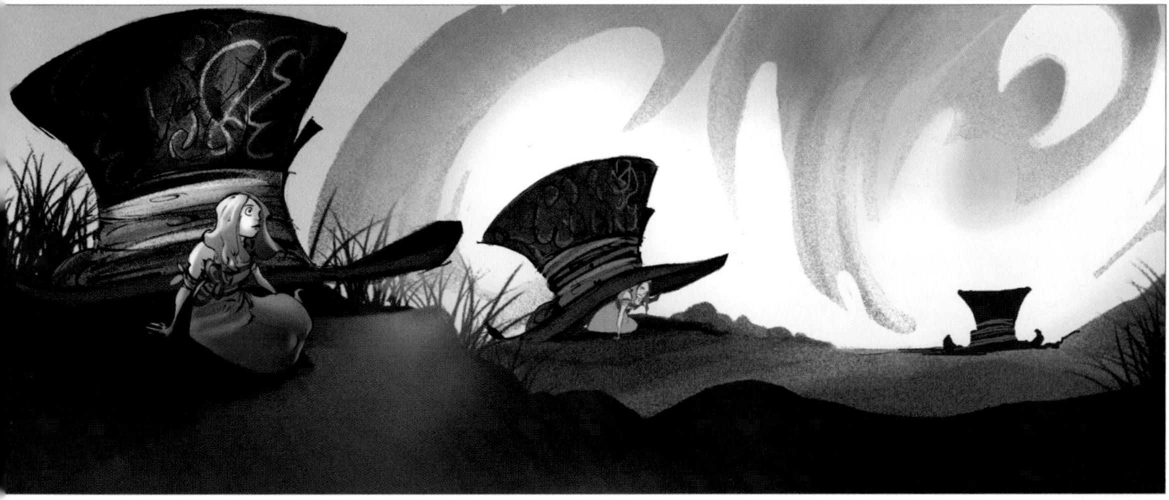

BIOGRAPHIES

Alessandro Ferrari

After attending a script-writing course at the Accademia Disney in Milan in 2005, Alessandro Ferrari penned the adventures of a host of Disney characters, including those from such hits as *Mickey Mouse, Witch, Pirates of the Caribbean* and *High School Musical.* Prior to his work on *Alice in Wonderland*, he adapted, for the graphic novel format, Pixar films *Wall•E* (2008), *Up* (2009), *Toy Story, Toy Story 2* and *Toy Story 3* (2009). His first book, *Facebook: Domani Smetto (Facebook: Tomorrow I Quit)*, was published in 2009 by Castelvecchi Editore.

After falling into the rabbit's hole years back, he never really made it out...

Max Narciso

Massimiliano Narciso studied animation for many years before attending an Accademia Disney comics course. Since then, he's been a Disney comics illustrator (*Mickey Mouse Magazine, PK Magazine, Pirates of the Caribbean Magazine*), and has illustrated three graphic novels based on Disney films: *Lilo & Stitch* (2001), *Brother Bear* (2003), and *The Wild* (2006). He has also been working with the German publisher Mosaik since 1993. In 2003 he started Kawaii Creative Studio together with Marieke Ferrari.

They say he's mad, but he says it's only his weird hat!

Marieke Ferrari

After graduating from the Academy of Fine Arts, Marieke Ferrari attended various courses at the Accademia Disney, including 3D computer graphics, illustration, layout, and scriptwriting. Since 1998, she has been working as an illustrator and painter on many different Disney projects, and in the publishing and merchandise licensing areas in multimedia formats. She is creative director, as well as scriptwriter and painter, at Kawaii Creative Studio, which she co-founded with Massimiliano Narciso. She does not happen to be related to Alessandro Ferrari, but both enjoy the coincidence.

When she's in the mood, she dispenses cryptic advice while sitting on a huge blue mushroom.

Credits

Manuscript Adaptation: Alessandro Ferrari

Layout, clean-up and ink: Massimiliano Narciso

Paint: Marieke Ferrari

Paint supervision: Stefano Attardi

Editing: Kawaii Creative Studio, Absink

Contributors: Gioia Gabrielli, Marta De Cunto,
Paola Beretta, Elisa Checchi, Deborah Barnes

Based on the screenplay by Linda Woolverton
Produced by Richard D. Zanuck, Joe Roth,
Suzanne Todd and Jennifer Todd
Directed by Tim Burton

Created by Disney Publishing Worldwide

Designer: Erika Terriquez

Assistant Editors: Christopher Burns and Jason Long

Editors: Aaron Sparrow & Christopher Meyer

Special Thanks: Tim Burton, Derek Frey,
Dominique Flynn and Erik Schumdde

ROSS RICHIE
chief executive officer

MARK WAID
editor-in-chief

ADAM FORTIER
vice president,
new business

WES HARRIS
vice president,
publishing

LANCE KREITER
vice president,
licensing & merchandisi

CHIP MOSHER
marketing director

MATT GAGNON
managing editor

FIRST EDITION: JUNE 2010

10 9 8 7 6 5 4 3 2 1

PRINTED IN CANADA

Office of publication: 6310 San Vicente Blvd Ste 404, Los Angeles, CA 90048 -5457.

A catalog record for this book is available from OCLC and on our website www.boom-studios.com on the Librarians page.

11.49 $\leftarrow$ T 13.18.10